D1572191

GREAT
BATTLES
ON THE
EASTERN FRONT

Books by T. N. Dupuy:

To the Colors
with R. Ernest Dupuy

Faithful and True Military Heritage of America
with R. Ernest Dupuy

Campaigns of the French Revolution and of Napoleon

Brave Men and Great Captains
with R. Ernest Dupuy

Compact History of the Revolutionary War
with R. Ernest Dupuy

Civil War Land Battles

Civil War Naval Actions

Military History of World War II (19 vols.)

Compact History of the Revolutionary War
with R. Ernest Dupuy

Military History of World War I (12 vols.)

The Battle of Austerlitz

Modern Libraries for Modern Colleges

Ferment in College Libraries

Military History of the Chinese Civil War

The Encyclopedia of Military History from 3500 B.C. to the Present
with R. Ernest Dupuy

Military Lives (12 vols.)

Revolutionary War Land Battles
with Gay M. Hammerman

Revolutionary War Naval Battles
with Grace P. Hayes

Holidays

Documentary History of Arms Control and Disarmament
with Gay M. Hammerman

Almanac of World Military Power
with John A. C. Andrews and Grace P. Hayes

An Outline History of the American Revolution
with R. Ernest Dupuy

People & Events of the American Revolution
with Gay M. Hammerman

A Genius for War: The German Army and General Staff, 1807–1945

Elusive Victory: the Arab-Israeli Wars, 1947–1974

Numbers, Predictions and War

The Evolution of Weapons and Warfare

GREAT
BATTLES
ON THE
EASTERN FRONT

The Soviet-German War, 1941–1945

by

Colonel T. N. DUPUY, USA, Retired,

and

Paul MARTELL

THE BOBBS-MERRILL COMPANY, INC.
Indianapolis/New York

Copyright © 1982 by T. N. Dupuy

All rights reserved, including the right of reproduction
in whole or in part in any form
Published by The Bobbs-Merrill Company, Inc.
Indianapolis   New York

Library of Congress Cataloging in Publication Data
Dupuy, Trevor Nevitt, 1916–
  Great battles on the eastern front.

   1. World War, 1939–1945—Campaigns—
Eastern.   I. Title.
D764.D86   940.54′21   81–17983
ISBN 0–672–52674–3   AACR2

Designed by Jacques Chazaud
Manufactured in the United States of America

First printing

Dedicated with great appreciation
to our respected colleague,
Grace P. Hayes

Acknowledgments

The authors are grateful and wish to express their thanks to several members of the HERO staff for their contributions to the book. We are especially in debt to Grace P. Hayes for many useful comments, for organizing confused figures into tables, converting complicated maps into simple ones, and for the final proofreading. Gay Hammerman checked the entire manuscript for consistency and accuracy, and Edward Oppenheimer prepared the first draft of the narratives of the Stalingrad and Kursk battles.

We are extremely thankful to Laura Fentin Duvall and Alane Arehart for the many hours put into the typing of the manuscript and tables.

And last, but not least, we appreciate the efforts made by Mary Henze, who carefully read and corrected the galleys.

Contents

List of Tables	*xi*
List of Maps	*xvii*
Introduction	*1*
Operation Barbarossa	*7*
The Defense of Moscow	*27*
Soviet Counteroffensive at Moscow	*46*
The Soviet Counteroffensive at Stalingrad	*59*
The Battle for Kursk	*75*
Kursk Counteroffensive	*91*
The Race to the Dnieper	*106*
The Melitopol Operation	*119*
The Korsun-Shevchenkovskiy Operation	*129*
The Crimea Operation	*139*
The Byelorussian Offensive	*150*
The Lvov-Sandomierz Offensive	*167*
The Yassy-Kishinev Operation	*183*
The Battle for East Prussia	*193*
The Vistula-Oder Offensive	*205*
The Battle for Berlin	*219*
Soviet Campaign in Manchuria	*235*
Appendix 1 Units of Fire for Principal Soviet Weapons	*248*
Appendix 2 Glossary of Abbreviations	*249*

List of Tables

Operation Barbarossa

1	Deployment of German Forces, Eastern Front	20
2	Deployment of Soviet Forces	21
3	Men and Equipment	22
4	Soviet Air Forces on the Western Border	23
5	German Air Forces	23
6	Personnel Strength of the Soviet Armed Forces	23
7	Strength of Soviet Combat Ground and Air Forces	24
8	Strength of German Allies	24
9	Soviet Armament and Ammunition Production	25
10	German Infantry and Artillery Weapons Production	25
11	German Production of Tanks and Assault Guns	25
12	Strength of Front Line German Ground and Air Forces	26
13	Personnel and Equipment Strength	26

The Defense of Moscow

1	Composition of Soviet Forces Deployed in Defense of Moscow	32
2	Soviet Strengths	33
3	Composition and Strength of the Soviet Air Force, October 1, 1941	34
4	Composition and Strength of the Soviet Air Force, November 10, 1941	35
5	Composition of German Army Group Center	36
6	Operational Deployment of Soviet Forces, October 1, 1941	37
7	Operational Deployment of Soviet Forces, November 15, 1941	38
8	Operational Density of German Forces	39
9	Frontage and Operational Density of Soviet Forces, October 1, 1941	40
10	Frontage and Operational Density of Soviet Forces, November 15, 1941	42
11	Tactical Density of Soviet Forces, October 1, 1941	43
12	Tactical Density of Soviet Forces, November 15, 1941	44
13	Rates of Advance, German Army Group Center	45

Soviet Counteroffensive at Moscow

1	Composition of Soviet Forces	50
2	Composition and Strength of the Soviet Air Force	51

3   Reinforcements Received by Soviet Forces   *52*
4   Combat Strength of Soviet Forces   *53*
5   Defense Frontage and Density of German Forces   *54*
6   Frontage and Density of Advancing Soviet Armies   *55*
7   Tactical Density of Soviet Forces   *56*
8   German Combat Strength   *57*
9   Average Rate of Advance of Soviet Forces   *58*

The Soviet Counteroffensive at Stalingrad

Soviet Order of Battle   *64*
1   Planned and Actual Scope of Soviet Operation   *66*
2   Soviet Strength   *67*
3   Composition of Southwestern, Don, and Stalingrad Army
       Groups   *69*
4   Composition and Strength of the Soviet Air Force   *70*
5   German and Allied Forces   *71*
6   Attack Frontage and Density of Soviet Forces   *72*
7   Operational Density of Artillery and Tanks   *73*

The Battle for Kursk

1   Soviet Strengths   *79*
2   Composition of Soviet Forces   *80*
3   Steppe Army Group Strength   *81*
4   Soviet Air Strength   *82*
5   Composition of German Forces   *82*
6   Deployment of Soviet Forces   *83*
7   Operational Density of Soviet Forces   *84*
8   Fortification of Central and Voronezh Army Groups   *85*
9   Comparison of Soviet and German Forces   *85*
10   Comparison of Soviet and German Forces on Axes of Main
       Effort   *86*
11   Tactical Density and Comparison of Soviet and German Forces
       in the Breakthrough Sectors   *87*
12   Status of Soviet Ammunition Supplies (Units of Fire)   *88*
13   Average German Advance per Day   *89*

Kursk Counteroffensive

Soviet Order of Battle   *96*
1   Composition of Soviet Army Groups   *97*
2   Soviet Army Group Strengths   *99*
3   Planned vs. Actual Scope of Operations   *101*
4   Soviet Air Forces   *102*

5 German Forces on Orel and Belgorod-Kharkov Axes   *103*
6 Comparison of Soviet and German Forces at Start
       of Counteroffensive   *104*
7 Operational Density of Soviet Forces   *105*

The Race to the Dnieper

1 Composition of Soviet Forces, September 1, 1943   *111*
2 Composition of Soviet Forces, October 1, 1943   *112*
3 Composition of Soviet Forces, November 1, 1943   *113*
4 Composition of German Forces   *114*
5 Scope of Operation from Jump-Off Area to Dnieper River   *115*
6 Soviet Bridgeheads on West Bank of the Dnieper   *116*
7 Voronezh Army Group Units and Equipment in the Bridgehead   *117*
8 Means of Crossing of Voronezh Army Group   *118*

The Melitopol Operation

Soviet Order of Battle   *121*
1 Soviet Strengths   *122*
2 Composition of Soviet Forces   *123*
3 Composition and Strengths of the Soviet Air Force   *124*
4 Soviet and German Strength Ratio   *124*
5 Operational Density of the Southern Army Group   *125*
6 Supply Status of the Soviet Forces   *126*
7 Operational Deployment of Army Group and Armies   *127*
8 Rates of Advance of Soviet Forces   *128*

The Korsun-Shevchenkovskiy Operation

1 Composition of Ground Forces of 1st and 2d Ukrainian
       Army Groups   *133*
2 Soviet Air Forces Attached to the 1st and 2d Ukrainian
       Army Groups   *134*
3 Operational Deployment in the Main Effort Zone of the 1st
       and 2d Ukrainian Army Groups   *135*
4 Soviet Personnel and Materiel   *136*
5 Intensity of Soviet and German Air Activities   *137*
6 Soviet-German Force Ratio   *138*

The Crimea Operation

1 Composition of Soviet Forces   *143*
2 Soviet-German Force Ratio   *144*
3 Personnel and Materiel   *145*
4 Composition and Strength of the Soviet Air Force   *146*

5   Partisan Personnel Strength   *146*
6   Soviet and German Naval Strength   *147*
7   Soviet and German Force Ratios Along the Advance Axes   *147*
8   Operational Density of Soviet Forces   *148*
9   Statistical Summary   *148*
10 Soviet Personnel and Materiel in Assault on Sevastopol   *149*
11 Soviet and German Force Ratio in Assault on Sevastopol   *149*

The Byelorussian Offensive

Soviet Order of Battle   *154*
1   Composition of Soviet Army Groups   *155*
2   Composition of German Forces   *156*
3   Men and Equipment of Soviet Army Groups   *157*
4   Operational Density of Soviet Troops   *158*
5   Composition and Strength of Soviet Air Armies   *158*
6   Deployment and Operational Density of German Forces   *159*
7   Soviet Reinforcements   *160*
8   Frontage and Density of Artillery, Tanks, and Assault Guns   *162*
9   Average Daily Rate of Advance   *163*
10 Rates of Advance of Mobile Groups   *164*
11 German Formations Defeated or Destroyed   *165*
12 German Reinforcements   *166*

The Lvov-Sandomierz Offensive

Soviet Order of Battle   *171*
1   Composition of the 1st Ukrainian Army Group   *172*
2   1st Ukrainian Army Group: Men and Weapons Strengths   *173*
3   1st Ukrainian Army Group: Tanks and Assault Guns   *174*
4   Composition and Strength of the Soviet Second Air Army   *175*
5   German Forces Facing the 1st Ukrainian Army Group   *177*
6   Soviet and German Force Ratio   *178*
7   1st Ukrainian Army Group Force Densities in the
    Breakthrough Sectors   *178*
8   Operational Deployment of First Echelon Armies, 1st
    Ukrainian Army Group   *179*
9   Reinforcements Sent to the 1st Ukrainian Army Group   *180*
10 Reinforcements Sent to German Forces   *181*
11 Soviet Second Air Army Sorties   *181*
12 Average Daily Rates of Advance of the 1st Ukrainian Army
    Group (km)   *182*

The Yassy-Kishinev Operation

Soviet Order of Battle   *186*
1   Composition of Soviet Forces   *187*
2   Effective Strength of Soviet Forces   *188*
3   Composition and Density of German and Romanian Forces   *189*
4   Operational Density of Soviet Forces   *189*
5   Average Density of Weapons   *190*
6   Ratio of Forces   *190*
7   Daily Average Advance (km)   *191*
8   Ammunition and Fuel Availability   *191*
9   Ammunition Consumption (Units of Fire)   *191*

The Battle for East Prussia

Soviet Order of Battle   *196*
1   Composition of Soviet Forces   *197*
2   Soviet Personnel Strengths, Weapons, and Equipment   *198*
3   Operational Density of Soviet Forces   *198*
4   Soviet Operational Aircraft   *199*
5   Composition and Operational Density of German Forces   *199*
6   Soviet Army Group Buildup Before January 10, 1945   *200*
7   Soviet Artillery Buildup Before January 10, 1945   *201*
8   Operational Density of Soviet Forces   *202*
9   Width of Front and Density of Artillery and Tanks   *203*
10 Soviet Advance Rates   *203*
11 Soviet Supply Levels   *204*
12 German Divisions Destroyed and Defeated   *204*

The Vistula-Oder Offensive

Soviet Order of Battle   *209*
1   Composition of the Soviet Forces   *210*
2   Men and Equipment   *211*
3   Operational Density of Soviet Forces   *211*
4   Composition and Strength of Soviet Air Force   *212*
5   Composition of German Army Group A   *212*
6   Operational Deployment of Soviet Armies   *213*
7   Reinforcements Sent to 1st Byelorussian Army Group   *214*
8   Reinforcements Sent to 1st Ukrainian Army Group   *215*
9   German Reinforcements   *216*
10 Ammunition, Fuel and Rations   *216*
11 Minimum/Maximum Daily Advance Rates (km)   *217*

The Battle for Berlin

Soviet Order of Battle   223
1   Composition of Soviet Forces   224
2   Soviet Equipment and Strengths   225
3   Composition of German Forces   226
4   German Reinforcements   227
5   First Echelon Deployment of Soviet Army Groups   228
6   Soviet Ammunition, Fuel, and Rations   229
7   Density of Soviet Forces   230
8   Deployment of Soviet Forces   231
9   Tactical Density of Soviet Artillery and Tanks   232
10 Tactical Density of Soviet MRLs, AAA, and AT Artillery   233
11 Number of Soviet Sorties   234

Soviet Campaign in Manchuria

1   Soviet Forces in the Far East   240
2   Combat Strength of the Soviet Forces in the Far East   241
3   Men and Materiel Transferred from Europe to the Far East   241
4   Composition of the Soviet Ground Forces   242
5   Soviet Men and Materiel   242
6   Composition, Strength, and Performance of the Soviet Air
      Force   243
7   Composition of the Soviet Naval Forces   244
8   Composition and Strength of the Japanese Force   245
9   Rate of Advance   246
10 Ammunition, Fuel and Food Supplies   247
11 Prisoners of War and Materiel Captured by the Soviet Forces   247

List of Maps

German Campaign Plan for Operation Barbarossa   6

The Defense of Moscow   28

Soviet Counteroffensive at Moscow   47

Soviet Counteroffensive at Stalingrad   60

The Battle for Kursk—German Offensive   74

The Battle for Kursk—Soviet Counteroffensive   90

The Race to the Dnieper   107

The Melitopol Operation   120

The Korsun-Shevchenkovskiy Operation   130

The Crimea Operation   140

The Byelorussian Offensive   151

The Lvov-Sandomierz Offensive   168

The Yassy-Kishinev Operation   184

The Battle for East Prussia   192

The Vistula-Oder Offensive   206

The Battle for Berlin   218

Soviet Campaign in Manchuria   236

Introduction

The Soviet-German War of 1941–1945 involved more men, more guns, and more casualties and was fought over a more extended battle front than any other war in history. The Soviet-German front line stretched for 4,500 kilometers at the outbreak of war and was increased to some 6,000 kilometers in the fall of 1942, when the Wehrmacht came close to overrunning the Caucasus. Even in January 1945, not long before the war ended, when the Germans were pulling back in almost all areas, the front was still 2,000 kilometers long. In comparison, the front in western Europe in 1945 was 400 kilometers. Even the combined frontage on which Western forces fought, in North Africa, Sicily, Italy, and southern France, was not nearly so extensive as that on which Soviet troops were engaged, and the numbers of Germans whom the Soviets faced were also significantly greater.

Without question, the Soviet Union's contribution to the Allied victory over Nazi Germany in World War II was, at the very least, commensurate with the contributions of the United States and Great Britain. One can only conjecture how the war might have turned out if the 150-odd German divisions and three air fleets that were deployed in the east in 1941 and the following years had been available in Africa to beef up Rommel's forces, or in western Europe to meet the Allied invasion, or, indeed, to mount a German invasion of the British Isles.

Yet outside the Soviet Union little has been published about the Soviet-German front in World War II, compared with the rich literature about the war in the west. A major reason for this, of course, is that official historical data concerning the military operations of the Western Allies and of Germany is easily available, whereas the Soviet archives are closed to Western researchers, and it takes an enormous effort to collect Soviet data from the various and numerous sources in Russian open literature and to glean hard data from the propaganda and the unidentified estimates that typically accompany it.

The data in this book is necessarily selective. It does not cover all the operations on the Eastern Front. For a number of important battles no data was found that was both reasonable and comprehensive. And since Soviet policy forbids publication of Soviet loss data, a large gap exists throughout. We gave some thought to including German estimates of Soviet losses, taken from contemporary German records. But since this data is based primarily on intelligence sources and is impossible to verify, we decided against using it. On the other hand, we have included Soviet figures on German strengths and losses, because these were taken by the Soviet authors from the German records captured either by the Red Army or by US forces, the latter available on microfilm at the US National Archives.

Two things about performance in this war are most noteworthy. The first is the superb combat performance of the German forces, with battlefield accomplishments at least matching the best of any other army in military history. Second, and most significant, is the fact that despite this German military excellence, despite being outclassed on the battlefield, Soviet Russia won. And the principal reason Russia won was the seemingly inexhaustible supply of manpower at the disposal of frequently mediocre Soviet commanders. Hardly less important is space—the vast country that provided that manpower, and whose great reaches exhausted the more limited manpower of the invader. Within that space, of course, was a war industry which, under the most adverse circumstances but with considerable assistance from the United States and Britain, was able to provide enough weapons for the Red Army.

At the beginning of 1941 the population of the Soviet Union and areas under Soviet control numbered more than 199,000,000. Germany's population (counting the people of Alsace-Lorraine, but not including non-Germans in occupied Poland and Slovakia) was almost exactly 100,000,000. But nearly four-fifths of the Russian males had not reached age 40; and only three-fifths of the German males were in the age group under 40. The proportions and numbers in each major group are shown in Table 1.

Not only was the number of young Russian men available for service more than double that in Germany; the ratio increased during the war. Russia, moreover, was not the only area where German forces were engaged. German troops were occupying most of western Europe, with substantial garrisons prepared to resist possible Allied landings along the extensive Atlantic and Mediterranean coasts of the continent, and additional forces committed to operations in North Africa.

During the first few weeks of the war the Soviets mobilized nearly 5,000,000 men, which allowed them to absorb the several million losses

Table 1
Comparison of Male Populations

	USSR		Germany	
	Number (millions)	Percent	Number (millions)	Percent
Under 20	43.0	45	15.5	31.9
20–39	31.5	33	15.5	31.9
40–59	14.7	15.4	11.5	23.8
60 and older	6.2	6.6	5.6	12.4
TOTALS	95.4	100.0	48.1	100.0

suffered in the summer of 1941. From the end of June to December 1941 Moscow organized 287 new rifle divisions and 159 rifle and 76 tank brigades. At the end of the war, despite nearly 10,000,000 casualties, the Soviets still had 11,365,000 men in their armed forces. By October 1943 the total manpower superiority of the Soviets over the Germans on the Eastern Front reached 2.2:1. In subsequent months the superiority increased, as the Red Army continually managed to replace its losses or bring up new units, while the Germans were unable to maintain their strength.

The toughness and the fighting capability of the Soviet soldier and his capacity to endure hardships and ceaseless combat under atrocious conditions of weather and terrain were respected by the Germans. Fighting in defense of his homeland against a foreign invader, the Soviet soldier was formidable.

Military manpower was only one facet of the problem that the Soviets faced and handled with remarkable speed and organization. Civilian labor was put to use in armament production, barrier construction, and other fields of home-front activity, work for which in Germany manpower was provided by people displaced from invaded territory and forced to work for the Reich. And of the utmost importance was the enormous accomplishment of moving vital industries east, just ahead of the German invaders. The territory occupied by the Germans during 1941–1942, representing 40% of the population (80,000,000), had contained 78% of Soviet pig iron production, 58% of steel, 63% of coal, 42% of electricity, 38% of grain and cattle, and 84% of sugar. Relocation of the people and the industry in a relatively short time was a major achievement and a tremendous contribution to the ability of the Soviet Union to maintain its military effort. The average annual Soviet output of armaments during the war surpassed that of Germany, and the lavish American and British lend-lease program, particularly the abundance of trucks and jeeps supplied by the United States, made it possible for the Red Army to meet its needs.

Of armor and artillery the Soviet Army had from the beginning a greater supply. This numerical superiority was maintained by standardization of relatively simple equipment, which allowed the Soviets to increase production rates in spite of the loss of two-thirds of their factory space. The development of the Katyusha multiple rocket launcher, the diesel-powered T-34 medium tank—which was faster and more heavily armed and armored than most German tanks—and the 60-plus-ton KV heavy tank gave the Russians at least selective qualitative equality, and sometimes qualitative superiority. The efficiency of the Soviet production program, focused on manufacturing limited types of weapons in very large quantities, not only facilitated supplying the army in the field but contrasted sharply with the confusion that reigned in the German armament industry until it was reorganized by Albert Speer and General Fritz Fromm in late 1942.

Had it not been for the size of the Soviet Union, the volume of Russian manpower and the quantity of weapons would probably not have been sufficient to halt the German offensives. As it was, the Soviet leaders were able to trade space and sacrifice lives, not only to gain time in which to mobilize manpower, but also to wear down the Germans as they struggled to maintain momentum along a lengthening line of communications. Primitive roads and an inadequate railroad net added to the Germans' problems.

Then there was the weather. In winter the temperature dropped as low as $-30°$ Celsius ($-22°$ Fahrenheit). The first winter paralyzed the poorly prepared Germans, while the Red Army, its acclimated men wearing quilted uniforms and its cavalry riding Siberian horses, performed effectively. While physically the Germans were prepared for the subsequent winters, they were never psychologically able to match Russian winter performance.

Hardly less paralyzing to the Germans, inhibiting their blitzkrieg tactics, was the effect of the long-lasting spring thaws and the fall rains on the Russian dirt roads. One might think these natural problems would have affected the Russians as much as they did the Germans, and to some extent of course they did. But during those months of 1941 and 1942 when there seemed to be a possibility of a German victory, time was precious to the invaders, because unless they could use the weeks of good operational weather to gain a victory, the Russians would have time to recover from their setbacks and to mobilize more of their manpower. And that is what happened. Once the initiative had passed to the Russians, they were under no time pressure; the passage of time simply made their victory more inevitable.

Considering the Soviet advantages in terms of manpower, equipment, space, and weather, it is difficult to understand how either Hitler or his efficient General Staff could have expected victory in Russia. But—having correctly assessed the weakness of the Red Army—not only did they expect it, they came very close to achieving victory.

The "might have beens" of history are intriguing, but to explore them is usually an exercise in futility. However, it is not difficult to visualize a different course of events in Russia in the summer and early fall of 1941, for if Hitler had not insisted on a series of mistaken strategic decisions, his armies would probably have taken Moscow and possibly even reached the line of the Volga River. Even in the summer of 1942 the Germans had a good chance of fastening a secure grip on the lower Volga.

A German victory of such magnitude in 1941 might well have meant the collapse of Stalin and his regime—or else a cessation of hostilities on German terms. A German success on the Volga in 1942, rather than the disaster at Stalingrad, might also have meant Russian defeat—particularly if Hitler had been playing his other cards correctly.

But these potential victories eluded the grasp of the Germans. The Soviet advantages—manpower, quantity of materiel, space, and weather—finally prevailed. Yet while they lost the war, in the process of coping, just short of success, with those tremendous Soviet advantages, the German armies gave a performance of military virtuosity that has never been excelled—perhaps never even matched—by any other army of history.

The superb combat performance of the Wehrmacht was not lost on the Russians. It is evident from Soviet postwar literature that the Soviets have learned a great deal from their experience in World War II and—to a degree unmatched by the Western Allies—have taken those lessons to heart. Clear evidence of this surfaces in their final campaign of the war, in August 1945 in Manchuria. That blitzkrieg campaign can easily be compared to classic German models. Yet it had a typically Russian flavor: massive concentrations of men and guns on a scale more reminiscent of Kursk in 1943 than the German performance at Smolensk and Kiev in 1941 or in the Caucasus in 1942.

The tables in this book, which are based primarily on materials in various issues of the Soviet monthly magazine *Military-Historical Journal,* testify to the Soviet concern with statistical data concerning their operations in World War II and bear witness to their careful study of all conceivable aspects of these operations. We would do well to do more such historical studies ourselves.

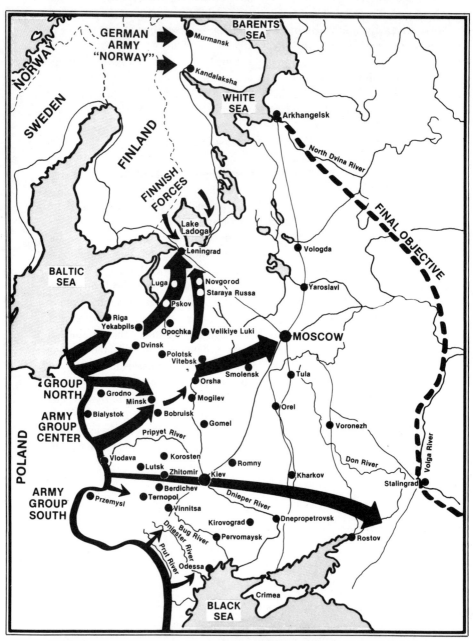

GERMAN CAMPAIGN PLAN FOR OPERATION BARBAROSSA

Operation Barbarossa

*The German Campaign in the Soviet Union,
Summer 1941*

In July 1940, a month after the triumphant conclusion of the German campaign in France, Hitler decided that in the spring of 1941 he would invade
the Soviet Union. He ordered the Army General Staff to prepare plans for the
campaign. The military objective was to defeat the Soviet armed forces in a
blitzkrieg of three to five months—or at least to advance far enough in that
time to capture the important production centers of European Russia, and to
seize so much Soviet territory that the industrial and armament plants of
eastern Germany and the oilfields of Romania would be beyond the range of
Soviet bombers.

The General Staff recognized the magnitude of the problems it faced: the
Red Army's numerical strength, the tremendous manpower potential of the
USSR, Russia's vast expanse and difficult terrain, and the severity of Russia's
winter, intensified by the problems of alternately very dry and very rainy
weather. It was obvious that a quick victory was essential.

At the same time, there were factors that could help achieve that victory.
The Red Army had performed so badly in the campaign against Finland in the
winter of 1939–40 that the German General Staff had a very low opinion of
the USSR's military capabilities. Moreover, it was generally assumed that the
people in the areas occupied by the Soviet Union in 1939 and 1940 (Poland,
the Baltic countries, and Bessarabia) were anti-Soviet, and that dissatisfaction
with the Communist system in the Ukraine, Byelorussia, the Crimea, and the
Caucasus was also widespread.

The ratio of strength between Soviet and German forces was certainly not
at all favorable. Against the equivalent of some 220 Soviet divisions, plus
ample reinforcements, the Germans could at best put 151 divisions, including

19 panzer divisions, into the field. Small contingents of Romanian and Finnish forces could be added to this total, but their equipment, capabilities, and combat efficiency were below German standards. Achievement of surprise could compensate somewhat for the disadvantage in numbers, but concealing an operation of this magnitude would be difficult, and in the final analysis the Germans could count on surprise only with respect to the direction and timing of the attack.

German Plans

The German planners realized that it was essential to engage Soviet forces decisively as close to the border as possible, in order to prevent them from taking advantage of Russia's great depth. Lacking sufficient forces to mount an offensive in strength along the entire front, the Germans decided to open gaps in the Soviet line at crucial points, to envelop and encircle Soviet forces, and to try to annihilate them before they had a chance to fall back.

The plan developed by the German General Staff called for a three-pronged attack: one army group would attack from East Prussia toward Leningrad; another would advance via Minsk toward Smolensk and Moscow; the third would drive south of the Pripyet Marshes toward Kiev, the coalfields of the Donets Basin, and the faraway oil of the Caucasus. The objective of the entire operation was to reach the Volga and the northern Dvina River.

In June 1941 the Wehrmacht's intelligence branch estimated Soviet strength at about 170 infantry divisions, 33.5 cavalry divisions, and 46 motorized and tank brigades. Of these, 118 infantry and 20 cavalry divisions and all of the motorized and tank brigades were assumed to be deployed in the western part of the USSR. The rest were in the interior—in Siberia, central Asia, and the Far East. Actually, according to Soviet sources, in June 1941 the Red Army had 170 divisions in the western part of the USSR, including 55 tank and mechanized divisions.

The total strength of the Soviet Air Force was estimated at about 7,000 aircraft, over 5,000 of them deployed in the western military districts close to the German border. These included: 2,700 fighters, 400 of them modern; 2,266 bombers, 750 of them modern; and 69 obsolete reconnaissance planes. In addition, the Baltic and Black Sea fleets had about 700 obsolete aircraft.

In early June 1941 the bulk of the Soviet forces were concentrated in three main areas: in the Baltic states; to the west of Minsk and near Bialystok and Grodno; and in the Ukraine in the Lvov-Lutsk-Ternopol area. There were strong operational reserves around Shepetovka, Proskurov, and Zhitomir, and also southwest of Minsk and in the Pskov area.

War Directive No. 21: Operation BARBAROSSA

On December 18, 1940, in War Directive No. 21, Adolf Hitler set forth the formal plan for his grand assault on the Soviet Union, code-named "Barbarossa." This directive embodied Hitler's desire to crush the USSR in a lightning campaign and to reach the Volga River and swing north to Arkhangelsk before the winter set in. If necessary, the easternmost Soviet industrial region—located in the Urals and beyond—would be destroyed by the Luftwaffe.

The German forces that were to participate in Barbarossa were organized in three army groups, designated Army Groups North, Center, and South, plus the German Army of Norway. The Finnish Army was to invade Russia after the start of the operation.

With its main forces massed on its right flank, Army Group North was to launch a powerful attack from central East Prussia through Kovno toward the area south of Pskov, to cut off Soviet forces in the Baltic states and push them back to the sea. Establishing itself around Lake Ilmen, Army Group North would then be in a favorable position for an advance toward Leningrad. The Fourth Panzer Group, in cooperation with the Sixteenth and Eighteenth armies, was to break through the Soviet border, advance along the Gumbinnen-Kovno highway, reach the area south of Pskov as soon as possible, and then continue to push toward the north or the northeast. The Sixteenth Army was to follow the panzer group via Dvinsk toward Pskov, making its main effort on its right flank. The Eighteenth Army was to concentrate its forces east of and along the Tilsit-Riga highway, break through the Soviet border defense positions, advance toward the northeast, cross the Dvina River near Yekabpils, and encircle and destroy Soviet forces southwest of Riga. Then the army was to push toward Pskov, thus preventing the withdrawal of the Red Army from the area southwest of Lake Peipus, and set the stage for the seizure of Estonia and the islands of Hiiumaa and Saaremaa.

Army Group Center was to mass extremely strong forces on both flanks. On the left, the Ninth Army and the Third Panzer Group were to break through the Soviet lines near Suwalki and push toward Molodechno and Orsha. On the right, the Fourth Army and Second Panzer Group were to advance along the main Baranovichi-Minsk-Orsha highway. The objective of the two forces was the encirclement and destruction of all Soviet forces between the border and Minsk. Thereafter the Second and Third Panzer groups would move on Smolensk from the southwest and northwest, to prevent Soviet forces from reorganizing along the upper Dnieper and Dvina rivers. The Fourth Army was to advance behind the Second Panzer Group through Bobruisk and Borisov toward Mogilev. At the same time, the Ninth

Army, taking advantage of the Third Panzer Group's advance, was to reach the Dvina around Polotsk.

Army Group South, committed south of the Pripyet Marshes, was to concentrate its main effort on its left flank, attacking in the direction of Kiev. After reaching the Dnieper River and taking Kiev, a strong panzer force would thrust deep into Soviet territory and envelop the Red forces west of the Dnieper by thrusting south along the lower Dnieper. The mixed German-Romanian forces in the south would tie down the opposing Soviet forces during the advance of the army group's left wing, and then launch an attack to prevent the Soviets from making an organized withdrawal across the Dnieper.

On the left, the Sixth Army was to screen the north flank of the army group along the Pripyet Marshes and follow the First Panzer Group closely to Zhitomir. Then the army would shift strong forces southeastward along the west bank of the Dnieper and join the First Panzer Group in the destruction of the Soviet forces fighting in the western Ukraine. The First Panzer Group was to thrust via Berdichev and Zhitomir toward the Dnieper River and Kiev, and then, bearing southeast along the Dnieper, block Soviet routes of withdrawal toward the east and destroy the enveloped or encircled Red troops. The Seventeenth Army was to attack from the vicinity of Przemysl toward Lvov and Vinnitsa, concentrating its main effort on the left flank. The Eleventh Army was to prevent possible Soviet penetration into Romania, tie down the Soviet forces opposite the Romanian border, and upon receiving specific orders from the army group launch an offensive, thus preventing the Soviet troops from making an organized withdrawal toward the Dnieper.

The Finnish Army would attack west of or on both sides of Lake Ladoga and seize the island of Hanko. The Finns were to time their offensive to coincide with Army Group North's crossing of the Dvina River. In the far north the German Army of Norway was to seize Murmansk, denying it to the Soviets as a base for attack against northern Finland and Norway. An attack toward Kandalaksha would cut Soviet lines of communication to Murmansk.

The plans prepared by the General Staff provided for a force buildup in four echelons. The first echelon was to begin to move into assembly areas in February. The second would start in mid-March and would be concentrated in rear areas away from the border. At the beginning of April, as late as possible in order to maintain secrecy, Hungary would have to be approached regarding the transit of troops. The third echelon was to begin its movement in mid-April. From then on concealment would become difficult. The transfer of the fourth echelon was planned for the period April 25–May 15.

The target date for Barbarossa was set at May 15. On March 27, 1941, however, an unexpected coup by Serbian officers in Yugoslavia caused Hitler to order an emergency operation in the Balkans that resulted in postponing the launching date to June 22, a delay of five and a half weeks.

Distribution of German Forces

Hitler and his top military commanders believed that they could defeat the Soviet Union in three or four months. There were 151.5 German divisions, including 19 panzer divisions, available for the invasion, distributed among the individual army groups and armies. (See Table 1.) The total strength was:

Officers and enlisted personnel	3,050,000
Tanks	3,350
Artillery pieces	7,184*
Motor vehicles (including armored reconnaissance cars)	600,000

Each army group was supported by an air fleet, with a total of about 2,000 planes, of which 1,160 were bombers and dive bombers, 720 were fighter planes, and 120 were reconnaissance planes.

Distribution of Soviet Forces

While the Germans were massing their troops in the east in the spring of 1941, the Soviet General Staff drew up a defense plan and began reorganizing the defenses of the western frontier, which was 4,500 kilometers long, including 1,125 kilometers of seacoast. Extensive mobilization was carried out in May and June. By the beginning of June, 790,000 reservists had been called up, increasing the total strength of the Soviet armed forces to nearly 5,400,000 effectives. Before the outbreak of war, Soviet official sources state, the Soviet Union had concentrated in its western regions 170 rifle, cavalry, tank, and motorized divisions and 2 rifle brigades, plus supporting units, with a total strength of 2,900,000 men. These forces possessed 1,800 heavy and medium tanks (including 1,475 modern KVs and T-34s), in addition to about two or three times as many light and obsolete tanks, 34,695 artillery guns and heavy and medium mortars, and some 5,000 aircraft, of which the Soviets considered only 1,540 to be of modern design.

The defense of the land frontier was organized in a zone 300 to 400 kilometers in depth. Close to the border, in the first echelon of defense, 56 divisions and 2 brigades were deployed up to 50 kilometers in depth. Behind them, divisions of the second echelon were 50 to 100 kilometers from the border. All tank divisions were deployed in the second and third echelons. Divisions of the first echelon had only a few units—up to one regiment— holding a broad front along the border, while the main force was kept in

---

* Soviet sources mention 48,000 guns and mortars. S. S. Lototskiy, *The Red Army* (Moscow, 1971). p. 114.

barracks or camps 10 to 50 kilometers to the rear. Average frontage per division was about 50 kilometers, and along the Prut River and in the Carpathians, 100 to 120 kilometers.

Official Soviet doctrine provided for 8 to 12 kilometers of front per division, or 25 to 30 kilometers in fortified areas. The actual frontages, however, were stretched longer and thinner; they had to permit coverage of the long frontier by available forces while still retaining density in a defense in depth. Also, in the frontier areas fortifications were still under construction. Even in those few areas where defensive structures had already been built, armament and equipment had not yet been installed.

This situation was aggravated by the fact that the Soviets, while building a new defensive line closer to the new frontier, had stripped the old fortifications some 150 kilometers to the east—the so-called Stalin Line—of all their armament and dismantled all other equipment. Thus when the war started the Red Army found itself practically without fortifications either near the frontiers or in the interior. This was one of the great blunders of World War II.

The Soviet forces in the western part of the USSR were organized in five military districts, to be called fronts (or army groups) on the outbreak of the war. The Leningrad Military District (Northern Army Group) covered the area north of Narva to Polyarnyy. The Baltic Special Military District (Northwestern Army Group) defended the south shore of the Gulf of Finland, the Baltic coast, and 300 kilometers of the East Prussian frontier. The Western Special Military District (Western Army Group) covered 450 kilometers from south of Suvalki to Vlodava. The Kiev Special Military District (Southwestern Army Group) stretched from Vlodava to Mogilev Podolskiy. The Odessa Military District (Southern Army Group) stretched from Kamenets Podolskiy to the Black Sea. The forces assigned to each military district (army group) are shown on Table 2.

On the eve of the war the planned concentration of Soviet forces was not yet completed. The so-called Reserve Army Group, a total of 32 divisions, had not yet been deployed on the line of the Western Dvina and Dnieper rivers as a second echelon. Soviet lack of preparedness was due to two principal causes: misjudgment of the possible time of German attack, despite plenty of warnings; and Stalin's conviction that it would be possible to avoid war in the summer of 1941, and thus win time. Therefore strict orders were given not to "provoke" the Germans by strengthening border defenses.

Toward the evening of June 21, however, it became obvious to the Soviet military leaders that Germany would attack the USSR within the next 24 hours. An immediate alert was ordered so that troops could be withdrawn from the frontier outposts to defendable positions, air units relocated to reserve airfields, the troops of the first echelon deployed along the lines of defense, and the deployment of the second echelon and reserves initiated.

However, the People's Commissariat of Defense was unable to communicate with the military districts until just after midnight on June 22. The Red Army therefore had less than three hours to prepare itself for the German assault.

The German Offensive

The German offensive began at 0315 on June 22, 1941, taking the Soviet forces along the border by surprise. In most places Soviet troops were caught in their camps and barracks. The Luftwaffe inflicted heavy initial losses on the Soviet Air Force, catching most of the planes on the ground and destroying about 2,000 in the first two days. Heavy bombers struck at Soviet towns, communications centers, rear installations, and naval bases, even before the Soviets officially announced the outbreak of war. The field fortifications in the border areas, either incomplete or unmanned, were quickly pierced by German troops.

By the end of June, the German High Command had good reason to be satisfied with the progress of the operation. In the Army Group North area the Dvina River had been crossed at Dvinsk and Yekabpils by June 26, and the Germans estimated that nearly 15 Soviet divisions had been destroyed in Lithuania and Latvia. However, the Soviets were offering strong resistance in a series of delaying actions.

In the Army Group Center area, Soviet forces west of Minsk had been encircled. The Second and Third panzer groups had linked up near Minsk on June 28. The surrounded units made an uncoordinated effort to break out of the pocket, with very limited success. Eventually some 20 Soviet divisions were wiped out in the Minsk pocket, and the Germans captured 300,000 prisoners, 1,500 tanks (most of them obsolete), and 1,400 guns.

In the Army Group South sector, the First Panzer Group reached the area east of Rovno, its advance having been repeatedly held up by Red Army counterattacks. Farther to the south, the advance of the Seventeenth Army had progressed to the area around the south of Lvov, but against strong resistance. Formations of the Soviet Southwestern Army group, having recovered from the initial shock, were showing considerable skill in blocking the advance.

The offensive of Army Group South hinged on the progress made by the Sixth Army and the First Panzer Group on the left flank. To achieve a decisive success the latter would have to penetrate the Red Army defenses that blocked the German axis of advance in the direction of Vinnitsa and Korosten. The mounting pressure exerted by the Soviet Fifth Army, which was threatening the German north flank from the Pripyet Marshes, also had to be eliminated. Moreover, to prepare the way for the encirclement of Soviet troops southwest of Berdichev, the Eleventh Army would have to advance northeastward toward Vinnitsa and assist the First Panzer Group.

By mid-July the Soviet Fifth Army had diverted much of the German Sixth Army from its original missions, but the First Panzer Group was advancing southeastward toward Uman; and the Seventeenth Army, despite stubborn Soviet resistance and heavy rain, had penetrated the Vinnitsa area. The Eleventh Army had reached the Dniester River.

After destroying Soviet forces in the Grodno-Minsk area, the objective of Army Group Center was to bring about the collapse of the vital Soviet defensive triangle anchored on Orsha, Smolensk, and Vitebsk. This would assure control of a corridor between the Dnieper and Dvina rivers through which the Germans could continue their advance toward Moscow. The Soviets were preparing a strong defense in this area, using fresh units and forces that had escaped from the Minsk pocket. Another Soviet concentration was being built up near Velikiye Luki, for future commitment against either Army Group Center or Army Group North. To accomplish its mission, Army Group Center planned a double envelopment, with the Second Panzer Group advancing in the general direction of Bobruisk-Roslav and the Third Panzer Group along the upper Dvina via Polotsk and Vitebsk. The infantry divisions of the Fourth and Ninth armies were to close up and support the armor.

The Soviet Orsha-Smolensk-Vitebsk defense line was crushed by mid-July, and the encirclement ring near Smolensk was closed when General Heinz Guderian's Second Panzer Group, coming from the southwest, met General Hermann Hoth's Third Panzer Group, advancing from the north. The Germans captured another 100,000 prisoners, some 1,000 tanks, and 1,900 guns. The Soviet forces, although split into isolated and encircled or enveloped groups, continued to resist stubbornly, slowing Army Group Center's advance toward Moscow, and occasionally even striking back. To divert the German forces from the Smolensk sector, a counteroffensive operation was carried out at Bobruisk by General F. I. Kuznetsov's Twenty-first Army. The Twentieth Army, under General P. A. Kurochkin, had pinned down several German divisions by enveloping both German flanks at Smolensk. Between July 10 and July 15 this army launched 22 counterattacks in division or corps strength.

In Army Group North, the Sixteenth Army fought its way eastward against stubborn resistance in the difficult terrain east of Opochka, while the Fourth Panzer Group turned northward, advancing between Lakes Ilmen and Peipus toward Leningrad. The two panzer corps of the Fourth Panzer Group became separated during the course of their advance. The corps on the right moved toward Novgorod with the aim of isolating Leningrad from the east. The corps on the left advanced along the eastern shore of Lake Peipus and toward Narva, to close the corridor between Lake Peipus and the Baltic and resume the advance toward Leningrad from the west.

This splitting of the Fourth Panzer Group was highly undesirable from the German point of view. The Army High Command had planned to keep the group intact until it reached the area southeast of Leningrad. The city would thus have been cut off from the east, and the way paved for the advance of the Finns along the shores of Lake Ladoga.

After one month of fighting, the effective strength of the average German infantry division had been reduced by approximately 20 percent, and that of panzer and motorized divisions by about 50 percent. By that time, German intelligence estimated that the number of Soviet divisions had decreased to 93, of which 78 were rifle, 13 tank, and 2 cavalry. However, Soviet sources indicate that a total of 324 divisions were dispatched to the front in the summer of 1941.

At the end of July the German Army High Command (Oberkommando des Heeres, or OKH) estimated that Army Group South would cross the Dnieper River by mid-August, and that Army Group Center, after mopping up Soviet pockets of resistance, might resume its advance around August 5. The Soviets were building up strength west of Moscow, where very strong opposition might be expected. Army Group North would probably have to regroup before it could launch a final drive on Leningrad.

Although Army Group South fought intense battles at Kiev and Korosten in July, it could not take Kiev. General Potapov's Soviet Fifth Army fought stubbornly northwest of Korosten, pinning down the entire German Sixth Army. In a month of bitter fighting, German troops managed to advance no more than 60 or 70 kilometers. However, to the south, the First Panzer Group had broken through the Soviet Sixth and Twelfth armies and was headed toward Pervomaysk.

During the first half of August, Army Group South partially succeeded in destroying Soviet forces on the western bank of the Dnieper River, where the main forces of the Soviet Southwestern Army Group were drawn into large-scale fighting. On August 5 the First Panzer Group and Seventeenth Army encircled the Soviet Sixth and Twelfth armies (about 16 divisions) near Uman. Thereupon the Soviet Supreme Headquarters ordered the bulk of the armies of the Southwestern and Southern army groups to retreat across the Dnieper and hold its left bank, while continuing to hold Kiev, Dnepropetrovsk, and several bridgeheads on the right bank. By the end of August the entire Dnieper bend was cleared of Soviet forces.

On July 20 the Soviet forces of the Western Army Group were ordered to counterattack, retake the region of Smolensk, and throw the Germans of Army Group Center back to Orsha. Although the Soviets' counteroffensive was not well organized, they struck in force at Smolensk, Yelna, and Yartsevo. Fierce fighting went on at Yelna, which the Germans were temporarily forced to give up, and Yartsevo changed hands several times. By August 10 the Germans had regained the initiative, but their plans had been seriously affected. Whereas in the first days of the war the Germans had advanced at an average daily rate of 30 kilometers, in late July and August their advance had dwindled to 6 or 7 kilometers a day.

During the early summer, Army Group North made progress on the right, and most of the infantry divisions succeeded in closing with two panzer corps along the Luga River and near Novgorod. By August 7 the German Eighteenth Army had split the two corps of the Soviet Eighth Army in northern Estonia, driving one corps back toward the city of Tallin and its naval base, which it defended for another three weeks, and the other Soviet corps to the Luga River line beyond Narva. On August 10, Field Marshal Wilhelm von Leeb's Army Group North launched a three-pronged attack on Leningrad. The main axes were (1) Narva-Kingisepp-Leningrad, (2) Luga-Leningrad, and (3) Keksholm-Leningrad. The Soviets responded by rushing three new armies to Leningrad and ordering the Northwestern Army Group to counterattack the German forces near Staraya Russa.

Meanwhile, the German Army of Norway had initiated its operations. Petsamo was occupied, but some units were bogged down near the Litsa River, and others, driving toward the Murmansk railroad, made very slow progress in the forests and swamps. The Karelian Army, under the Finnish High Command, advanced along the eastern shore of Lake Ladoga toward the pre-1940 Soviet-Finnish border. On the Karelian Isthmus the Finnish forces launched their offensive against Viipuri on July 31, after Soviet forces in the area had been weakened by the withdrawal of some units needed for the defense of Leningrad.

As the Germans pushed deeper into the Soviet heartland, the Soviet Government took steps to adjust the country's industry and armed forces to the situation. All defense matters were placed under a State Defense Committee, which mobilized industry, and among other measures moved more than 1,500 factories east beyond the Ural Mountains. Changes were made in the organization and command of the army, to strengthen control over its operations. To coordinate operations of the various army groups, commands were set up for the Northwestern, Western, and Southwestern theaters. Overall command was centralized in the General Headquarters of the Supreme High Command (Stavka), under Stalin as the Supreme Commander.

Hitler, convinced that the most important objectives were the Crimea and Leningrad, was insistent on peeling off the panzer forces from Army Group Center as soon as the fighting around Smolensk subsided. Hoth's Third Panzer Group was to be sent to assist Army Group North in its assault on Leningrad, and Guderian's Second Panzer Group would turn south and southeast to join Army Group South in destroying the Soviet Fifth Army and breaking into the rear of the Soviet Southwestern Army Group. Army Group Center would proceed toward Moscow as best it could with infantry alone.

Hitler's plans were opposed by many of the German top commanders, including General Franz Halder, Chief of the General Staff, and Field Marshal Walther von Brauchitsch, Commander in Chief of the German Army. The generals argued that to prevent the Soviets from building a defense line all the way from the Baltic to the Black Sea, along which they would attempt to stop the German advance before the onset of winter, the Red Army's resistance should be smashed by a concentrated thrust to Moscow. Since there was a maze of defensive positions to the west of the city, no quick advance to Moscow could be expected without panzer forces. On the contrary, such an operation would be costly and difficult, and might bog down altogether. By a concentrated combined-arms attack on Moscow the German Army could destroy the bulk of the Red Army, split the Soviet theater into two parts, and seriously impair Soviet unity of command. All secondary operations should be abandoned or at least curtailed unless they contributed to the basic concept of a powerful offensive against Moscow.

But Hitler was not interested in Moscow. To him the prime objectives remained capture of the Crimea and the industrial region of the south and cutting off the Soviets from the oil wells in the Caucasus, while at the same time encircling Leningrad and linking up with the Finns in the north. On August 21 he ordered a concentric attack by Army Group South and part of Army Group Center against the Soviet Southwestern Army Group.

Part of Guderian's Second Panzer Group was already near Gomel, on the southern flank of Army Group Center, and Guderian was ordered to divert his whole group south toward the Ukraine. The leading panzers attacked toward the Ukraine on August 25. On the third day they broke through the lines of the Soviet Thirteenth Army and captured intact the 700-meter-long bridge over the Desna River east of Novgorod Severskiy. On September 9 a weak spot in the Soviet defenses was found between Baturin and Konotop. Through it the panzers pushed southward toward Romny, where the Soviet defenders were so completely surprised that they were unable to take advantage of their well-prepared positions. Meanwhile the First Panzer Group and the Seventeenth Army had broken through the exhausted Soviet Thirty-eighth Army near Cherkassy and Kremenchug and headed northeast toward Romny. The two panzer groups made contact near Lekhvitsa, about 100 kilometers east of Kiev, on September 16, closing the outer encirclement of four armies of the Soviet Southwestern Army Group. The Second and Seventeenth Armies subsequently joined in an inner encirclement, capturing Kiev and part of the Ukraine east of the Dnieper.

German troops had reached the approaches to the Crimea, and nearly 600,000 Soviet troops had been encircled. Within the pocket, disorganization of the Soviet units was complete, and no concerted attempt was made to break out. The way was open for a sustained German drive eastward toward

Kharkov and Rostov, as the remnants of the Soviet Southwestern Army Group tried to establish a defense on the line Belopolye-Lebedin-Shishaki-Krasno-dar-Novomoskovsk.

Farther to the south, Romanian forces had blockaded and besieged Odessa, one of the main bases of the Soviet Black Sea Fleet. On August 10 they attacked the Soviet positions. Bloody fighting continued for over two months. Finally, with the Soviet position in the Ukraine and the Crimea extremely grave, Soviet troops abandoned the city on October 17.

Meanwhile, Army Group North had reached the outskirts of Leningrad by September 8, cutting all Soviet surface communications with the city except across Lake Ladoga. Attacks on the city were halted after several days, however, to avoid a long and savage battle through a city of immensely strong buildings, with a maze of canals and small waterways. Leeb, transferring his panzer forces to Army Group Center for the push to Moscow (which Hitler had now belatedly approved), tightened the ring around Leningrad, strengthened his eastern flank near the Valdai Hills, and improved his positions along the Volkhov River. Insufficient forces, bad weather, and fierce Soviet resistance prevented him from advancing east of Lake Ladoga to link up as planned with Finnish units.

German victories in the Ukraine and at the outskirts of Leningrad opened the way for a major thrust toward Moscow which commenced on September 30, 1941.

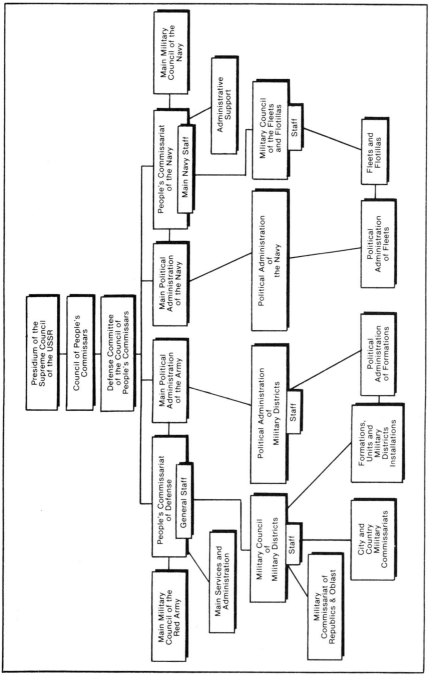

Organization of the Soviet Armed Forces (1940)

Table 1

Deployment of German Forces, Eastern Front
June 21, 1941

Army/Group	Location	Inf Div	Mtn Div	Pz Div	Mot Div	Cav Div	SS Div	Sec Div	Total	Air Fleet	Bombers	Ftr/Recon
Army Group South (FM Gerd von Rundstedt)												
Eleventh	Romania	7							7			
Seventeenth	Poland	10	1					2	13			
Sixth	Poland	5						1	6	Fourth	360	210/30
First Pz Group	Poland	6		5	2		1		14			
Reserve	Poland	1							1			
TOTALS		29	1	5	2		1	3	41			
Army Group Center (FM Fedor von Bock)												
Fourth	Poland	12						2	14			
Second Pz Group	Poland	6		5	2	1	1		15			
Ninth	Poland	7							7	Second	490	390/30
Third Pz Group	Poland	4		4	3				11			
Reserve	Poland	2						1	3			
TOTALS		31		9	5	1	1	3	50			
Army Group North (FM Wilhelm von Leeb)												
Sixteenth	East Prussia	8							8			
Fourth Pz Group	East Prussia	2		3	2		1		8	First	270	110/50
Eighteenth	East Prussia	7							7			
Reserve		3							3			
TOTALS		20		3	2		1		26			
OKH Reserve		21	1	2	1		1	2	28			
OKH TOTALS		101	2	19	10	1	4	8	145			
German Army of Norway (Gen. Nikolaus von Falkenhorst)												
Finnish III Corps									2			
German XXXVI Corps									2.5	Fifth	40	10/10
German Mtn Corps									2			
TOTALS									6.5			
EAST FRONT GRAND TOTAL									151.5		1,160	720/120

Source: OKH, *Kriegstaebuch*, I (Frankfurt, 1965)

Table 2

Deployment of Soviet Forces
June 21, 1941

Army/Corps	Location	Divisions				
		Rifle	Tank	Mechanized	Cavalry	Total
Leningrad Military District (Northern Army Group) (Lt. Gen. M. M. Popov)						
Twenty-third	Viipuri-Keksholm					
Seventh	N&NE Lake Ladoga					
Fourteenth	Belomorsk-Murmansk					
X Mechanized Corps	Karelian Isthmus					
TOTALS		19	—	1	—	20
Baltic Special Military District (Northwestern Army Group) (Col. Gen. F. I. Kuznetsov)						
Eighth	East Prussian frontier					
Eleventh	East Prussian frontier					
Twenty-seventh	South of Pskov					
TOTALS		19	4	2	—	25
Western Special Military District (Western Army Group) (Army Gen. D. G. Pavlov)						
Third Army	Grodno area					
XI Mechanized Corps	Grodno area					
Tenth Army	Bialystok area					
VI Mechanized Corps	Bialystok area					
XIII Mechanized Corps	Bialystok area					
Fourth Army	Brest-Pinsk area					
XIV Mechanized Corps	Brest-Pinsk area					
Thirteenth Army	Minsk (reserve)					
Sixteenth Army	Bobruisk					
V Mechanized Corps	Bobruisk					
VII Mechanized Corps	Bobruisk					
Twenty-first Army	Gomel					
Twenty-second Army	Vitebsk					
TOTALS		24	12	6	2	44
Kiev Special Military District (Southwestern Army Group) (Col. Gen. M. P. Kirponos)						
Fifth Army	Lutsk area					
XXII Mechanized Corps	Lutsk area					
Sixth Army	Lvov area					
IV Mechanized Corps	Lvov area					
Twenty-sixth Army	Borislav					
VIII Mechanized Corps	Striy					

Table 2—(continued)
Deployment of Soviet Forces
June 21, 1941

| Army/Corps | Location | Divisions | | | | Total |
		Rifle	Tank	Mechanized	Cavalry	
Twelfth Army	Kamenets Podolskiy- Chernovtsy					
XV Mecha- nized Corps	Radekhov- Ostrog					
XIX Mecha- nized Corps (+ 1 rifle corps)	Zhitomir (reserve)					
TOTALS		32	16	8	3	59
Odessa Military District (Southern Army Group) (Army Gen. I. V. Tyulenev)						
Ninth Army	Moldavia					
Eighteenth Army	Northwest of Odessa					
IV Independent Rifle Corps	Crimea					
TOTALS		13	4	2	3	22
GRAND TOTALS		107	36	19	8	170

Table 3
Men and Equipment
June 20, 1941

Men and Equipment	German	Soviet
Officers and men	3,050,000	2,900,000
Tanks	3,350	1,800
Artillery pieces	7,184	34,695
Motor vehicles (including armored reconnaissance cars)	600,000	not available

Table 4
Soviet Air Forces on the Western Border
June 20, 1941

Military District Air Forces[1]	Bombers	Fighters	Reconnaissance	Total
Leningrad	558	585	12	1,155
Baltic	300	315	15	630
Western	640	770	20	1,430
Kiev	448	625	12	1,085
Odessa	320	405	10	735
TOTAL	2,266	2,700	69	5,035[2]

[1] On June 22 the Leningrad, Baltic, Western, Kiev, and Odessa military districts were reorganized respectively into Northern, Northwestern, Western, Southwestern, and Southern army groups.

[2] About 70% of the planes were obsolete.

Table 5
German Air Forces
June 20, 1941

Air Force	Bomber	Fighter	Reconnaissance	Total
Fourth (Army Group South)	360	210	30	600
Second (Army Group Center)	490	390	30	910
First (Army Group North)	270	110	50	430
Fifth (Finland)	40	10	10	60
TOTAL	1,160	720	120	2,000

Table 6
Personnel Strength of the Soviet Armed Forces
May 1940–June 1941

Armed Forces Services	May 1940		June 1941	
	Number	Percent of Total	Number	Percent of Total
Ground forces	3,542,300	84.2	4,383,000	81.6
Air Force	244,000	5.8	476,000	8.8
Navy	315,500	7.5	344,000	6.4
Air Defense of the Country	105,100	2.5	170,000	3.2
TOTAL	4,206,900	100.0	5,373,000	100.0

Table 7

Strength of Soviet Combat Ground and Air Forces
December 1, 1941

Troops and Combat Equipment	Western Front	Other Areas	Supreme Headquarters Reserve	Total
Men	3,394,000	1,568,000	531,000	5,493,000
Tanks				
Total	1,954	2,541	—	4,495
Medium and heavy	533	27	—	560
Aircraft				
Total	2,238	2,951	85	5,274
Modern	1,289	165	64	1,518

Table 8

Strength of German Allies
July 1941

	Infantry and Motorized Divisions	Infantry and Motorized Brigades	Cavalry Brigades	Tanks	Guns and Mortars	Combat Aircraft	Ships
Finland	16	2	1	86	c. 2,000	307	52
Romania	13	6	3	60	c. 3,000	623	57
Hungary	—	3	1	116	c. 200	48	—

Table 9
Soviet Armament and Ammunition Production
July 1–December 31, 1941

Type	Number
Tanks	4,800
Combat aircraft	8,200
Other aircraft	1,600
Guns and howitzers	
76mm and larger	9,900
Less than 76mm	20,300
Mortars	
82mm and larger	19,100
Less than 82mm	23,200
Machine guns	1,062,000
Submachine guns	897,000
Rifles and carbines	1,600,000
Ammunition (bombs, mines, shells)	62,900,000

Table 10
German Infantry and Artillery Weapons Production
1940 and 1941

Types	1940	1941
Rifles and carbines	1,352,000	1,359,000
Submachine and machine guns	171,000	325,000
Mortars	4,000	4,200
Guns and howitzers (75mm and larger)	6,100	7,200

Table 11
German Production of Tanks and Assault Guns
January 1–June 30, 1941

Period	Type and Number of Tanks						Number of Assault Guns	Total Tanks and Assault Guns
	M-II	T-38 (Czech)	M-III	M-IV	Command	Total		
Jan 1–Mar 31	7	148	288	85	60	588	104	692
Apr 1–Jun 30	42	192	400	103	41	778	151	929
TOTAL	49	340	688	188	101	1,366	255	1,621

Table 12

Strength of Front Line German Ground and Air Forces
December 1, 1941

Troops and Combat Equipment	Soviet-German Front	North Africa	Total	Occupied Countries and Germany	Grand Total
Men	3,200,000	50,000	3,250,000	2,748,000	5,998,000
Division equivalent	155.5	3	158.5	60.5	219
Tanks and assault guns	1,650	300	1,950	3,665	5,615
Combat aircraft	2,040	450	2,490	2,688	5,178

Table 13

Personnel and Equipment Strength
December 1941

Men and Equipment	USSR	Germany
Ground forces	5,493,000	5,998,000
Air Force	563,000	1,710,000
Navy	514,000	490,000
TOTAL	6,570,000	8,198,000
Tanks and assault guns	4,495	5,615
Combat aircraft	7,409	5,178
Combat ships		
Battleships	2	5
Cruisers	7	7
Destroyers	42	27
Submarines	190	253
TOTAL	241	292

The Defense of Moscow

October–November 1941

The first three months of the Soviet-German war had brought stunning victories to the Wehrmacht. Army Group North took the Baltic states and reached the gates of Leningrad. Army Group South captured almost the entire Ukraine and opened the roads to the Crimea and the Caucasus.

In the center of the huge German-Soviet front, pointed directly toward Moscow, was Army Group Center under Field Marshal Fedor von Bock. In September, it was deployed along the general line Rogachev-Roslavl-Yartsevo-Belyy-Andreapol, about 300 kilometers west of the Soviet capital.

The capture of Moscow was one of the most important German objectives of the war. The German Army High Command (OKH) believed that with its capture Soviet resistance would cease and the Soviet state would collapse. It was imperative to take the city before the onset of winter, and both OKH and the commander of Army Group Center believed that, despite delays caused by Hitler's decision in August to take the Ukraine first, the mission would be accomplished.

The offensive toward Moscow was code-named Operation Typhoon. It was to commence late in September and be concluded in four to six weeks. Offensively deployed, Army Group Center was organized in three field armies (Second, Fourth, and Ninth) and three panzer groups and was composed of 76 divisions, including 14 panzer and 8 motorized. It had over 1,000,000 men, nearly 2,000 tanks, almost 14,000 artillery pieces and mortars, and some 1,000 aircraft. The main effort was concentrated on the northern and southern flanks of the army group, where panzer and mobile elements were committed.

Facing the German onslaught were, from north to south, the Western,

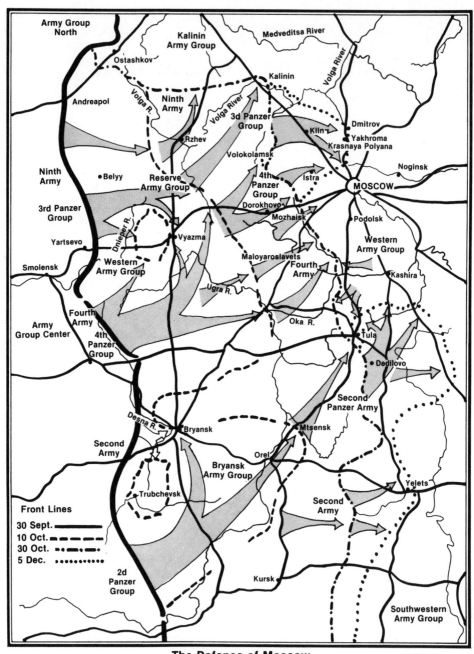

**The Defense of Moscow
October-November 1941**

Reserve and Bryansk army groups. Together they numbered 1,250,000 men and had 850 tanks (of which 700 were light), some 7,000 guns and mortars, and fewer than 600 combat-ready aircraft.

The German drive on Moscow started early in the morning of September 30, with attacks by the Second Panzer Group and the Second Army against the Soviet Bryansk Army Group. Two days later, on October 2, the Fourth and the Ninth armies, supported by the Third and Fourth panzer groups, launched an assault against the Western and Reserve army groups.

At the outset the German operation was very successful. In the southern sector, the Second Panzer Group took Orel, a major industrial city, and by October 8, in cooperation with the Second Army, had encircled the Soviet Bryansk Group of forces and overwhelmed or destroyed three Russian armies.

In the center, the Fourth and Ninth armies, spearheaded by panzer elements, broke through strong Soviet defenses to the north and south of Vyazma, then quickly advanced eastward. Their outer wings converged at a point east of Vyazma. By doing so, the Germans formed a pocket that sealed the fate of eight Soviet armies.

Altogether, in the battles of Bryansk and Vyazma eleven Soviet armies were destroyed, and Army Group Center captured about 650,000 officers and men and took or destroyed nearly 800 tanks, 3,700 artillery pieces and mortars, 480 antitank guns, 400 antiaircraft guns, and 49 aircraft.

Although the liquidation of the encircled Soviet forces in the Bryansk area took more time than expected, by mid-October the bulk of Army Group Center found itself some 100 kilometers west of Moscow. OKH expected to take the city itself before the Russian winter set in for good.

For the Soviets, the situation grew more precarious day by day, if not by the hour. The Mozhaisk defense line west of Moscow was penetrated in several places. Almost all of the already meager Soviet reserves were committed to the battle. All ministries, agencies, and diplomatic missions were evacuated to the east. Even the General Staff left Moscow, leaving only an operational group in the city.

To alleviate this dangerous situation, directives were issued to prepare two defense perimeters on the close approaches to Moscow, the first 15 to 20 kilometers from the center of the city, and the second just outside the limits of the city proper. The Reserve Army Group was disbanded and its forces transferred to the Western Army Group, which came under the command of one of the ablest Soviet generals, Georgiy Zhukov. To defend the northwestern approaches to the capital, a four-army Kalinin Army Group was organized, under General Ivan Konev.

Toward the end of October and early in November, as the rainy season turned the roads into impassable quagmires, Soviet resistance stiffened. The advance of the Fourth Army and the Fourth Panzer Group bogged down at the Oka and Nara rivers and east of the Ruza River. To the north, the Ninth Army, supported by the Third Panzer Group, attempting to envelop Moscow from the northwest and north, was unable to reach Kalinin.

The Second Panzer Army (the Second Panzer Group was renamed Second Panzer Army on October 6, 1941) encountered heavy resistance south of Tula, and despite intense efforts could not make any progress.

Unable to continue the advance under these circumstances, the German command decided to take advantage of the stalemate by bringing up reserves and increasing the flow of supplies. Then the offense would be resumed at the onset of frost in mid-November. There would be rapid drives to envelop Moscow from the north and south and to close the ring at Noginsk, east of Moscow.

Anticipating such a renewed German attack, the Stavka too continued to build up the front-line forces, reinforcing the Western Army Group by some 100,000 men, 300 tanks, and 2,000 artillery pieces and mortars. Nearly 1,500 aircraft were concentrated in the Moscow area.

The Soviets had one great advantage over the Germans. Their troops were equipped and prepared for winter warfare. The Germans were not. The German soldiers, inadequately clad, were freezing; their motorized equipment was hampered by inadequate lubricants.

The final German offensive toward Moscow started on November 15. On the German left flank, northwest of Moscow, elements of the Ninth Army and the Third Panzer Group broke through the defense lines of the Kalinin Army Group, took Kalinin, and cut the Moscow-Leningrad highway and railroad line.

In the center, the Fourth Army and the Fourth Panzer Group encountered stubborn Soviet resistance and advanced very slowly. Especially heavy fighting developed along the Volokolamsk highway. Nevertheless, in ten days the Germans advanced nearly 60 kilometers. On November 26 they were on the Moscow-Klin highway, less than 50 kilometers from the Kremlin.

On the German right flank, the Second Panzer Army, which had resumed its operations south and southeast of Tula, was able to advance only a few kilometers per day.

The German offensive seemed to have the best chance of success in the northern sector. There, elements of the Third Panzer Group took Yakhroma, while the Fourth took Krasnaya Polyana, approaching within 25 kilometers of Moscow. On November 29, the 7th Panzer Division of the Third Panzer Group captured a bridge across the Moscow-Volga Canal and established a bridgehead on the east bank of the Canal.

This was the height of the German progress. While General Hans Reinhard, commander of the Third Panzer Group, tried to reinforce his troops at the bridgehead in order to continue the advance, the Russians committed the

First Strike Army from GHQ reserve and forced the Germans to withdraw from the bridgehead.

German efforts to develop success in the Krasnaya Polyana area also failed. In fierce fighting with fresh Soviet troops, the Fourth Panzer Group was halted, and some of its units had to retreat.

In the south, sudden Soviet counterattacks by two armies pushed back Guderian's Second Panzer Army. General Guderian called a halt to the offensive and, in defiance of Hitler's explicit directive, ordered his main forces to withdraw to the Tula-Uzlovaya railroad line.

As the German advance on the flanks suffered serious reverses, Bock came to realize that he could be successful only if the Fourth Army made a simultaneous major effort in the center. This would not only pin down Soviet forces; it would induce the Soviet Command to throw some of its fresh troops against the Fourth Army, and in this way facilitate the panzer attacks on the flanks.

On December 1, the Fourth Army launched an attack across the Nara River between Panino and Dorokhovo. Fighting with determination, German units managed to penetrate Soviet defenses to various depths. However, after one day of fighting the German attack bogged down. Only one small unit, an advance detachment of the 258th Infantry Division, advanced as far as Aprelevka, a suburb of Moscow. But there, counterattacked by Soviet tanks, it was forced to retreat.

On December 3, when it became obvious that the attack could not succeed, the offensive was ordered to cease, and the Fourth Army withdrew to the original jump-off positions behind the Nara River without serious Soviet interference. At the same time orders to halt the offensive and take up defensive positions were issued to all remaining armies of Army Group Center.

This was the end of German efforts to take the Soviet capital. Hitler's hopes of knocking out the Soviet Union in 1941 collapsed. The blitzkrieg came to an end, and the initiative passed to the Red Army, which started a major counteroffensive on December 5.

Table 1

Composition of Soviet Forces Deployed in Defense of Moscow[1] October–November 1941

	October 1, 1941 Army Groups				November 15, 1941 Army Groups			
	Western	Reserve	Bryansk	Total	Kalinin	Western	Southwestern (Third and Thirteenth) armies	Total
Combined arms armies	6	6	3	15	3	7[2]	2	12
Air corps						1		1
Rifle divisions	30	28	25	83[3]	14	35	12	61[4]
Motorized rifle divisions	2			2		3		3
Tank divisions			1	1		3		3
Cavalry divisions	3	2	4	9	1	12	4	17
Motorized rifle brigades	1			1	1			1
Tank brigades	4	5	4	13	1	16	2	19
Independent rifle, cavalry, and motorcycle regiments	2		1	3	2	8	1	11
Independent tank battalions			3	3		2		2
Artillery regiments	23	16	13	52	10	32	2	44
Antitank artillery regiments	5	11	3	19	1	22	2	25
Independent artillery battalions	1	3		4	1	1		2
Independent mortar battalions	2	1		3	1	2		3
Independent MRL regiments	3		2	5		2	1	3
Independent MRL battalions		1		1		22		22
Antiaircraft defense brigades	1			1				1
Antiaircraft brigade defense areas	5			5	1	2		3
Independent AAA battalions	11	5	7	23	5	21	1	27
Independent engineer battalions	30	12	7	49	10	32	5	47

[1] Does not include the I AAA Defense Corps and the Tula AA Defense Brigade. While protecting military and industrial targets in Moscow and the Moscow area, they were not part of the army groups.

[2] The Thirtieth Army shown in the Western Army Group, since it was transferred November 17, 1941, from the Kalinin Army Group to the Western Army Group.

[3] Average actual strength of rifle divisions: in the Western Army Group—10,500; in the Reserve Army Group—8,000; in the Bryansk Army Group—6,600 men.

[4] Average actual strength of rifle divisions: in the Western Army Group—6,500; in the Kalinin Army Group—5,600; in the Southwestern Army Group—2,500.

Table 2
Soviet Strengths
October 1, 1941

	Western Army Group		Reserve Army Group		Bryansk Army Group		Three Army Groups	
	Total	In Combat Units Only	Total	In Combat Units Only	Total	In Combat Units Only	Total	In Combat Units Only
Personnel	540,375	320,606	471,912	358,843	240,304	188,363	1,252,591	867,812
Rifles	339,862	245,340	322,581	267,854	169,156	147,213	831,599	660,407
Submachine guns	2,678	2,289	3,490	3,370	2,826	2,597	8,994	8,256
Light machine guns	5,418	4,015	6,025	4,376	2,372	2,084	13,815	10,475
Heavy machine guns	2,167	1,848	3,288	3,147	1,440	1,362	6,895	6,357
Antiaircraft machine guns	350	152	285	184	104	83	739	419
Tanks:								
Heavy	19	19	10	10	18	18	47	47
Medium	32	32	29	29	33	33	94	94
Light	413	389	262	220	33	32	708	641
TOTAL	464	440	301	259	84	83	849	782
Artillery guns:								
107mm and larger	956	947	723	723	318	318	1,997	1,988
76mm	613	586	758	354	366	365	1,737	1,305
45mm	408	386	386	369	198	196	992	951
76–85mm antiaircraft	266	251	287	264	34	34	587	549
25–37mm antiaircraft	108	93	151	129	65	65	324	287
TOTAL	2,351	2,263	2,305	1,839	981	978	5,637	5,080
Mortars:								
107–120mm	227	209	183	179	82	82	492	470
82mm	547	521	624	616	122	121	1,293	1,258
50mm	911	864	1,699	1,656	566	566	3,176	3,086
TOTAL	1,685	1,594	2,506	2,451	770	769	4,961	4,814
Armored cars	92	54	84	71	38	35	214	160
Cars and trucks	30,386	12,182	22,745	13,671	9,520	5,760	62,651	31,613
Horses	96,842	66,028	82,258	74,866	47,504	43,531	226,604	184,425

Table 3

Composition and Strength of the Soviet Air Force
October 1, 1941

	Army Groups			Long Range Bombers	Total
	Western	Reserve	Bryansk		
Air divisions					
Bomber	1	—	—	5	6
Mixed	4	3	3	—	10
TOTAL	5	3	3	5[1]	16
Air regiments[2]					
Bomber	4	3	4	18	29
Ground attack	2	1	2	—	5
Fighter	8	7	4	—	19
TOTAL	14	11	10	18	53
Aircraft					
Bombers—total	99	43	68	368	578
Combat ready	80	20	47	154	301
Ground attack—total	14	6	16	—	36
Combat ready	7	1	5	—	13
Fighters—total	146	77	62	—	285
Combat ready	114	44	43	—	201
Reconnaissance—total	13	—	24	—	37
Combat ready	13	—	17	—	30
TOTAL AIRCRAFT	272	126	170	368	936
TOTAL COMBAT READY	214	65	112	154	545

[1] 40th, 42d, 51st, 52d, and 81st long range bomber divisions.

[2] Includes independent air regiments and those in air divisions.

Table 4

Composition and Strength of the Soviet Air Force
November 10, 1941

	Army Groups			AF Moscow Military District (The Sbytov Task Force)	Long Range Bombers	VI Fighter Air Corps Antiair Defense Forces	Total
	Kalinin	Western	Right Wing Southwestern				
Air divisions							
Bomber	—	2	—	—	7[1]	—	9
Mixed	—	6	3	—	—	—	9
TOTAL	—	8	3	—	7	—	18
Air regiments[2]							
Bomber	1	10	4	1	23	—	39
Ground attack	—	4	1	1	—	—	6
Fighter	2	10	4	2	1	24	43
TOTAL	3	24	9	4	24	24	88
Combat aircraft							
Bombers							
Total	12	125	21	—	265	—	423
Combat ready	2	104	10	—	87	—	203
Ground attack							
Total	5	25	7	9	—	—	46
Combat ready	5	12	6	5	—	—	28
Fighter							
Total	36	87	33	25	6	471	658
Combat ready	18	61	15	21	4	378	497
Reconnaissance							
Total	—	6	5	—	—	—	11
Combat ready	—	6	4	—	—	—	10
TOTAL AIRCRAFT	53	243	66	34	271	471	1,138
TOTAL COMBAT READY	25	183	35	26	91	378	738

[1] 26th, 40th, 42d, 51st, 52d, 81st, and 133d long range bomber divisions.
[2] Includes independent regiments and those in air divisions.

Table 5

Composition of German Army Group Center
Fall 1941

	October 1	November 1	November 15
Field armies	3	3	3
Panzer armies	—	1	1
Panzer groups	3	2	2
Army corps	15[1]	14	14
Motorized corps	8	8	8
Divisions[2]			
Infantry	50	49	47
Panzer	14	14	14
Motorized	8	8	8
Security	3	3	3
Cavalry	1	1	1
Total	76	75	73
Brigades			
Infantry	—	1	1
Motorized	2	2	2
Cavalry	1	1	1
Total	3	4	4
TOTAL DIVISIONS AND BRIGADES	79	79	77
TOTAL DIVISION EQUIVALENT	77.5	77	75
Percentage of divisions deployed on the Soviet-German front			
a) infantry and security divisions	31.6	33.7	34.2
b) panzer and motorized divisions	63.8	63.0	63.0

[1] Includes the II Army Corps (three infantry divisions) of Sixteenth Army, Army Group North.
[2] Average strength of the divisions:

a) infantry	15,200	14,300	13,500
b) panzer	14,400	13,600	12,800
c) motorized	12,600	11,900	11,200

Table 6

Operational Deployment of Soviet Forces
October 1, 1941

	Total		First Echelon		Second Echelon		Reserve	
	Divisions	Brigades	Divisions	Brigades	Divisions	Brigades	Divisions	Brigades
Western Army Group								
Twenty-second Combined Arms Army	6	—	5	—	1	—	—	—
Twenty-ninth Combined Arms Army	4	1	3	1	1	—	—	—
Thirteenth Combined Arms Army	4	—	3	—	1	—	—	—
Nineteenth Combined Arms Army	5	1	4	—	1	1	—	—
Sixteenth Combined Arms Army	4	—	3	—	1	—	—	—
Twentieth Combined Arms Army	4	—	2	—	2	—	—	—
Army Group's Reserve	8	3	—	—	—	—	8	3
TOTAL	35	5	20	1	7	1	8	3
Reserve Army Group								
a) First Line								
Twenty-fourth Combined Arms Army	6	2	4	—	2	2	—	—
Forty-third Combined Arms Army	4	2	3	—	1	2	—	—
5th Rifle Division, Thirty-first Combined Arms Army	1	—	1	—	—	—	—	—
TOTAL	11	4	8	—	3	4	—	—
b) Second Line (Thirty-first, Thirty-second, Thirty-third, and Forty-ninth combined arms armies)	19	1	12	—	7	1	—	—
TOTAL	30	5	20	—	10	5	—	—
Bryansk Army Group								
Fiftieth Combined Arms Army	8	—	8	—	—	—	—	—
Third Combined Arms Army	6	1	6	—	—	1	—	—
Thirteenth Combined Arms Army	8	2	8	—	—	—	—	—
Yermakov's Task Force	5	1	4	—	—	—	1	2
Army Group's Reserve	3	—	—	—	—	—	3	1
TOTAL	30	4	26	—	—	1	4	3
OVERALL TOTAL	95	14	66	1	17	7	12	6

Table 7

Operational Deployment of Soviet Forces
November 15, 1941

	Total		First Echelon		Second Echelon		Reserves	
	Divisions	Brigades	Divisions	Brigades	Divisions	Brigades	Divisions	Brigades
Kalinin Army Group								
Twenty-second Combined Arms Army	6	1	5	1	—	—	1	—
Twenty-ninth Combined Arms Army	5	—	3	—	2	—	—	—
Thirty-first Combined Arms Army	4	—	4	—	—	—	—	—
TOTAL	15	1	12	1	2	—	1	—
Western Army Group								
Thirtieth Combined Arms Army	7	2	5	2	2	—	—	—
Sixteenth Combined Arms Army	8	3	4	—	4	3	—	—
Fifth Combined Arms Army	5	5	4	1	1	4	—	—
Thirty-third Combined Arms Army	5	1	3	1	2	—	—	—
Forty-third Combined Arms Army	4	6*	4	4	—	2	—	—
Forty-ninth Combined Arms Army	6	—	4	—	2	—	—	—
Fiftieth Combined Arms Army	10	2	7	—	2	1	1	1
Army Group's Reserve	6	—	—	—	—	—	6	—
TOTAL	51	19	31	8	13	10	7	1
Right wing of the Southwestern Army Group								
Third Combined Arms Army	7	2	7	—	—	—	—	2
Thirteenth Combined Arms Army	8	—	6	—	2	—	—	—
TOTAL	15	2	13	—	2	—	—	2
OVERALL TOTAL	81	22	56	9	17	10	8	3

* Two airborne brigades and four tank brigades.

Table 8
Operational Density of German Forces

Formations	October 1, 1941						November 15, 1941		
	Frontage (kms)		Division Equivalent[1]		Frontage/Div (kms)		Frontage (kms)	Division Equivalent	Frontage /Div (kms)
	Total	Breakthrough Sector	Total	Breakthrough Sector	Entire Front	Breakthrough Sector			
Army Group North									
II Army Corps, Sixteenth Field Army	60	—	3.0	—	20.0	—	—	—	—
Army Group Center									
Ninth Field Army and Third Tank Army	250	50	24.5	12.0	10.2	4.2	250	20.0	12.5
Fourth Field Army and Fourth Tank Group	125	50	23.0	13.0	5.4	3.8	230	29.0	8.0
Second Field Army and Second Tank Group	125	30	9.5	6.0	13.2	5.0	160	9.0	17.8
Second Tank Army (from October 6)	200	80	14.5	12.0	13.8	6.7	230[2]	14.0	14.3
Army Group's Reserve	—	—	3.0	—	—	—	—	3.0	—
TOTAL	760	210	77.5	43.0[3]	9.8[4]	4.9	870	75.0[5]	11.6

[1] In tabulation, two brigades equal one division.

[2] Excluding the 30 kms sector on the right flank of the Second Tank Army to the west of Yefremov, not occupied by troops.

[3] Including 21 panzer and motorized divisions instead of 23 divisions, which were in the Army Group Center. During the first two days of October, the 9th Panzer and the 25th motorized divisions were still on the march toward the combat zone.

[4] Operational density includes reserve of Army Group Center. Without reserves the density was 10.2 kms/div on October 1 and 12.1 kms/div on November 15.

[5] Including 23 panzer and motorized divisions.

Table 9

Frontage and Operational Density of Soviet Forces
October 1, 1941

	Divisions	Brigades	Div Equivalents[1]		Frontage (kms)	Kms/ Division
			Tank, Motorized	Total		
Western Army Group						
Twenty-second Combined Arms Army	6	—	—	6.0	85	14.2
Twenty-ninth Combined Arms Army	4	1	0.5	4.5	75	16.7
Thirtieth Combined Arms Army	4	—	—	4.0	70	17.5
Nineteenth Combined Arms Army	5	—	—	5.0	40	8.0
Sixteenth Combined Arms Army	4	1	0.5	4.5	25	5.6
Twentieth Combined Arms Army	4	—	—	4.0	45	11.3
Army Group's Reserve	8	3	3.5	9.5	—	—
TOTAL	35	5	4.5	37.5	340	9.1
Reserve Army Group						
a) First line						
5th Rifle Division, Thirty-first Combined Arms Army	1	—	—	1.0	30	30.0
Twenty-fourth Combined Arms Army	6	2	1.0	7.0	40	5.7
Forty-third Combined Arms Army	4	2	1.0	5.0	60	12.0
TOTAL	11	4	2.0	13.0	130	10.0
b) Second line						
Thirty-first Combined Arms Army (less 5th Rifle Division)	4	—	—	4.0	90	22.5
Thirty-second Combined Arms Army	4	—	—	4.0	60	15.0
Thirty-third Combined Arms Army	5	1	0.5	5.5	—	—
Forty-ninth Combined Arms Army	6	—	—	6.0	40	6.7
TOTAL	19	1	0.5	19.5	190	9.7

Table 9—(continued)

Frontage and Operational Density of Soviet Forces
October 1, 1941

	Divisions	Brigades	Div Equivalents[1]		Frontage (kms)	Kms/ Division
			Tank, Motorized	Total		
Bryansk Army Group						
Fiftieth Combined Arms Army	8	—	—	8.0	100	12.5
Third Combined Arms Army	6	—	—	6.0	70	11.7
Thirteenth Combined Arms Army	8	1	0.5	8.5	60	7.1
Yermakov's Task Force	5	2	1.0	6.0	60	10.0
Army Group's Reserve	3	1	1.5	3.5	—	—
TOTAL	30	4	3.0	32.0	290	9.1
TOTAL of three army groups[2]	76	13	9.5	82.5	760	9.2

[1] In tabulation two tank, motorized, or rifle brigades equal one division.

[2] Excluding second line divisions of the Reserve Army Group.

Table 10

Frontage and Operational Density of Soviet Forces
November 15, 1941

			Div Equivalents[1]			
	Divisions	Brigades	Tank, Motorized	Total	Frontage (kms)	Kms/ Division
Kalinin Army Group						
Twenty-second Combined Arms Army	6	1	0.5	6.5	120	18.4
Twenty-ninth Combined Arms Army	5	—	—	5.0	40	8.0
Thirty-first Combined Arms Army	4	—	—	4.0	40	10.0
TOTAL	15	1	0.5	15.5	200	12.9
Western Army Group						
Thirtieth Combined Arms Army	7	2	3.0	8.0	70	8.8
Sixteenth Combined Arms Army	8	3	1.5	9.5	70	7.4
Fifth Combined Arms Army	5	5	3.5	7.5	50	6.7
Thirty-third Combined Arms Army	5	1	1.5	5.5	30	5.5
Forty-third Combined Arms Army	4	6	2.0	7.0	30	4.3
Forty-ninth Combined Arms Army	6	—	—	6.0	80	13.3
Fiftieth Combined Arms Army	10	2	2.0	11.0	70	6.4
Army Group's Reserve	6	—		1.0	6.0	—	—
TOTAL	51	19	14.5	60.5	400	6.6
Right wing of the Southwestern Army Group						
Third Combined Arms Army	7	2	1.0	8.0	120	15.0
Thirteenth Combined Arms Army	8	—	—	8.0	150	18.8
TOTAL	15	2	1.0	16.0	270	16.9
OVERALL TOTAL	81[2]	22	16.0	92.0	870	9.5

[1] In tabulation, two tank, motorized or rifle brigades equal one division.

[2] Includes 15 cavalry, 3 tank, and 3 motorized.

Table 11

Tactical Density of Soviet Forces
October 1, 1941

Army Groups	Frontage (km)	Combat Troops	Men/Km	Field Artillery and Mortars			AT and AA Artillery		Total Guns and Mortars	Tanks
				Guns 76mm and Larger	Mortars 82–120mm	Total	AT Guns	AA Guns		
Western Army Group Twenty-second, Twenty-ninth, Thirtieth, Nineteenth, Sixteenth, and Twentieth combined arms armies	340	320,620	943	4.5	2.2	6.7	1.5[1]	0.7	8.9	1.3
Reserve Army Group Twenty-fourth and Forty-third combined arms armies and one division of the Thirty-first Combined Arms Army[2]	130	152,880	1,176	4.5	4.3	8.8	2.0[3]	0.7	11.5	1.3
Bryansk Army Group Third, Thirteenth, Fiftieth combined arms armies and the Yermakov Task Force	290	188,355	649.5	2.4	0.6	3.0	0.7	0.3	4.0	0.3
TOTALS	760	661,855	—							
Average	—	—	870.9	3.7	1.9	5.7	1.3	0.5	7.6	0.9

[1] Including 112 antiaircraft guns used as antitank guns and attached to antitank units. Subsequently, the number of antiaircraft guns in antiaircraft units was decreased by 112.

[2] The Thirty-first, Thirty-second, Thirty-third, and Forty-ninth combined arms armies were deployed defensively behind the Western Army Group and are not included in the above table.

[3] Includes 88 antiaircraft guns used as antitank guns. Subsequently the number of antiaircraft guns was decreased by 88.

Table 12

Tactical Density of Soviet Forces
November 15, 1941

Army Groups	Frontage (km)	Combat Troops	Men/ Km	Men and Weapons/Km of Frontage						
				Field Artillery and Mortars			AT and AA Artillery		Total Guns and Mortars	Tanks
				Guns 76mm and Larger	Mortars 82–120mm	Total	AT Guns	AA Guns		
Kalinin Army Group Twenty-second, Twenty-ninth, and Thirtieth combined arms armies	200	98,820	494.1	2.4	1.1	3.5	0.70	0.30	4.5	0.2
Western Army Group Fifth, Sixteenth, Thirty-third, Forty-third, Forty-ninth, and Fiftieth combined arms armies	400	363,880	909.7	3.2	1.6	4.8	1.00	1.30	7.1	1.6
Right wing of the Southwestern Army Group Third and Thirteenth combined arms armies	270	46,278	171.4	0.6	0.2	0.8	0.05	0.04	0.9	0.1
TOTALS Average	870 —	508,978 —	585.0	2.2	1.1	3.3	0.60	0.67	4.6	0.8

Table 13

Rates of Advance, German Army Group Center
October–December 1941

Army Group Center	Sept 30–Oct 15, 1941				October 16–30, 1941				Nov 15–Dec 5, 1941				Sep 30–Dec 5, 1941		
	Dates[1]	Days	Adv (kms)	Kms/Day	Dates	Days	Adv (kms)	Kms/Day	Dates[2]	Days	Adv (kms)	Kms/Day	Days	Adv (kms)	Kms/Day
Ninth Field Army	Oct 2–15	14	140	10.0	Oct 16–30	15	80	5.3	—	—	—	—	29	195	6.7
Third Panzer Group	Oct 2–15	14	270	19.3[3]	—	—	—	—	Nov 16–29	14	90	6.4	28	360	12.9
Fourth Field Army	Oct 2–15	14	200	14.4	Oct 16–30	15	60	4.0	—	—	—	—	29	260	9.0
Fourth Panzer Group	Oct 2–15	14	240	17.1[4]	Oct 17–26	10	30	3.0	Nov 16–28	13	60	4.6	37	360	9.7
Second Field Army	Sep 30–Oct 15	16	180	11.2	Oct 16–30	15	80	5.3	Nov 16–Dec 5	20	90	4.5	51	350	6.9
Second Panzer Group[5]	Sep 30–Oct 5	6	200	33.3[6]	Oct 16–30	15	120	8.0	Nov 18–Dec 5	18	90	5.0	38	410	10.8

[1] On Sept. 30 and Oct. 1, the Ninth Field Army and Third Panzer Group faced the Soviet Western Army Group; the Fourth Field Army and Fourth Panzer Group faced the Soviet Twenty-fourth, Forty-third and Thirty-first combined arms armies of the Reserve Army Group; the Second Field Army and Second Panzer Group faced the Soviet Bryansk Army Group.

[2] On Nov. 15, the Ninth Field Army and part of the Third Panzer Group advanced against the Soviet Kalinin Army Group; most of the forces of the Third Panzer Group, the Fourth Panzer Group, the Fourth Field Army, and the Second Panzer Army advanced against the Soviet Western Army Group; the Second Field Army continued its offensive against the right wing of the Soviet Southwestern Army Group.

[3] Between Oct. 11 and 15, the Third Panzer Group's advance averaged 30 kms/day.

[4] From Oct. 2 to 5, the Fourth Panzer Group advanced 120 kms (30 kms/day).

[5] After Oct. 6, 1941, renamed the Second Panzer Army.

[6] From Sept. 30 to Oct. 2, the Second Panzer Group advanced 180 kms (60 kms/day).

Soviet Counteroffensive at Moscow

December 1941–January 1942

The Soviet counteroffensive at Moscow was planned and prepared while the Germans were still attacking the Soviet capital in the hope of breaking through the last Russian defense lines and capturing the city.

The immediate aim of the counteroffensive was to eliminate the two wedges made by German panzers to the north and south of Moscow and then push the German forces back as far as possible along the entire Moscow front. The Russians were racing against time. It was imperative to strike before the Germans could organize their winter defenses and bring up reserves and supplies.

Thus, the counteroffensive was mounted without a pause for regrouping, under very difficult conditions. The winter was in full blast. The cold was bitter. Snow was deep; it was very difficult to move on the roads. Despite the arrival of considerable numbers of Soviet replacements, the ratio of forces was still slightly in the Germans' favor. As a consequence of the shortage of manpower and equipment, Soviet forces were strung out in a single echelon with little in reserve to exploit any breakthrough that might be achieved. The Soviets still had the great advantage, however, of being clothed and equipped for winter warfare; the frozen, exhausted Germans were not.

The counteroffensive was launched on December 5 by the Kalinin Army Group (under General I. Konev), followed the next day by the Western Army Group and the right wing of the Southwestern Army Group, commanded respectively by General Zhukov and Marshal S. K. Timoshenko. The Kalinin Army Group struck the German lines south of Kalinin, where a fierce battle developed. After three days of heavy fighting, the Soviet Thirty-first Army broke through the German defenses, and on December 9 it straddled the

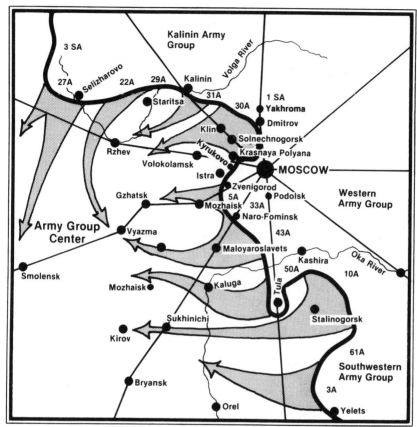

Soviet Counteroffensive at Moscow
December 1941

━━━━━━━━ Front Line December 5, 1941

Moscow-Kalinin railway. There it was temporarily halted. It was not until December 16, after the right wing of the Western Army Group had defeated the Germans near Solnechnogorsk and Klin, that the Kalinin Army Group continued its advance. But by that time the main German forces were already in retreat, and Konev had only the rear guard units to fight.

The Western Army Group struck north and south of Moscow after heavy air and artillery preparation. In two days of stubborn fighting, its right (northern) wing pierced the German defenses and captured the towns of Rogachev, Yakhroma, and Krasnaya Polyana. On December 13 the city of Klin, an important German stronghold, was encircled. Two days later it fell.

In the center, equally stubborn fighting developed along the Kryukovo-

Istra axis. Kryukovo was taken on the night of December 7–8 by elements of General Konstantin K. Rokossovskiy's Sixteenth Army. The Germans attempted to halt the advance at favorable defensive positions near the Istra Reservoir, but under the threat of double envelopment by two mobile groups they hastily retreated to Volokolamsk, leaving behind most of their heavy armament and vehicles. This operation was greatly facilitated by the push of the Fifth Army, which defeated the Germans near Zvenigorod, and by a daring raid against the German rear by the II Guards Cavalry Corps under General L. Dovator. On December 17 Dovator's horses reached Lake Trosten-skoye, opening the way for the further advance of the Fifth and Sixteenth armies.

By December 25 the center of the Western Army Group had reached the Lama and Ruza rivers, where it encountered strong German resistance in well-organized defensive positions. Attempts to break through failed, and General Zhukov decided to halt the advance, regroup, and bring up reserves before resuming the attack.

On the left (southern) flank of the army group, in the Tula area, troops of the Forty-ninth and Fiftieth armies, in a pincer attack coordinated with the Tenth Army and I Guards Cavalry Corps, delivered a strong blow at Guderian's Second Panzer Army, took Mikhaylov and Serebryaniye Prudy, and forced the Germans to fall back. East of Tula, German panzers, threatened with deep envelopments of their flanks, retreated rapidly through Bogorodsk, abandoning heavy weapons, trucks, and even tanks. The Second Panzer Army retreated to the Upa River.

To the left of the Western Army Group, the right wing of the Southwestern Army Group (on December 18 it was reconstituted into a three-army Bryansk Army Group under General Y. T. Cherevichenko) struck against the German Second Army. After taking Yelets, the Soviet forces advanced some 80 to 100 kilometers and on December 16 reached the line Lyubovschina-Pavlovka-Livny, and penetrated further south to points on the eastern bank of the Kshev River. There, the army group regrouped and launched an attack toward the northwest, in order to destroy the German Second Army. Early in January, unable to break through the stubborn German resistance along the line Belev-Mtsensk-Verkhovye-Livny, the Soviet advance stopped, and preparations for the next phase of the offensive commenced.

Meanwhile, in the north, the Kalinin Army Group captured Kalinin and continued to develop its offensive. Advancing toward Rzhev, by the end of December the army group had reached the line Staritsa-Lotoshina. On January 2, after regrouping, the Russians attacked again and forced another German withdrawal. By January 7, the Kalinin Army Group had reached the line Selizharovo-Zubtsov, where it took up advantageous positions, ready to strike at the exposed northern flank of Army Group Center.

The withdrawal of German forces under pressure from the Kalinin and Bryansk army groups contributed markedly to the success of the Western Army Group. The German Fourth Army, weakened and worn down by fighting, retreated westward. On December 26 it gave up Volokolamsk, and a few days later it lost Maloyaroslavets and Borovsk. After fierce fighting, Kaluga was taken by the Fiftieth Army on December 30.

The Moscow counteroffensive ended in early January, with the Soviet forces holding a line that ran through Selizharovo, Rzhev, Volokolamsk, and Ruza, and then west of Kaluga, and through Mosalsk, Belev, Mtsensk, and Novosil. Within a month the Red Army, carrying out its first large-scale offensive operation, had thrown the Germans 100 to 250 kilometers back from Moscow. German Army Group Center had suffered a severe setback. Losses in men and materiel were high and the morale of the troops low. The German situation became critically dangerous as the Soviet Supreme Command decided to continue the general offensive on all fronts. In February this offensive brought the Soviets close to Vyazma, pushing the Wehrmacht farther away from Moscow.

Table 1

Composition of Soviet Forces
December 1, 1941

	Army Groups			
	Kalinin	Western	South-western[1]	Total
Combined arms armies	3	10	2	15
Cavalry corps	—	2	1	3
Airborne corps	—	1	—	1
Rifle divisions	15	48	12	75
Motorized rifle divisions	—	3	—	3
Tank divisions	—	3	—	3[2]
Cavalry divisions	1	16	6	23[3]
Rifle brigades	1	16	1	18
Independent rifle, motorcycle, and cavalry regiments	1	9	1	11
Tank brigades	—	21	2	23[4]
Independent tank battalions	—	6	—	6
Independent armored train battalions	—	2	—	2
Independent ski battalions	—	11	—	11
Artillery regiments	10	29	3	42
AT artillery regiments	1	24	1	26
Independent artillery battalions	1	1	—	2
Independent mortar battalions	1	2	—	3
MRL regiments	—	2	1	3
Independent MRL battalions	1	30	4	35
AA defense brigades	—	1	—	1
AAA regiments	—	1	—	1
Independent AAA battalions	4	16	1	21
Independent engineer and sapper battalions	11	33	5	49

[1] Right wing only consisted of the Third and Thirteenth combined arms armies, and General F. Ya. Kostenko's Task Force.

[2] The 108th Tank Division shown in the Western Army Group was reorganized as the 108th Tank Brigade at the start of the counteroffensive.

[3] Excluding the 29th Cavalry Division, withdrawn for reorganization in mid-December.

[4] Excluding the 11th, 27th, and 33d tank brigades, withdrawn for reorganization in mid-December.

Table 2

Composition and Strength of the Soviet Air Force
December 5, 1941

	Kalinin Army Group	Western Army Group	Moscow Defense Zone	Right Wing, South-western Army Group	Long Range Bombers	VI Air Corps, AA Defense Forces	Total
Air divisions	—	11[1]	—	2[2]	7[3]	—	20
Bomber	—	2	—	—	7	—	9
Mixed	—	9	—	2	—	—	11
Air regiments[4]							
Bomber	1	10	1	2	19	—	33
Ground attack	1	5	1	2	—	—	9
Fighter	3	11	3	3	—	26	46
Light bomber	—	13	—	—	—	—	13
Total	5	39	5	7	19	26	101
Combat aircraft							
Bombers							
Total	11	124	3	30	237	—	405
Operational	9	39	2	12	111	—	173
Ground attack							
Total	15	46	8	13	—	—	82
Operational	9	22	2	9	—	—	42
Fighters							
Total	40	114	47	31	10	432	674
Operational	31	74	20	17	7	331	480
Reconnaissance							
Total	—	4	—	—	—	28	32
Operational	—	1	—	—	—	23	24
Night bombers							
Total	—	172	11	—	—	—	183
Operational	—	131	9	—	—	—	140
TOTAL AIRCRAFT	66	460	69	74	247	460	1,376
TOTAL OPERATIONAL	49	267	33	38	118	354	859

[1] 23d Bomber Division; 12th, 28th, 38th, 43d, 47th, 77th, 146th mixed air divisions; General Ivan V. Petrov's Air Group (10th, 46th mixed and 31st Light Bomber divisions).

[2] 10th and 61st mixed air divisions.

[3] 26th, 40th, 42d, 51st, 52d, 81st, and 133d long range bomber divisions.

[4] Includes air regiments which formed the air divisions.

Table 3

Reinforcements Received by Soviet Forces December 1941

	Kalinin Army Group		Western Army Group		Bryansk Army Group*		Total
	Number	Designation	Number	Designation	Number	Designation	
Combined arms armies	1	Thirty-ninth	—	—	1	Sixty-first	2
Rifle divisions	10	355th, 357th, 359th, 361st, 363d, 369th, 373d, 375th, 379th, 381st	4	201st, 329th, 336th, 338th	6	287th, 342d, 346th, 350th, 356th, 387th	20
Rifle brigades	—	—	10	17th, 19th, 26th, 30th, 34th, 41st, 43d, 46th, 60th, 62d	1	57th (NKVD)	11
Cavalry divisions	—		—		2	83d, 91st	2
Tank brigades	1	35th	—	—	1	142d	2
Independent tank battalions	5	143d, 145th, 148th, 159th, 165th	3	123d, 133d, 140th	—	—	8
Independent glider battalions	1	21st	2	7th, 23d	—	—	3
Independent ski battalions	8	21st, 73d, 74th, 75th, 76th, 81st, 82d, 83d	3	17th, 23d, 24th	—	—	11
Artillery regiments	—	—	1	517th	2	40th, 201st	3
Independent MRL battalions	4	39th, 102d, 103d, 202d	1	42d	—	—	5
Air force regiments	2	6th Guards Ground Attack, 593d Light Bomber	8	601st, 692d, 698th, 700th, 701st, 703d, 706th, 710th light bomber	—	—	10
Engineer brigades	—	—	2	37th, 38th	—	—	2

* Formerly Right Wing of the Southwestern Army Group; renamed on December 18.

Table 4

Combat Strength of Soviet Forces
December 1, 1941

	Army Groups							
	Kalinin		Western		Southwestern (right wing)[1]		Total in Army Groups	
	Total	Combat Troops	Total	Combat Troops	Total	Combat Troops	Total[2]	Combat Troops
Men	192,198	118,394	787,184	577,726	80,998	63,398	1,060,380	759,518
Rifles	109,388	85,452	404,113	330,665	40,766	36,749	554,267	452,866
Submachine guns	1,078	1,015	12,106	11,784	1,151	1,127	14,335	13,926
Heavy machine guns	436	387	3,134	2,938	225	218	3,795	3,543
Light machine guns	1,478	1,288	6,872	6,149	509	458	8,859	7,895
AA machine guns	83	46	653	397	50	44	786	487
AT rifles	—	—	353	353	—	—	353	353
AT guns (45mm)	118	117	634	622	69	69	821	808
Field guns (76mm)	330	327	1,010	1,005	85	83	1,425	1,415
Field guns (107mm and larger)	249	249	784	781	99	99	1,132	1,129
Mortars (50mm)	303	290	1,415	1,412	71	71	1,789	1,773
Mortars (82mm)	135	129	1,217	1,209	59	59	1,411	1,397
Mortars (120mm)	89	87	341	335	48	48	478	470
MRLs (M–8 and M–13)	22	22	311	311	82	82	415	415
AA guns	59	59	606	604	26	26	691	689
Tanks	17	17	618	607[3]	43	43	678	667
Vehicles	8,911	3,536	40,848	22,510	3,145	1,988	52,904	28,034
Horses	32,611	24,532	144,529	119,300	22,984	21,936	200,124	165,768

[1] Third and Thirteenth combined arms armies and General F. Ya. Kostenko's Task Force.

[2] Excluded due to the lack of data, strength, and equipment are the 126th, 173d, and 239th rifle divisions; 17th Cavalry Division; 9th, 17th, and 24th tank brigades.

[3] Included are 205 heavy KV and medium T-34 tanks; the rest were light and were obsolete.

Table 5

Defense Frontage and Density of German Forces December 1941 and January 1942

	December 5–6, 1941			December 16–17, 1941			December 24–25, 1941			January 8, 1942		
	Frontage (kms)	Divs	Kms/Div	Frontage (kms)	Divs	Kms/Div	Frontage (kms)	Divs	Kms/Div	Frontage (kms)	Divs	Kms/Div
Ninth Field Army	250	13.5	18.5	230	13.5	17.0	210	13.5	15.5	245	13.5	18.1
Third Panzer Group	120	5.5	21.8	90	9.5	9.5	55	9.5	5.8	45	9.5	4.7
Fourth Panzer Group	90	16.0	5.6	100	12.0	8.3	70	14.0	5.0	70	17.0	4.1
Fourth Field Army	130	14.0	9.3	145	15.0	9.6	170	16.0	10.6	235	15.0	15.6
Second Panzer Army	250	14.0	17.8	165	14.0	11.8	130	12.0	10.8	185	10.5	17.6
Second Field Army	220	8.0	27.5	145	8.0	18.1	145	9.0	16.1	155	10.5	14.8
Reserve, Army Group Center	—	3.0	—	—	1.0	—	—	1.0	—	—	—	—
Sectors not defended (gaps)	—	—	—	35[1]	—	—	40[2]	—	—	75[3]	—	—
TOTAL	1,060	74.0	14.3	910	73.0	12.5	820	75.0	10.9	1,010	76.0	13.30

[1] In the sector Ivanovka-Suprut (southwest of Tula).

[2] In the sector Kaluga-Belev, between the Second Panzer and Fourth Field armies (on the Oka River line).

[3] One gap, 60 kilometers wide, between the Second Panzer and Fourth Field armies in the sector Masalska-Ignatovka (west of Sukhinichi); another gap, 15 kilometers wide, in the sector Vodrino-Troitskoye (northwest of Maloyaroslavets).

Table 6

Frontage and Density of Advancing Soviet Armies December 1941–January 1942

	December 5–6, 1941			December 16–17, 1941			December 24–25, 1941			January 8, 1942		
	Frontage (kms)	Divs[1]	Kms/Div	Frontage (kms)	Divs[1]	Kms/Div	Frontage (kms)	Divs[1]	Kms/Div	Frontage (kms)	Divs[1]	Kms/Div
Kalinin Army Group[2]												
Twenty-second Combined Arms Army	135	5.5	25.0	135	5.0	27.0	105	4.0	26.2	90	4.0	22.5
Twenty-ninth Combined Arms Army	75	5.0	15.0	60	5.0	12.0	25	5.0	5.0	20	5.0	4.0
Thirty-first Combined Arms Army	40	5.0	8.0	35	8.0	4.4	20	8.0	2.5	35	8.0	4.4
Thirtieth Combined Arms Army	—	—	—	40	12.0	3.3	40	12.0	3.3	40	10.0	4.0
Thirty-ninth Combined Arms Army	—	—	—	—	—	—	35	7.0	5.0	75	8.0	9.4
Army Group Reserve	—	1.0	—	—	2.0	—	—	1.0	—	—	4.0	—
TOTAL	250	16.5	15.1	270	32.0	8.4	225	37.0	6.1	260	39.0	6.7
Western Army Group												
Thirtieth Combined Arms Army	80	13.0	6.1	—	—	—	—	—	—	—	—	—
First Strike Army	35	8.0	4.4	35	8.5	4.1	20	9.0	2.2	30	8.5	3.5
Twentieth Combined Arms Army	35	4.5	7.7	20	5.0	4.0	20	4.5	4.4	25	6.5	3.8
Sixteenth Combined Arms Army[3]	25	15.0	1.7	25	6.5	3.8	25	8.5	2.9	30	9.0	3.3
Fifth Combined Arms Army	65	7.0	9.3	80	15.0	5.3	50	12.0	4.2	50	11.0	4.5
Thirty-third Combined Arms Army	35	5.0	7.0	35	6.5	5.4	35	6.5	5.4	70	8.5	8.2
Forty-third Combined Arms Army	35	5.5	6.4	30	4.5	6.6	30	4.5	6.6	30	4.5	6.6
Forty-ninth Combined Arms Army	80	7.0	11.4	70	11.0	6.4	75	10.0	7.5	30	9.0	3.3
Fiftieth Combined Arms Army	100	6.5	15.4	100	7.5	13.3	85	8.5	10.0	80	8.5	9.4
Tenth Combined Arms Army	130	11.0	11.8	20	10.0	2.0	35	6.0	5.8	170	6.0	28.3
Task Force Belov	30	3.5	8.6	15	3.5	4.3	20	7.5	2.6	20	7.5	2.7
Army Group Reserve	—	5.0	—	—	3.0	—	—	4.0	—	—	—	—
TOTAL	650	91.0	7.1	430	81.0	5.3	395	81.0	4.9	550[4]	79.0	6.9
Bryansk Army Group[5]												
Third Combined Arms Army	90	6.0	15.0	40	6.0	6.6	40	6.0	6.6	60	6.0	10.1
Thirteenth Combined Arms Army	110	6.5	16.9	—	8.0	—	—	8.0	—	—	8.5	—
Task Force Kostenko	40	6.0	6.6	110	5.0	22.0	110	5.0	22.0	90	5.0	18.0
Sixty-first Combined Arms Army	—	—	—	60	7.0	8.6	50	7.0	7.1	50	7.0	7.1
TOTAL	240	18.5	13.0	210	26.0	8.1	200	26.0	7.7	200	26.0	7.7
TOTAL in three army groups	1,140	126.0	9.0	910	139.0	6.5	820	144.0	5.7	1,010	145.0	7.0

[1] Division equivalent.

[2] Thirtieth Army under Kalinin Army Group from December 16, 1941; Thirty-ninth from December 22.

[3] The 7th and 8th Guards rifle divisions are not included. These two divisions were transferred to GHQ Reserve on December 17.

[4] Includes a 15km gap northwest of Maloyaroslavets in the Vodrino-Troitskoye sector not covered by Soviet troops.

[5] Formerly right wing of Southwestern Army Group; renamed December 18, 1941.

Table 7

Tactical Density of Soviet Forces
December 5, 1941

			Men and Weapons/Kilometer Frontage						
			Field Artillery and Mortars			AA and AT Guns		Total Guns	
	Frontage (kms)	Men	76mm Guns and Larger	82mm and 120mm Mortars	Total	AT Guns	AA Guns	and Mortars	Tanks
Kalinin Army Group									
Twenty-second, Twenty-ninth, Thirty-first combined arms armies	250	786.8	2.3	0.7	3.0	0.4	0.2	3.6	0.06
Western Army Group									
Right wing First Strike Army, Thirtieth, Twentieth, Sixteenth combined arms armies and part of the Fifth Combined Arms Army	220	2,026.0	3.5	4.0	7.5	1.6	1.3	10.4	1.40
Center* Thirty-third, Forty-third combined arms armies and part of the Fifth and Forty-ninth combined arms armies	150	1,198.0	3.5	1.7	5.2	0.8	1.3	7.3	1.20
Left wing Tenth, Fiftieth combined arms armies, part of the Forty-ninth Combined Arms Army; Task Force Belov	280	577.6	1.7	1.4	3.1	0.5	0.5	4.1	0.40
TOTAL	650	1,211.0	2.7	2.3	5.0	1.0	0.9	6.9	0.90
Right wing of the Southwestern Army Group									
Third, Thirteenth combined arms armies; Task Force Kostenko	240	339.9	0.7	0.5	1.2	0.3	1.0	2.5	0.10
OVERALL TOTAL	1,140	930.6	2.2	1.5	3.7	0.7	0.5	4.9	0.60

* Left wing of the Fifth Army: 32d Rifle and 82d Motorized Rifle divisions; right wing of the Forty-ninth Army: 5th Guards; 60th, 194th, and 415th Rifle divisions.

Table 8

German Combat Strength
December 1941–January 1942

	December 5, 1941	December 16, 1941	December 24, 1941	January 8, 1942
Field armies	3	3	3	3
Panzer armies	1	1	1	3
Panzer groups	2	2	2	—
Army corps	13	13	14	14
Motorized corps	8	8	8	8
Divisions				
Infantry	47	46	48	49
Panzer	14	14	14	14
Motorized	8	8	8	8
Security	3	3	3	3
TOTAL	72	71	73	74
Brigades				
Infantry	1	1	1	1
Motorized	2	2	2	2
Cavalry	1	1	1	1
TOTAL	4	4	4	4

Table 9

Average Rate of Advance of Soviet Forces
December 5, 1941–January 8, 1942

Formations	First Period December 5-16, 1941				Second Period December 17-25, 1941				Third Period Dec 25, 1941-Jan 8, 1942				Total Dec 5, '41-Jan 8, '42		
	Dates	Days	Adv (kms)	Kms/day	Dates	Days	Adv (kms)	Kms/Day	Dates	Days	Adv (kms)	Kms/Day	Days	Adv (kms)	Kms/Day
Kalinin Army Group Twenty-second, Twenty-ninth, Thirtieth, Thirty-ninth combined arms armies*	Dec 5–16	12	12	1.0	Dec 17–25	9	45	5.0	Dec 26 –Jan 8	14	45	3.2	35	102	2.9
Western Army Group Right wing First Strike Army, Thirtieth, Twentieth combined arms armies, and right wing of Fifth Combined Arms Army	Dec 6–16	11	65	6.0	Dec 17–25	9	45	5.0			—		20	115	5.7
Left wing Tenth and Fiftieth combined arms armies, left wing of Forty-ninth Combined Arms Army, Task Force Belov	Dec 6–16	11	100	9.0	Dec 17–24	8	90	11.2	Dec 25 –Jan 8	15	110	7.3	34	300	8.8
Center Left wing of Fifth Combined Arms Army, Thirty-third and Forty-third combined arms armies, right wing of Forty-ninth Combined Arms Army	—				Dec 18–24	7	20	2.9	Dec 25 –Jan 8	15	40	2.7	22	60	2.7
Right wing of the Southwestern Army Group (Bryansk Army Group from Dec. 18, 1941) Third, Thirteenth, Sixty-first combined arms armies, and Army Groups Mobile Task Force	Dec 6–16	11	60	5.4	Dec 17–24	8	25	3.1	Dec 25 –Jan 8	15	25	1.7	34	110	3.2

* The Thirtieth Combined Arms Army under Kalinin Army Group to December 16; Sixty-first Combined Arms Army under Southwestern Army Group from December 16, 1941.

The Soviet Counteroffensive at Stalingrad

November 1942–February 1943

Background

By the spring of 1942 the Germans had completed plans for a summer offensive. Lacking forces and weapons sufficient to undertake a renewed advance on the entire Soviet-German front, as in the offensive of 1941, Hitler decided that his armies should attack in the southern section on two axes: one from Kharkov toward Stalingrad and the Volga River, and the other from the Mius River toward the oil-rich Caucasus and Iran.

The attack toward Stalingrad was to be carried out by the Sixth Army under General Friedrich Paulus, with support from elements of the Second Army and the Fourth Panzer Army. By late June, when the operation began, the Germans had massed 250,000 men, 740 tanks, 7,500 pieces of artillery and mortars, and 1,200 aircraft. The Soviets, anticipating such an offensive, were determined to prevent the Germans from reaching the Volga and splitting the Red Army in two. On July 12 the Supreme Command organized the Stalingrad Army Group and deployed it in defensive positions along a 530-kilometer front west of Stalingrad, from Pavlovsk and Serafimovich in the north to Suroviko and Verkhne-Kurmoyarskaya in the south. Commanded by Marshal Timoshenko, the army group consisted of 38 understrength divisions, with 187,000 men, 350 tanks, 337 operational aircraft, and 7,900 guns and mortars.

On July 17, following preliminary drives to Voronezh by the Second and Fourth panzer armies, the Sixth Army launched its Stalingrad operation. A few days later German panzer and mechanized troops smashed through the defenses of the Soviet Sixty-second Army and reached the Don near Kamensky. On August 2, elements of the Fourth Panzer Army took Kotelnikovsky, some 150 kilometers southwest of Stalingrad, and then continued northeast

toward Abganerovo and Plodovitoye, which were taken the next day. The
Germans were within 50 kilometers of the outskirts of Stalingrad.

By mid-August most of the area inside the Don River bend had been
overrun. Elements of the Fourth Panzer Army were attempting to envelop the
Soviet Sixty-fourth Army from the south and reach Stalingrad through Gav-
rilovka. The German XIV Panzer Corps advanced from the west toward the
Volga and reached Latoshinka-Rynok, just north of Stalingrad. August 23
saw the heaviest air raid on the city. Six hundred German bombers attacked
Stalingrad, leaving 40,000 casualties in their wake. Heavy air raids continued
day after day. Most of the inhabitants—some 300,000 people—were evacuated, leaving only essential personnel. The last civilians left the city in September, when street fighting began.

Early in September German forces attacking from the west and northwest
reached the outskirts of the city and poised for the final assault on the Soviet

Soviet Counteroffensive at Stalingrad
November 1942 - January 1943

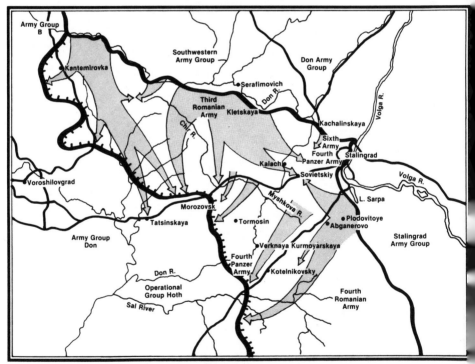

━━━━━━━━━━━━━━━ Front Line November 19, 1942

▲▲▲▲▲▲▲▲▲▲▲▲▲▲ Front Line December 31, 1942

Sixty-second Army, which had been charged with the defense of Stalingrad. On September 13, the Germans attacked the inner city from two directions. Four divisions moved from the Gumrak area and three more from Verkhnaya Yelshanka. The Soviet Sixty-second Army, under General V. I. Chuikov, yielded most of the central part of Stalingrad, including the railroad station and Mamai Hill, the highest point in the city, in the first assault. Nevertheless, the Germans were unable to break the defenders. Despite tremendous losses, the Sixty-second Army, its front line only a few hundred yards from the Volga, fought for each street, each house, each bit of land. The railroad station changed hands thirteen times during the battle, and neither side held Mamai Hill for long. By the end of the month fighting was concentrated around the Krasny Oktyabar and Barrikady factories.

The Soviet Counteroffensive

As the weary Sixty-second Army desperately defended Stalingrad during the fall of 1942, in Moscow plans were formed for a Soviet counteroffensive that was to alter drastically the strategic situation on the Soviet-German front. This plan called for encirclement of the German Sixth Army and parts of the Fourth Panzer Army at Stalingrad. Then, in a second phase, the Soviets would move southwestward toward Rostov and Novorossiysk to cut off the Germans in the Caucasus, who in the summer and fall had penetrated deep into the mountains and almost reached the oil-producing fields of Baku.

The Soviets committed three army groups to the operation. North of Stalingrad were the Southwestern Army Group under General N. F. Vatutin, and the Don Army Group under General K. Rokossovskiy. To the south was the Stalingrad Army Group under General A. I. Yeremenko. The three army groups had a combined strength of 1,015,300 men, 1,560 tanks, 13,535 guns and mortars, and 1,350 aircraft. According to Soviet sources, German forces in the Stalingrad sector and nearby areas consisted of 1,011,000 men, 675 tanks, 10,290 guns and mortars, and 1,200 aircraft. These forces included two Romanian armies and one Italian army.

The Germans were surprised when, early in the morning of November 19, 1942, Soviet artillery opened up along the entire front. Soon afterward the Southwestern Army Group moved out from the areas around Serafimovich and Kletskaya, flanked the Third Romanian Army, and drove quickly through its defensive positions, reaching Kalach-Sovietsky by November 23. The Don Army Group attacked the Germans defending around Kachalinskaya, crashed through the defense area, and advanced southeast toward Stalingrad. Its objective was to take Vertyachy and cut off German troops in Stalingrad. The Germans put up such a strong resistance that the Don Army Group failed to accomplish its mission. The Stalingrad Army Group went into action a day later, on November 20. It advanced from the Sarpa Lakes region south of Stalingrad, concentrating against the Fourth Romanian Army, and soon breached the German-Romanian lines. Mobile troops sent into the breach began to envelop German forces deployed between the Volga and Don rivers. At mid-day on November 23 forward elements of the Northwestern and Stalingrad army groups met at the village of Sovietsky, closing the encirclement ring. Some 300,000 German troops of the Sixth Army and elements of the Fourth Panzer Army were trapped in the pocket.

Realizing that the Germans would make an all-out effort to break out of the encirclement, or to break through to relieve the Sixth Army, the Soviet Supreme Command took precautionary measures. It ordered part of its forces to turn inward toward Stalingrad and attack the Germans inside the pocket, while the remaining troops were to push the outer ring of the encirclement westward and southwestward to prevent any German rescue mission from relieving the trapped force.

As it turned out, the Soviet assumption was correct. To rescue the encir-cled troops, Army High Command (OKH) organized Army Group Don, with the prime mission of reaching General Paulus's army and restoring the situa-tion.

The new army group, under Field Marshal Erich von Manstein, initially had a force of some 30 infantry, panzer, and motorized divisions, of which 12 were quickly concentrated in two areas near Kotelnikovsky and Tormosin, southwest of Stalingrad.

On December 12, the Kotelnikovsky force attacked toward the northeast, routed the Soviet defenders, and after three days of heavy fighting advanced over 50 kilometers, reached the Asai-Yesaulovsky River, and continued toward the Myshkova River. According to Manstein's plans, upon reaching the Myshkova River the second German force would attack from Tormosin, squeeze the Soviets, make a gap in their defenses, and join with Paulus. However, these plans had to be drastically changed. In the first place, Hitler vetoed Manstein's instructions to Paulus to evacuate Stalingrad and attack westward. The Sixth Army was to hold its positions.

On December 16, as the Germans were advancing toward Stalingrad on their ill-fated rescue mission, the Soviet Southwestern Army Group and the left wing of the Voronezh Army Group attacked in the Middle Don sector, in order to hit the rear of Manstein's Tormosin force and envelop the German and Italian troops in the Bokovo and Morozovsk regions.

This new development forced Manstein to parry the Soviet assault with troops assigned to the rescue mission. It was too late. The Germans suffered defeat on the Chir and Don rivers. On December 25 the Soviets reached the towns of Tatsinskaya and Morozovsk, threatening the left flank and rear of the German Kotelnikovsky force. German efforts to stabilize the situation failed, and Manstein ordered the withdrawal of his army group to new defensive positions. By the end of December the Germans were some 160 kilometers from the beleaguered forces and had given up any attempt to assist them. The situation of the Sixth Army had become hopeless. However, the Germans continued to fight desperately—to hold down the Soviet forces near Stalingrad.

Now the Soviets concentrated all their efforts on the destruction of the encircled troops. German forces were bombed and shelled almost continuously. The Soviet air blockade was very effective. Luftwaffe transport planes flying supply missions were shot down by dozens, and only a few were able to deliver their precious cargoes of food and ammunition. Hunger was severe inside the ring. Hospitals overflowed with wounded and sick. Little ammunition and less food were available.

On January 8 Paulus was given an ultimatum to surrender or be destroyed. Acting on Hitler's direct orders, he refused to capitulate. At that time he had nearly 250,000 men, some 300 tanks (almost without fuel), and over 4,000 guns and mortars—still a formidable force. But his men were exhausted, weapons and equipment were in bad shape, ammunition was scarce, and morale was very low.

On January 10 the Soviets launched their final assault. After an hour-long artillery preparation, Soviet tanks and infantry attacked. The Germans offered ferocious resistance, often counterattacking. However, despite desperate efforts, they could not stop the Soviet advance. Soon the German area was split into two. Germans began to surrender, and even entire units capitulated. By the end of January the Germans were holding out in only two pockets in Stalingrad and the nearby suburbs. On January 31 General Paulus, who had just been promoted by Hitler to the rank of field marshal, surrendered. Two days later all organized resistance ended.

According to Soviet statistics, nearly 150,000 German dead were picked up on the battlefield; and 91,000 prisoners, including 2,500 officers and 24 generals—headed by Field Marshal Paulus—were taken.

Soviet Order of Battle
November 20, 1942

Southwestern Army Group
First Guards Army
  First echelon
    1st Rifle Division
    153d Rifle Division
    197th Rifle Division
    203d Rifle Division
    278th Rifle Division
  Army reserve
    226th Rifle Division
    22d Motorized Rifle Brigade
Fifth Tank Army
  First echelon
    14th Guards Rifle Division
    47th Guards Rifle Division
    50th Guards Rifle Division
    119th Guards Tank Brigade
    8th Guards Tank Brigade
    510th Independent Tank Battalion
    511th Independent Tank Battalion
  Second echelon
    VIII Cavalry Corps
      21st Cavalry Division
      55th Cavalry Division
      112th Cavalry Division
    I Tank Corps
      89th Tank Brigade
      117th Tank Brigade
      159th Tank Brigade
      44th Motorized Rifle Brigade
      159th Rifle Division
      8th Motorcycle Regiment
  Army reserve
    346th Rifle Division (less 1166th
      Rifle Regiment)
Twenty-first Combined Arms Army
  First echelon
    63d Rifle Division
    76th Rifle Division
    96th Rifle Division
    293d Rifle Division
    1st Independent Tank Regiment
    2d Independent Tank Regiment
    3d Independent Tank Regiment
    4th Independent Tank Regiment
  Second echelon
    III Guards Cavalry Corps
      5th Cavalry Division
      6th Cavalry Division
      32d Cavalry Division
    IV Tank Corps
      277th Rifle Division
      333d Rifle Division
      45th Tank Brigade
      69th Tank Brigade
      102d Tank Brigade
      4th Motorized Rifle Brigade

Army group reserve
  I Guards Mechanized Corps
    1st Guards Mechanized Brigade
    2d Guards Mechanized Brigade
    3d Guards Mechanized Brigade
    16th Guards Tank Regiment
    17th Guards Tank Regiment
Don Army Group
Sixty-fifth Combined Arms Army
  First echelon
    4th Guards Rifle Division
    27th Guards Rifle Division
    40th Guards Rifle Division
    23d Rifle Division
    24th Rifle Division
    304th Rifle Division
    321st Rifle Division
    91st Tank Brigade
    121st Tank Brigade
  Second echelon
    252d Rifle Division
    258th Rifle Division
Twenty-fourth Combined Arms Army
  First echelon
    49th Rifle Division
    120th Rifle Division
    173d Rifle Division
    214th Rifle Division
    260th Rifle Division
    298th Rifle Division
    10th Tank Brigade
  Second echelon
    XVI Tank Corps
      107th Tank Brigade
      109th Tank Brigade
      164th Tank Brigade
      15th Motorized Rifle Brigade
    84th Rifle Division
    233d Rifle Division
  Army reserve
    273d Rifle Division
    54th Fortified Area
Sixty-sixth Combined Arms Army
  First echelon
    99th Rifle Division
    116th Rifle Division
    226th Rifle Division
    343d Rifle Division
  Army reserve
    64th Rifle Division
    299th Rifle Division
    58th Tank Brigade
Army group reserve
  159th Fortified Area
  64th Tank Brigade (no tanks)
  148th Tank Brigade (no tanks)

Soviet Order of Battle
November 20, 1942—(continued)

Stalingrad Army Group
Sixty-second Combined Arms Army
  First echelon
    13th Guards Rifle Division
    37th Guards Rifle Division
    39th Guards Rifle Division
    45th Rifle Division
    95th Rifle Division
    112th Rifle Division
    138th Rifle Division
    193d Rifle Division
    284th Rifle Division
    308th Rifle Division
    42d Rifle Brigade
    92d Rifle Brigade
    115th Rifle Brigade
    124th Rifle Brigade
    149th Rifle Brigade
    160th Rifle Brigade
  Army reserve
    84th Tank Brigade
Sixty-fourth Combined Arms Army
  First echelon
    VII Rifle Corps
      93d Rifle Brigade
      96th Rifle Brigade
      97th Rifle Brigade
    29th Rifle Division
    38th Rifle Division
    157th Rifle Division
    204th Rifle Division
    66th Marine Rifle Brigade
    13th Tank Brigade
    56th Tank Brigade
  Second echelon
    36th Guards Rifle Division
    154th Marine Rifle Brigade
  Army reserve
    118th Fortified Area
    20th Independent Assault Brigade
Fifty-seventh Combined Arms Army
  First echelon
    169th Rifle Division
    422d Rifle Division
    143d Rifle Brigade
    90th Tank Brigade
    235th Tank Brigade

  Second echelon
    XIII Tank Corps
      17th Mechanized Brigade
      61st Mechanized Brigade
      62d Mechanized Brigade
Fifty-first Combined Arms Army
  First echelon
    15th Guards Rifle Division
    91st Rifle Division
    126th Rifle Division
    302d Rifle Division
    76th Fortified Area
    254th Tank Brigade
  Second echelon
    IV Cavalry Corps
      61st Cavalry Division
      81st Cavalry Division
    IV Mechanized Corps
      36th Mechanized Brigade
      59th Mechanized Brigade
      60th Mechanized Brigade
      55th Tank Regiment
      158th Tank Regiment
  Army reserve
    38th Motorized Rifle Brigade
Twenty-eighth Combined Arms Army
  First echelon
    34th Guards Rifle Division
    152d Rifle Brigade
    6th Guards Tank Brigade
  Second echelon
    248th Rifle Division
    52d Rifle Brigade
    159th Rifle Brigade
  Army reserve
    78th Fortified Area
    116th Fortified Area
    565th Independent Tank Battalion
Army group reserve
  300th Rifle Division
  77th Fortified Area
  115th Fortified Area
  156th Fortified Area
  85th Tank Brigade
  35th Tank Regiment
  166th Tank Regiment

Table 1

Planned and Actual Scope of Soviet Operation November–December 1942

Army Groups	Depth of Operation (km)		Duration of Operation (days)		Average Daily Rates of Advance (km)			
					Planned		Actual	
	Planned	Actual	Planned	Actual	Rifle Formation	Mobile Formation	Rifle Formation	Mobile Formation
Southwestern	140	140–160	3	5	20–25	40–45	15–20	28–35
Don	60	30–60	3	5	15–20	20	6–12	6–12
Stalingrad	90	85	2	4	10–15	45	12–15	20–35

Table 2
Soviet Strength
November 20, 1942

	Southwest Army Group*		Don Army Group		Stalingrad Army Group		Total	
	Total	In Combat Units	Total	In Combat Units	Total	In Combat Units	Total	In Combat Units
Men	338,631	275,504	292,707	185,565	383,961	258,633	1,015,299	719,702
Rifles	191,020	166,234	159,330	124,846	176,957	142,867	527,307	433,947
Submachine guns	27,081	25,634	19,902	18,144	37,799	35,366	84,782	79,144
Machine guns								
Light	5,143	4,791	4,160	3,647	5,587	5,037	14,890	13,475
Heavy	1,802	1,741	1,843	1,756	2,264	2,203	5,909	5,700
Super Heavy	622	581	374	348	463	395	1,459	1,324
TOTAL	7,567	7,113	6,377	5,751	8,314	7,635	22,258	20,499
AT Rifles	6,280	6,195	5,733	5,545	5,649	5,037	17,662	16,777
Artillery								
45mm AT gun	740	728	581	532	986	945	2,307	2,205
76mm gun/how	974	963	838	829	1,185	1,141	2,997	2,933
107mm+ gun/how	487	486	419	412	372	368	1,278	1,266
TOTAL	2,201	2,177	1,838	1,773	2,543	2,454	6,582	6,404
Mortars								
120mm	541	532	444	418	624	599	1,609	1,549
82mm	1,828	1,793	2,010	1,885	1,506	1,449	5,344	5,127
50mm	1,932	1,846	1,483	1,336	1,178	1,077	4,593	4,259
TOTAL	4,301	4,171	3,937	3,639	3,308	3,125	11,546	10,935

(cont.)

Table 2—(continued)
Soviet Strength
November 20, 1942

	Southwest Army Group*		Don Army Group		Stalingrad Army Group		Total	
	Total	In Combat Units	Total	In Combat Units	Total	In Combat Units	Total	In Combat Units
AA guns								
76–85mm	45	45	53	53	245	245	343	343
25–37mm	278	276	133	133	287	273	698	682
TOTAL	323	321	186	186	532	518	1,041	1,025
MRLs								
BM-8 and BM-13	148	148	147	147	145	145	440	440
M-30 frames	480	480	288	288	192	192	960	960
TOTAL	628	628	435	435	337	337	1,400	1,400
Tanks								
Heavy	145	145	43	42	49	49	237	236
Medium	318	316	67	65	357	354	742	735
Light	267	262	70	59	244	218	581	539
TOTAL	730	723	180	166	650	621	1,560	1,510
Armored cars	99	93	38	20	181	164	381	277
Vehicles	14,529	8,599	12,003	4,383	14,881	7,750	41,413	20,732
Tractors	792	477	864	498	1,001	626	2,657	1,601
Horses	69,003	62,752	44,915	28,078	55,691	39,398	169,609	130,228

* Excluded are IV and VI Guards rifle corps (35th, 38th, 41st, 44th Guards and 195th rifle divisions; and 40th and 42d Guard artillery regiments, which did not start to arrive until after November 21, 1942.

Table 3

Composition of Southwestern, Don, and Stalingrad Army Groups November 20 and December 1, 1942

	November 20, 1942				December 1, 1942			
	South-western	Don	Stalin-grad	Total	South-western	Don	Stalin-grad	Total
Armies								
Combined arms	2	3	5	10	1	4	5	10
Tank	1	—	—	1	1	—	—	1
Air	2	1	1	4	2	1	1	4
Flotillas	—	—	1	1	—	—	1	1
Corps								
Rifle	—	—	1	1	3	—	1	4
Cavalry	2	—	1	3	2	—	1	3
Mechanized	1	—	1	2	2	—	1	3
Tank	3	1	1*	5	2	3	1	6
Corps AA defense area	—	—	1	1	—	—	1	1
Divisions								
Rifle	18	24	24	66	20	27	26	73
Cavalry	6	—	2	8	6	—	2	8
Artillery	1	—	—	1	1	2	1	4
AAA	2	—	1	3	3	1	1	5
Fortified areas	—	2	7	9	—	2	7	9
Independent brigades								
Rifle	—	—	15	15	1	—	15	16
Motorized rifle	1	—	1	2	1	—	1	2
Tank destroyer	1	—	1	2	1	—	1	2
Tank	1	6	8	15	2	6	7	15
Engineers	2	2	3	7	3	3	5	11
Independent regiments								
Rifle	—	—	1	1	—	—	1	1
Cavalry	—	—	1	1	—	—	1	1
Tank	3	—	2	5	4	8	6	18
Motorcycle	1	—	—	1	1	—	—	1
Artillery	12	13	14	39	8	9	8	25
Tank destroyer	20	4	18	42	12	7	16	35
Mortar	8	2	3	13	5	5	3	13
MRLs	7	12	14	33	4	15	14	33
AAA	12	9	14	35	4	11	7	22
Engineer	—	1	—	1	1	—	1	2
Independent battalions								
Tank	2	—	1	3	2	—	1	3
Armored train	—	4	4	8	—	4	4	8
Heavy artillery	—	—	1	1	—	—	—	—
MRLs	13	—	1	14	15	—	1	16
AAA	6	2	5	13	5	5	—	10

* Until January 9, 1943, the XIII Corps was considered a tank corps, although in reality it was organized like a mechanized corps (three mechanized brigades).

Table 4

Composition and Strength of the Soviet Air Force November 20, 1942

	Seventeenth Air Army, Southwestern Army Group		Second Air Army, Voronezh Army Group		Sixteenth Air Army, Don Army Group		Eighth Air Army, Stalingrad Army Group		102d Fighter Division, AA Defense Forces		Total	
Formations												
Mixed air corps	1		—		—		1		—		2	
Air divisions												
Bomber	1		—		—		1		—		2	
Ground attack	1		1		2		2		—		6	
Mixed	—		—		—		2		—		2	
Night bomber	1		1		1		1		—		4	
Fighter	2		2		2		4		1		11	
Regiments												
Bomber	3		—		1		4		—		8	
Ground attack	5		4		7		14		—		30	
Reconnaissance	—		1		—		1		—		2	
Fighter	6		4		8		17		4		39	
Night bomber	4		3		6		6		—		19	
Mixed	—		—		—		5		—		5	
	Total	Op*	Total	Op	Total	Op	Total	Op	Total	Op	Total	Op
Aircraft												
Bomber	57	46	7	4	20	11	68	29	—	—	152	90
Ground attack	133	118	64	57	103	68	255	177	—	—	555	420
Fighter	169	147	31	23	107	81	408	235	88	23	803	509
Reconnaissance	6	6	15	12	3	2	15	3	—	—	39	23
Night bombers	76	71	54	48	116	98	121	91	—	—	367	308
TOTAL	441	388	171	144	349	260	867	535	88	23	1,916	1,350

* Op = Operational.

Table 5

German and Allied Forces
November 20, 1942

Formations	Corps				Divisions				Brigades			Tot Div¹	Front (km)	
	Army	Panzer	Cav	Tot	Inf	Panzer	Mot	Cav	Light Inf	Inf	Mot		Tot	Per Div
Eighth Italian Army	3²	—	—	3	7³	—	—	—	—	1	—	7.5	160	21.3
Third Romanian Army	4	—	—	4	9⁴	—	—	2	1	—	—	11.0	140	12.7
Sixth German Army	3	1	—	4	11	3	2	—	—	—	—	17.0	230	13.5
Fourth German Panzer Army	1	—	—	1	—	2⁵	1	—	—	—	—	3.0	⎱ 110	11.0
Fourth Romanian Army	1	—	1	2	5	—	—	2	—	—	—	7.0	⎰	
16th Motorized Div, Fourth Panzer Army	—	—	—	—	—	—	1	—	—	—	—	1.0	210	210.0
Army Group Reserve	—	1	—	1	1	—	—	—	—	—	1	3.5	—	—
TOTALS	12	2	1	15	35	5	4	4	1	1	1	50.0	850	17.0

¹ One brigade = ½ division.
² Two Italian, one German.
³ Two German, five Italian.
⁴ One German, eight Romanian.
⁵ One German, one Romanian.

Table 6

Attack Frontage and Density of Soviet Forces
November 20, 1942

Number of Formations (grouped under Total / Attack Zone / Bkth* Sectors)

	Frontage (km)			Total					Attack Zone				Bkth* Sectors				Avg Density (km/Div)		
	Tot	Atk Zone	Bkth* Sect	Corps	Div	Bde	FA	Div Equ	Corps	Div	Bde	Div Equ	Corps	Div	Bde	Div Equ	Total	Atk Zone	Bkth* Sect
Southwestern Army Group																			
First Guards Army	175	10.0	—	—	6	1	—	6.5	—	2	—	2.0	—	—	—	—	26.9	5.0	—
Fifth Tank Army	35	27.0	10.0	3	9	—	—	9.0	3	9	—	9.0	2	4	—	4.0	3.9	3.0	2.5
Twenty-first Combined Arms Army	40	19.0	12.0	2	9	1	—	9.5	2	9	—	9.0	2	8	—	8.0	4.2	2.1	1.5
Army Group Reserve	—	—	—	1	—	—	—	—	—	—	—	—	—	—	—	—	—	—	—
TOTAL	250	56.0	22.0	6	24	2	—	25.0	5	20	—	20.0	4	12	—	12.0	10.0	2.8	1.8
Don Army Group																			
Sixty-fifth Combined Arms Army	80	16.0	6.0	—	9	—	—	9.0	—	5	—	5.0	—	4	—	4.0	8.9	3.2	1.5
Twenty-fourth Combined Arms Army	40	4.5	4.5	1	9	—	1	10.0	1	4	—	4.0	1	4	—	4.0	4.0	1.1	1.1
Sixty-sixth Combined Arms Army	30	—	—	—	6	—	—	6.0	—	—	—	—	—	—	—	—	5.0	—	—
Army Group Reserve	—	—	—	—	—	—	1	1.0	—	—	—	—	—	—	—	—	—	—	—
TOTAL	150	20.5	10.5	1	24	—	2	26.0	1	9	—	9.0	1	8	—	8.0	5.8	2.3	1.3
Stalingrad Army Group																			
Sixty-second Combined Arms Army	40	—	—	—	10	6	—	13.0	—	—	—	—	—	—	—	—	3.0	—	—
Sixty-fourth Combined Arms Army	35	12.0	12.0	1	5	6	1	9.0	1	4	—	4.0	2	4	—	4.0	3.9	3.0	3.0
Fifty-seventh Combined Arms Army	35	16.0	16.0	—	2	1	—	2.5	—	2	1	2.5	—	2	1	2.5	14.0	6.4	6.4
Fifty-first Combined Arms Army	130	12.0	12.0	2	6	1	1	7.5	2	5	—	5.0	1	5	—	5.0	17.3	2.4	2.4
Twenty-eighth Combined Arms Army	210	—	—	—	2	3	2	5.5	—	—	—	—	—	—	—	—	38.2	—	—
Army Group Reserve	—	—	—	—	1	—	3	4.0	—	—	—	—	—	—	—	—	—	—	—
TOTAL	450	40.0	40.0	3	26	17	7	41.5	3	11	1	11.5	3	11	1	11.5	10.8	3.5	3.5
TOTAL	850	116.5	72.5	10	74	19	9	92.5	9	40	1	40.5	8	31	1	31.5	9.2	2.9	2.3

* Bkth Sect = Breakthrough Sector.

Table 7

Operational Density of Artillery and Tanks
November 20, 1942

	Army Groups		
	Southwestern	Don	Stalingrad
Frontage (km)			
Total	250.0	150.0	450.0
Attack zone	56.0	10.5	40.0
Breakthrough sector	22.0	10.5	40.0
Guns and mortars[1]			
Front			
Total	4,320.0[2]	4,076.0	4,502.0
Per km	17.3	27.2	10.0
Attack zone			
Total	3,508.0	735.0	1,320.0
Per km	62.4	70.0	33.0
Breakthrough sector			
Total	1,452.0	735.0	1,320.0
Per km	66.0	70.0	33.0
MRLs			
BM-13 and BM-8			
Front total	148.0	147.0	145.0
Per km	0.6	1.0	0.3
Atk zone and bkth sect	134.0	105.0	90.0
Per km	2.4	10.0	2.2
M-30			
Front total	480.0	288.0	192.0
Per km	2.0	1.9	0.4
Atk zone and bkth sect	480.0	288.0	192.0
Per km	8.6	27.4	4.8
Tanks[3]			
Front			
Total	560.0[2]	166.0	621.0
Per km	2.2	1.1	1.4
Attack zone			
Total	560.0	161.0	397.0
Per km	10.0	15.3	9.9
Breakthrough sector			
Total	560.0	161.0	397.0
Per km	25.4	15.3	9.9

[1] AA guns and 50mm mortars not included.

[2] 182 guns and mortars and 163 tanks of the I Guards Mechanized Corps which did not take part in the initial phase of the counteroffensive not included.

[3] In combat formation only.

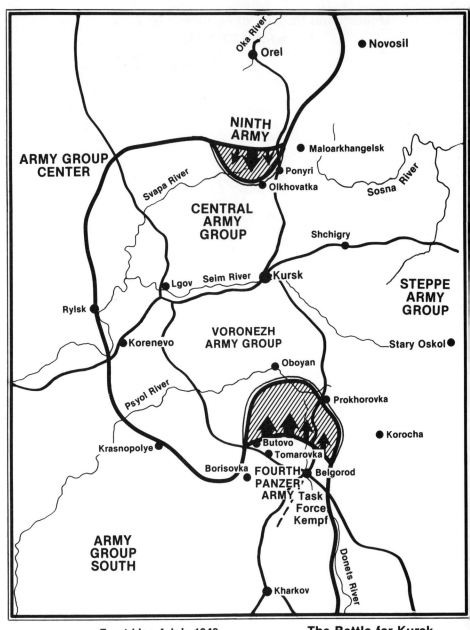

Oka River
Orel
● Novosil

NINTH
ARMY

ARMY GROUP
CENTER
● Maloarkhangelsk
Svapa River
● Ponyri
● Olkhovatka
Sosna River

CENTRAL
ARMY
GROUP

● Shchigry

Lgov
Seim River
● Kursk

STEPPE
ARMY
GROUP

Rylsk ●

VORONEZH
ARMY GROUP

● Korenevo

Stary Oskol ●

● Oboyan

Psyol River

● Prokhorovka

● Korocha

Krasnopolye ●

● Butovo
● Tomarovka

Borisovka
FOURTH
PANZER
ARMY
Belgorod
Task
Force
Kempf

ARMY
GROUP
SOUTH

Donets River

● Kharkov

	Front Line 4 July 1943
	Front Line 12 July 1943
‖‖‖‖‖‖‖‖‖‖‖‖	Area Captured by the Germans

**The Battle for Kursk
July 4-12, 1943
GERMAN OFFENSIVE**

The Battle for Kursk

July 1943

The Soviet counteroffensive during the winter of 1942–43 led to the Germans' defeat at Stalingrad and forced them to retreat from the Caucasus and along the Don River. Advancing westward in January of 1943, Soviet troops pushed out a large salient between Orel and Belgorod in the central region of the Eastern Front, just west of Kursk. As spring approached and the Soviet offensive was halted, the Soviet Supreme Command became aware that the existence of the salient would provide a temptation to the Germans to cut off and crush Soviet forces defending the bulge. After making an estimate of the situation, the Soviets decided to fortify the entire area extensively, meet the anticipated German offensive, and, after bleeding the advancing German forces white, turn to the counteroffensive.

As the Soviets expected, the German High Command decided that it would be to its advantage to strike at the Kursk bulge. Two army groups were to be committed: Army Group Center, commanded by Field Marshal Gunther von Kluge, to the north and west of the salient; and Army Group South, commanded by Field Marshal von Manstein, south of it. Early in April, Hitler signed Directive #6, which outlined the plan for the Kursk offensive, code-named Operation "Citadel." It called for launching two converging blows at Kursk, one to the south from the Orel area by Army Group Center, and the other from the vicinity of Belgorod toward the north, by Army Group South. These drives would encircle and annihilate the Soviet troops in the Kursk salient. Not only would such an operation end the Germans' fear that their forces in the Belgorod-Kharkov areas could be attacked from the flanks; it could also be followed by an offensive east of Kursk toward Moscow, and to the southeast toward the Don and Volga rivers.

The Germans massed 900,000 men, 10,000 guns and mortars, 2,700 tanks, and 2,000 aircraft for the operation. In the north, deployed in the Orel area, was the Ninth Army of Army Group Center, with fifteen infantry, six panzer, and one panzer grenadier divisions. In the south, north of Kharkov, was the Fourth Panzer Army and Task Force Kempf of Army Group South, with ten infantry, eight panzer, and one panzer grenadier divisions. The Second Army of Army Group Center was deployed between these two striking groups, along the western edge of the salient, ready to jump off and crush the Soviet defenders as soon as the encirclement was completed.

The Soviet Supreme Command, meeting in Moscow on April 8, 1943, ordered a buildup of defenses in the salient. Two army groups were assigned there, the Central Army Group in the northern and northwestern sectors (306 kilometers of front), and the Voronezh Army Group in the southern and southwestern sectors (244 kilometers of front). Each army group consisted of five combined arms armies, one tank army, one air army, two independent tank corps, and one independent rifle corps. Together they had more than 1,337,000 men, 19,300 guns and mortars, 3,300 tanks and self-propelled assault guns, and 2,650 aircraft.

Included in the Soviet defense system was the Steppe Army Group, deployed behind the Central and Voronezh army groups as the strategic reserve, and increasing the depth of the defense from west to east to some 250–300 kilometers. This group was composed of five combined arms armies, one tank army, one air army, three tank corps, three mechanized corps, and three cavalry corps. The group had 573,000 men, 8,500 guns and mortars, 1,630 tanks and self-propelled assault guns, and 550 aircraft. The mission of the Steppe Army Group was to stop the German offensive in the event of a German breakthrough; or, together with the first two army groups, to deliver a crushing blow to the German forces in a decisive counteroffensive.

During the spring and early summer, the Soviets built a formidable defense system. The first fortified defense zone was five to seven kilometers deep. It consisted of three parallel defense positions, each of which had two or three trenches linked by numerous communication passages. Where the terrain favored it, combat outposts, well fortified, were set up one to two kilometers in front of the first position. Ten to fifteen kilometers to the rear of the first fortified defense zone was the second zone. It also had three defense positions, and was five to eight kilometers deep. Between the two zones were obstacle centers, each covering an area about five by eight kilometers.

The Soviets made additional preparations. Realizing that in the coming battle the main German thrust would be delivered by panzer formations, they developed a new concept of antitank warfare, namely fortified antitank defense centers. These were constructed in tactically important areas on the most probable axes of tank approaches, at various depths behind the front line. Most of the centers were equipped with four to eight antitank guns, nine to twelve antitank rifles, two to four mortars, a platoon of engineers with mines, and a squad of submachine gunners. Sometimes several tanks and/or self-propelled assault guns were added.

The Germans launched their assault on the Kursk salient on the morning of July 5, after a strong artillery barrage. The Ninth Army of Army Group Center attacked in a 40-kilometer sector in the general direction of Olkhovatka-Ponyri. The Germans moved with nearly 500 tanks, including heavy Tiger tanks, and Ferdinand assault guns, expecting to drive a wedge into the Soviet defenses. But the well-dug-in Soviet defenders fought staunchly, and during the first day repelled four German attempts to break through. Toward evening, however, the Germans managed to break through the first defense zone, and advanced six to eight kilometers on a narrow front.

The next day the Germans brought in fresh troops and, despite numerous Soviet counterattacks, continued their offensive. As a result of fierce fighting they advanced slightly, but they still failed to break through the second defense zone.

Unable to advance through Olkhovatka, the Germans changed their plans. On July 7 they began to concentrate their main effort on the Ponyri axis. In response, the Soviet Command quickly transferred its reserves to this sector. Extremely heavy fighting developed, often becoming hand-to-hand combat. Despite resolute Soviet resistance, the Germans were able to push forward. By the end of the day they had taken the northern part of Ponyri. The Soviets, still holding the southern part of the village, mounted a counterattack and by early morning had thrown the Germans back.

On July 8 the Germans tried once more to move via Olkhovatka. This time they deployed almost all of their armored and mechanized forces on a 10-kilometer front, where they concentrated their main effort. In a bloody two-day battle the attacking group advanced only some five kilometers and could not break the defense. Facing insurmountable Soviet resistance, the Ninth Army was forced to halt its attacks and turn to the defense. Its men and tanks had penetrated Soviet defenses to a depth of only 12 kilometers in a narrow 10-kilometer sector between Olkhovatka and Ponyri, thus failing to accomplish their mission.

In the southern sector of the bulge the main effort was made by the Fourth Panzer Army and Task Force Kempf. They also attacked on July 5, from a jump-off area east and west of Belgorod.

The immediate objective of the Fourth Panzer Army was Oboyan. From there it was to advance toward Kursk. Task Force Kempf, deployed on the secondary axis, was to move northeast toward Korocha and Stary Oskol to cover the eastern flank of the army group.

From the start of the offensive the Germans met well-organized and heavy resistance from the deeply entrenched Soviet troops of the Voronezh Army Group. During the first day, the Fourth Panzer Army, supported by artillery barrages and by aircraft strafing and bombing, progressed very slowly. At nightfall the Germans finally broke through the Soviet first defense zone, drove a wedge about 10 kilometers wide in two sectors, and pushed close to the second defense zone.

Facing the danger of further German breakthrough, the commander of the Voronezh Army Group, General Vatutin, ordered the First Tank Army and two tanks corps to redeploy the night of July 5/6 south and southeast of Oboyan behind the second defense zone and meet the German onslaught.

On the morning of July 6 the Germans committed fresh forces and continued their push. Some gains were made by the II SS Panzer Corps, which advanced about six kilometers and in several points crossed the second defense zone. The XLVIII Panzer Corps made a gain of three to four kilometers and pierced the second defense zone on a narrow front.

During July 7 and 8 the Fourth Panzer Army tried hard to widen the breach and move toward Oboyan and Prokhorovka. In heavy fighting the Germans advanced from 5 to 13 kilometers on a 20-kilometer front.

To the east, Task Force Kempf was no more successful. During the first four days of fighting it advanced only about 10 kilometers in a sector less than 10 kilometers wide, and did not reach Korocha, its first objective.

In the following three days, between July 9 and 11, the Germans continued to make slow progress, advancing on the average 2.5 kilometers per day. Their desperate effort to break the backbone of the Soviet defense system and move quickly northward faded with each passing day as new Soviet troops appeared on the battlefield. However, after committing all their panzer divisions, they managed to make some headway, especially in the direction of Prokhorovka.

The 11th of July was the last day on which the Germans made progress, advancing 2 to 3 kilometers. In the course of seven days the German troops had advanced about 35 kilometers on a front that decreased from 30 kilometers on July 5 to 18 kilometers on July 11. It was a far cry from the original plan. Initially, the German Command had expected to reach Kursk in two or three days. In actuality, the Germans covered one-third of the distance in seven days, and were unable to rout the Soviet forces.

As the German attack faded, the Soviet Supreme Command decided to commit to the battle the Fifth Guards Tank Army and the Fifth Guards Combined Arms Army of the Steppe Army Group, to deliver a final blow against the already badly weakened German forces. The counterattack was launched along the entire front on July 12. Particularly heavy fighting developed around the village of Prokhorovka, with a pitched tank battle between the Fifth Guards Tank Army and the II SS Panzer Corps, involving some 1,200 tanks

and assault guns—about 800 Soviet and 400 German tanks. It was the largest
tank battle in history. Both sides suffered heavy losses, but it was the Germans
who were driven back. They took up defensive positions; and three days later,
under Soviet pressure, they began a total withdrawal that took them back to
the defensive positions they had occupied before the ill-fated offensive began.

Table 1
Soviet Strengths
July 1, 1943

	Central Army Group		Voronezh Army Group		Both Army Groups	
	Total	In Combat Formations	Total	In Combat Formations	Total	In Combat Formations
Men	711,575	510,983	625,591	466,236	1,337,166	977,219
Rifles and carbines	341,396	297,008	301,826	242,876	643,222	539,884
Submachine guns	114,431	110,734	111,261	106,953	225,692	217,687
Machine guns						
Light	15,872	14,411	15,642	14,548	31,514	28,959
Heavy	5,179	5,012	4,578	4,386	9,757	9,398
AT rifles	11,561	11,216	13,224	12,897	24,785	24,113
Tanks						
Heavy	100	74	105	105	205	179
Medium	1,007	924	1,114	1,109	2,121	2,033
Light	587	518	443	443	1,030	961
TOTAL	1,694	1,516	1,662	1,657	3,356	3,173
Assault guns						
Heavy	25	25	—	—	25	25
Medium	32	32	24	24	56	56
Light	34	34	18	18	52	52
TOTAL	91	91	42	42	133	133
Guns and mortars						
AT guns (45 and 57mm)	2,144	2,106	1,795	1,763	3,939	3,869
Field guns (76mm and larger)	3,140	3,107	2,327	2,279	5,467	5,386
Mortars (82 and 120mm)	5,792	5,512	4,596	4,539	10,388	10,051
TOTAL	11,076	10,725	8,718	8,581	19,794	19,306
AA guns						
76 and 85mm	447	446	311	310	758	756
20 and 37mm	684	678	450	434	1,134	1,112
TOTAL	1,131	1,124	761	744	1,892	1,868
MRLs (BM-8 and 13)	246	246	272	272	518	518
Vehicles	29,311	15,849	26,331	14,156	55,642	30,005

Table 2

Composition of Soviet Forces
July 1, 1943

	Central Army Group	Voronezh Army Group	Total
Combined arms armies	5	5	10
Tank armies	1	1	2
Air armies	1	1	2
Rifle corps	11	11	22
Rifle divisions[1]	41	35	76
TD artillery divisions	1	—	1
Rifle brigades	4	—	4
Fortified areas	3	—	3
Independent tank corps	2	2	4
Independent tank brigades	3	6	9
Independent tank regiments	15	7	22
Independent assault gun regiments	4	3	7
Artillery corps	1	—	1
Artillery divisions[2]	3	—	3
AAA divisions	5	4	9
Independent artillery brigades	1	4	5
TD artillery brigades	3	7	10
Independent mortar brigades	1	1	2
Independent artillery regiments	3	9	12
Independent TD artillery regiments	8	26	34
Independent mortar regiments	10	11	21
Independent AAA regiments	12	9	21
MRL divisions[3]	1	—	1
MRL regiments	10	11	21
Independent armored train battalions	1	3	4
Independent engineer, mine engineer, and pontoon bridge brigades	4	5	9
Independent engineer, mine engineer, and pontoon bridge battalions	21	14	35
Corps areas of Air Defense of the Country	—	1	1
Divisional areas of Air Defense	1	—	1

[1] Average strength: Central Army Group 7,400 men
   Voronezh Army Group 8,400 men.

[2] Included: 5th and 12th artillery divisions of the IV Artillery Corps (Thirteenth Army) and 1st Guards Artillery Division (Seventieth Army).

[3] Included: 5th MRL Division of the IV Artillery Corps.

Table 3
Steppe Army Group Strength
July 1, 1943

Men and Means	Total	Combat Formations
Men	573,195	449,133
Rifles and carbines	288,115	248,586
Submachine guns	125,886	121,839
Machine guns		
Light	20,148	19,402
Heavy	5,566	5,412
AT rifles	11,223	10,417
Tanks		
Heavy	25	25
Medium	1,039	1,034
Light	449	447
TOTAL	1,513	1,506
Assault guns		
Heavy	—	—
Medium	72	72
Light	54	54
TOTAL	126	126
Artillery and mortars		
AT guns (45 and 57mm)	1,852	1,821
Field guns (76mm and larger)	1,756	1,746
Mortars (82 and 120mm)	4,902	4,790
TOTAL	8,510	8,357
AA guns		
76 and 85mm	160	155
20 and 37mm	541	508
TOTAL	701	663
Vehicles		
Cars	1,123	651
Trucks	21,916	16,279
Special	3,596	1,633
TOTAL	26,635	18,563

Table 4
Soviet Air Strength
July 1, 1943

	Army Groups			
	Central	Voronezh	Southwestern	Total
Corps				
Fighter	1	2	—	3
Ground attack	—	1	—	1
Bomber	1	1	—	2
Mixed	1	—	3	4
TOTAL	3	4	3	10
Divisions				
Fighter	6	5	3	14
Ground attack	2	3	4	9
Bomber	4	3	2	9[1]
TOTAL	12	11	9	32
Aircraft				
Fighters[2]	455	389	218	1,062
Ground attack	241	276	383	900
Day bombers	260	172	70	502
Night bombers[3]	74	34	64	172
Reconnaissance	4	10	—	14
TOTAL	1,034	881	735	2,650

[1] Includes three divisions (208th, 262d and 271st) of night bombers.

[2] Fighters of the IX Fighter Corps and the 36th and 101st fighter air divisions of the Air Defense of the Country also participated.

[3] Participating night bombers of Long Range Aviation are not shown.

Table 5
Composition of German Forces
July 1, 1943

	Divisions				Width of Front Line (km)	Kilometers per Division
Armies and Groups	Infantry	Panzer	Motorized	Total		
Ninth	15	6	1	22	190	9
Second	9	—	—	9	170	19
Fourth Panzer	4	5	1	10	110	11
Task Force Kempf	6	3	—	9	170	19
TOTAL	34	14	2	50	640	13
% of total forces on the eastern front	17	70	30	22	14	—

Table 6
Deployment of Soviet Forces
July 1, 1943

	Army Group 1st Echelon				Army Group 2d Echelon	Army Group Reserve
	1st Echelon	2d Echelon	3d Echelon	Reserve		
Central Army Group						
Forty-eighth Army	3 rifle divs	4 rifle divs	—	—	—	—
Thirteenth Army	4 rifle divs	3 rifle divs	5 rifle divs	1 tank bde	—	—
Seventieth Army	4 rifle divs	4 rifle divs	—	—	—	—
Sixty-fifth Army	6 rifle divs 1 rifle bde	3 rifle divs	—	—	—	—
Sixtieth Army	3 rifle divs 2 rifle bdes	2 rifle divs 1 rifle bde	—	1 tank bde	—	—
Second Tank Army					2 tank corps 1 tank bde	
Independent formations						IX Tank Corps XIX Tank Corps
TOTALS	20 rifle divs 3 rifle bdes	16 rifle divs 1 rifle bde	5 rifle divs	2 tank bdes	2 tank corps 1 tank bde	2 tank corps
Voronezh Army Group						
Thirty-eighth Army	5 rifle divs	1 rifle div	1 rifle div	2 tank bdes	—	—
Fortieth Army	4 rifle divs	2 rifle divs	—	1 tank bde	—	—
Sixth Guards Army	4 rifle divs	3 rifle divs	—	1 tank bde	—	—
Seventh Guards Army	4 rifle divs	3 rifle divs	—	2 tank bdes	—	—
Sixty-ninth Army					5 rifle divs	—
First Tank Army					2 tank corps 1 mech corps	—
Independent formations						XXXV Gds Rifle Corps II Gds Tank Corps V Gds Tank Corps
TOTALS	17 rifle divs	9 rifle divs	1 rifle divs	6 tank bdes	5 rifle divs 2 tank corps 1 mech corps	1 rifle corps 2 tank corps

Table 7

Operational Density of Soviet Forces[1]
July 1, 1943

	Central Army Group	Voronezh Army Group
Width of defensive sector (km)		
Total	306	244
Potential German attack sector	40	114
Percent of total	13	46.7
Rifle divisions		
Total	41	35
Kilometers/division	7.4	7
In potential German attack sector	14	22
Kilometers/division	2.9	5
Percent of total	34	63
Guns and mortars[2]		
Total	10,725	8,581
Per kilometer	35	35.2
In potential German attack sector	5,000	5,780
Per kilometer	125	50.7
Percent of total	46.6	67.3
Tanks and assault guns		
Total	1,607	1,699
Per kilometer	52	7
In potential German attack sector	1,119	1,304
Per kilometer	27.8	11.4
Percent of total	70	77

[1] Combat troops only.

[2] Excludes MRLs, AAA, and 50mm mortars.

Table 8
Fortification of Central and Voronezh Army Groups
July 1, 1943

| | Defensive Zone | | |
	Main	Second and Rear	Total
Emplacements			
Rifle and machine gun	30,673	35,228	65,901
AT rifle	10,049	16,048	26,097
Trenches (km)	2,593	3,399	5,992
Command and observation posts	4,983	4,350	9,333
Firing positions			
Artillery	6,353	7,575	13,928
Mortar	13,924	20,221	34,145
Planted mines			
Antitank	434,667	68,996	503,663
Antipersonnel	410,980	28,368	439,348
Barbed wire (km)	c. 700	—	c. 700

Table 9
Comparison of Soviet[1] and German[2] Forces
July 1, 1943

	German Forces	Soviet Forces	Ratio (G/S)
Men	c. 900,000	1,337,000+	1:1.5
Combat troops only	c. 570,000	c. 977,000	1:1.7
Guns and mortars[3]	c. 10,000	19,300	1:1.9
Tanks and assault guns	c. 2,700	c. 3,306	1:1.2
Aircraft	c. 2,050[4]	2,650	1:1.3

[1] Central and Voronezh army groups.
[2] Ninth and Second armies of Army Group Center, Fourth Panzer Army, and Task Force Kempf of Army Group South.
[3] Excludes MRL, AAA, and 50mm mortars.
[4] Includes 600 fighter, 100 ground attack, 1,200 bomber, and 150 reconnaissance aircraft.

Table 10

Comparison of Soviet and German Forces on Axes of Main Effort
July 1, 1943

	Central Army Group Sector					Voronezh Army Group Sector				
	German Strength[1]		Soviet Strength[2]		Ratio (G/S)	German Strength[3]		Soviet Strength[4]		Ratio (G/S)
	Total	Per Km	Total	Per Km		Total	Per Km	Total	Per Km	
Men[5]	c. 270,000	6,750	c. 220,000	5,500	1.2:1	c. 280,000	2,456	c. 334,000	2,930	1:1.2
Guns and mortars[6]	c. 3,500	88	c. 5,000	125	1:1.4	c. 2,500	22	c. 5,780	51	1:2.3
Tanks and assault guns	c. 1,200	30	c. 1,120	28	1.1:1	c. 1,500	13	1,304	11	1.2:1

[1] Striking group of the Ninth Army and support elements (8 infantry divisions, 6 panzer divisions, 1 motorized division) on a 40km front.

[2] Thirteenth Army, Second Tank Army, IX and XIX tank corps, 2 divisions of right flank of Seventieth Army (14 rifle divisions, 4 tank corps) on a 40km front.

[3] Striking group of the Fourth Panzer Army and Task Force Kempf (5 infantry divisions, 8 panzer divisions, 1 motorized division) on a 114km front.

[4] Sixth Guards, Seventh Guards, Sixty-ninth armies, XXXV Guards Rifle Corps, First Tank Army, II Guards and V Guards tank corps (22 rifle divisions, 4 tank corps, 1 mechanized corps) on a 114km front.

[5] Includes rear elements.

[6] Excludes MRLs, AA, and 50mm mortars.

Table 11

Tactical Density and Comparison of Soviet and German Forces in the Breakthrough Sectors
July 1, 1943

| | Central Army Group Sector (40km) | | | | | Voronezh Army Group Sector (64km) | | | | |
| | German Forces[1] | | Soviet Forces[2] | | Ratio (G/S) | German Forces[3] | | Soviet Forces[4] | | Ratio (G/S) |
	Total	Per Km	Total	Per Km		Total	Per Km	Total	Per Km	
Men[5]	160,00	4,000	c. 90,000	2,250	1.8:1	140,000	2,188.0	c. 70,000	1,094.0	2:1
Guns and mortars (75mm and larger)	c. 2,050	51.2	c. 1,860	46.5	1.1:1	c. 1,800	28.1	c. 1,300	20.3	1.4:1
Tanks and assault guns	c. 600	15	c. 280	7	2.1:1	c. 1,000	15.6	c. 160	2.5	6.3:1

[1] Striking group of the first echelon of Ninth Army: 7 infantry divisions, 3 panzer divisions.
[2] Thirteenth Army and right flank of Seventieth Army deployed in tactical defense zone: 8 rifle divisions.
[3] Striking group of the first echelon of Fourth Panzer Army: 3 infantry divisions, 5 panzer divisions, 1 motorized division.
[4] Troops of Sixth Guards Army deployed in the tactical defense zone: 7 rifle divisions.
[5] Includes support elements.

Table 12

Status of Soviet Ammunition Supplies (Units of Fire)
July 1, 1943

Types of Ammunition	Central Army Group					Voronezh Army Group				
	Formations and Units	Army Depots	Army Total	Army Group Depot	Army Group Total	Formations and Units	Army Depots	Army Total	Army Group Depot	Army Group Total
Small arms	2.6	0.5	3.1	0.3	3.4	2.6	0.5	3.1	0.8	3.9
50mm mines	0.9	0.3	1.2	0.2	1.4	1.0	0.5	1.5	0.1	1.6
82mm mines	1.3	0.8	2.1	0.3	2.4	1.5	1.7	3.2	0.7	3.9
120mm mines	1.4	0.8	2.2	0.3	2.5	1.3	0.4	1.7	0.4	2.1
37mm AA	2.9	1.2	4.1	0.7	4.8	2.4	0.3	2.7	1.3	4.0
76mm AA	1.0	0.4	1.4	3.3	4.7	n/a	n/a	n/a	1.1	n/a
85mm AA	1.9	1.1	3.0	0.1	3.1	2.1	0.5	2.6	1.5	4.1
45mm AT	1.4	0.7	2.1	0.5	2.6	1.6	0.8	2.4	0.2	2.6
76mm (regimental artillery)	1.6	0.6	2.2	0.2	2.4	1.5	0.5	2.0	0.1	2.1
76mm (divisional artillery)	1.8	0.8	2.6	0.1	2.7	2.2	0.4	2.6	0.4	3.0
122mm howitzer	1.7	0.7	2.4	n/a	2.4	1.3	0.3	1.6	0.4	2.0
152mm gun	2.5	1.2	3.7	0.4	4.1	2.6	1.8	4.4	1.3	5.7
152mm howitzer/gun	1.6	0.7	2.3	0.2	2.5	1.6	0.5	2.1	0.8	2.9
203mm howitzer	2.5	2.7	5.2	n/a	5.2	n/a	n/a	n/a	2.8	2.8

Table 13

Average German Advance per Day

| Date | Central Army Group Sector | | Voronezh Army Group Sector | |
	Attack Sector Width (km)	Advance (km)	Attack Sector Width (km)	Advance (km)
July 5	45	4–5	30	7–9
July 6	40	3–4	25	5–6
July 7	15	1–2	20	5–7
July 8	10	0.5–1	20	3–5
July 9	8	0.3–0.5	15	1–2
July 10	—	—	15	1–3
July 11	—	—	15	2–3
July 12	—	—	—	—

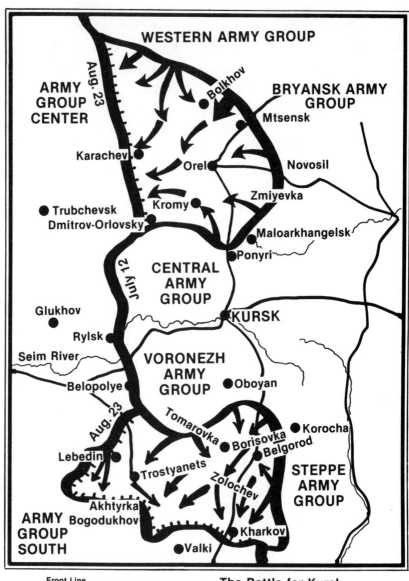

The Battle for Kursk
July 12-August 23, 1943
Soviet Counteroffensive

Front Line August 23 ▰▰▰▰▰▰▰▰

Front Line July 12 ▬▬▬▬▬

Kursk Counteroffensive

July–August 1943

As soon as the Soviets halted the German offensive at the Kursk salient, the Soviet Supreme Command launched a counteroffensive which it had conceived several months earlier. The counteroffensive was carried out as two separate operations, one code-named "Kutuzov" in the north in the Orel sector from July 12 to August 18, and the other code-named "Rumyantsev" in the south in the Belgorod-Kharkov sectors from August 3 to August 23.

The Soviet counteroffensive in the north was a combined operation of three army groups: the left wing of the Western Army Group, and the Bryansk and Central army groups. The Soviets massed over 1,250,000 men, 22,000 guns and mortars, 1,200 antiaircraft guns, nearly 3,000 tanks and assault guns, and some 3,100 aircraft.

Facing the Soviet onslaught were 27 infantry divisions, 8 panzer divisions, and 2 motorized divisions of the German Second Panzer Army and Ninth Field Army of Army Group Center, commanded by Field Marshal Günther von Kluge. Their strength included 600,000 men, 7,000 artillery pieces and mortars, 1,200 tanks and assault guns, and up to 1,100 planes.

According to the strategic plan worked out by the Soviet Supreme Command, the left wing of the Western Army Group under General V. D. Soko-lovskiy and the Bryansk Army Group under General M. M. Popov were to attack on July 12. The Western Army Group was to strike south against the German salient around Orel in order to cut the German forces and, together with the Bryansk Army Group, encircle and destroy the defenders. The Bryansk Army Group was to deliver two blows—one from west of Novosil westward, aimed at splitting the opposing troops and encircling the troops in Orel, and the other from the area east of Bolkhov to cut off the remaining German formations.

The Central Army Group, commanded by General Rokossovskiy, which had been greatly weakened by heavy fighting in defense, was to move on July 15, throw back the German forces that had penetrated into its position, press the offensive in the general direction of Kromy, and then continue northwest and southwest.

At three o'clock in the morning of July 12, the offensive of the Western and Bryansk army groups began, with two and three-quarters hours of intensive artillery and air preparation that demoralized, neutralized, and destroyed many of the German defenses. As the Soviet assault groups attacked, the Germans did not at first offer serious resistance. However, after they had recovered from the initial shock and had committed their close reserves to combat, the fighting became more and more intense.

Facing the possibility that their offensive might be bogged down before it started, the Soviets also committed second echelons and reserves. By the end of the day they had broken through the first German defense zone, advanced some 10 kilometers, and approached the second defense zone.

The next day, July 13, the fierce combat that had characterized the first day intensified. Both sides threw fresh forces, including tank formations, into the battle. Toward the end of the day German resistance weakened, and the Soviet troops broke through the second zone of defense, advancing 12 to 13 kilometers.

Although the Soviet drives shook the German defense in the entire Orel area, the Germans still offered strong, organized resistance, compelling the Western and Bryansk army groups to fight fiercely for every position. To strengthen their forces, the German Command rushed in reserves and transferred units from other sectors of the front, including several panzer divisions from the Ninth Army, which faced the Soviet Central Army Group.

On July 15 the Central Army Group jumped off. The battle resumed in the area which only a few days earlier had been the scene of stubborn defense against the German thrust toward Kursk. In the course of a three-day counteroffensive, the troops of the Central Army Group overcame German resistance and threw the Germans back to the lines they had held on July 5.

Meanwhile, the operations of the Western and Bryansk army groups also proceeded successfully. By July 19, after repulsing numerous counterattacks, the Soviet forces had advanced nearly 70 kilometers toward the southwest and were approaching Khotynets, creating a threat to the main German communication line, the railroad from Orel to Bryansk.

To avert the imminent danger, the German Command made an all-out effort to break up the Soviet offensive, hurriedly bringing additional forces into the breakthrough sector. This slowed the Soviet advance.

Toward the end of July the fighting became even more fierce. Only the commitment of GHQ reserves made it possible for the Soviets to make some progress. After days of inching their way forward, elements of the Western Army Group took Bolkhov, laying the groundwork for enveloping Orel from the northwest. The Bryansk Army Group, after enveloping the German troops in the Mtsensk area, forced them to retreat. Other formations of the Bryansk Army Group moved on Orel from the east.

Forces of the Central Army Group also made headway and, despite stubborn resistance, approached Kromy from the southeast, threatening the Germans in the Orel area with encirclement.

The German situation was growing steadily worse. Army Group Center had used up its reserves and was holding the Soviets with its last available forces. Soon it became clear that the Soviets intended to encircle the entire Orel group of forces, following the Stalingrad pattern. Consequently the German Command ordered a withdrawal from the endangered areas.

Pursuing the retreating Germans, the Western and Bryansk army groups hammered at the German rear guards and advanced doggedly westward. The units of the right wing of the Central Army Group also pushed forward, joining in the enveloping effort from the southwest. The combined operation of the three army groups resulted in German defeat and the capture of Orel on August 5.

The German Command was unable to stabilize the front. Its troops, retreating hastily, left the initiative to the Soviets, who continued to press their advance. On August 12 the Central Army Group took the important resistance center of Dmitrov-Orlovsky, and on August 15 the Bryansk Army Group captured Karachev.

By August 18 the Soviet forces had driven the Germans from the entire Orel salient and had reached the powerful German defense line "Hagen," where they were stopped. During the 37-day offensive the Soviets had advanced 150 kilometers, an average of four kilometers per day.

In the south, where the German offensive was not halted until July 12, the Germans were pushed back to their line of departure by July 23. Here the Soviet counteroffensive started on August 3.

The Voronezh and Steppe army groups, commanded by Generals Vatutin and Konev respectively and deployed offensively at the southern edge of the Kursk Bulge, were composed of eight combined arms armies, two tank armies and two air armies, with 980,000 men, over 13,000 artillery pieces and mortars, 2,400 tanks and assault guns, and about 1,300 aircraft.

The German forces in the area of the forthcoming Soviet attack consisted of the Fourth Panzer Army and Task Force Kempf of Army Group South, under Field Marshal von Manstein, numbering 14 infantry divisions and 4 panzer divisions, 300,000 men, about 3,000 guns and mortars, 600 tanks and assault guns, and 1,000 aircraft. They took up deeply echeloned defensive positions which they had prepared during the spring and early summer, while readying themselves for their ill-fated offensive.

The Soviet Supreme Command decided to launch the main attack with the adjacent flanks of the Voronezh and Steppe army groups from the area northwest of Voronezh toward Bogodukhov and Valki, and to envelop Kharkov from the west. The blow was directed at the junction between the Fourth Panzer Army and Task Force Kempf and was aimed at splitting the German forces into several groups and destroying them piecemeal. At the same time, a number of secondary attacks were to strike the defenders, and the Soviet Southwestern Army Group was to envelop Kharkov from the south.

On the morning of August 3, after a three-hour artillery and air preparation, the Soviet forces attacked. They soon pierced the German defense and, despite fierce resistance, advanced swiftly. By the end of the day they had broken through the first defense zone and had taken two pivotal strongholds at Tomarovka and Borisovka. Following the success of the infantry assault groups, General Vatutin committed his two tank armies, which moved rapidly forward, engaged German second echelons and reserves, and cut off the escape routes of the Belgorod group. This sealed the fate of Belgorod, which was taken by units of the Steppe Army Group on August 5, opening the way for a further advance toward Kharkov.

Despite German efforts to arrest it, the Soviet momentum continued. Soviet tank armies were advancing swiftly toward Kharkov. In five days the First Guards Tank Army advanced 100 kilometers, and on August 18 it captured Bogodukhov, some 50 kilometers west of Kharkov. Northwest of Kharkov the Fifth Guards Tank Army took Zolochev and Kazachya Lopan, closing in on Kharkov from that direction.

The German forces had been split into two groups, with the gap between them growing. One group was retreating toward the southwest, and the other toward the south. On August 11 the Steppe Army Group approached the outer defenses of Kharkov. On the same day, the Voronezh Army Group cut the Kharkov-Poltava railway. The breaking of this link was particularly disastrous for the Germans, for it threatened the destruction not only of the Kharkov forces but of the entire Donets Basin region.

Aware of the danger, Army Group South regrouped its forces and concentrated four infantry and seven panzer and motorized divisions west of Akhtyrka and south of Bogodukhov. On August 11 it launched a massive counterblow against the Voronezh Army Group, directing its main effort against the First and Fifth Guards tanks armies. Fierce fighting continued for over a week. Despite heavy losses which almost wiped out the First Guards Tank Army, the Soviets, after an initial retreat, stood their ground, parried the assault, and on August 20 defeated the attackers, forcing them to withdraw.

While the Voronezh Army Group was engaged in desperate fighting to repulse the furious attacks of the German panzer troops, the Steppe Army Group intensified its efforts to reach Kharkov. On August 13 it broke through the outer defenses of the city, and soon afterward it engaged the Germans at the outskirts of Kharkov.

An exceptionally grim battle developed. Threatened by encirclement, the Germans fought fiercely. By August 21 all the major highways and railways leading west were cut, leaving the Germans in control of only one railway and one highway to Merefa and Krasnograd, south of Kharkov.

The gravity of the German situation increased from hour to hour. There was no more hope for relief from the German Akhtyrka and Bogodukhov forces. The only chance to save the Kharkov troops from total annihilation was a quick withdrawal to the south, which was ordered on August 22.

This was the Germans' last opportunity. Advancing from north, west, and east, the Soviet forces were quickly closing the ring. Their pressure was overwhelming. The final assault on the city was mounted during the night of August 22/23. In savage street fighting the Soviet forces captured the key German resistance points, and on the morning of August 23 the city fell.

With the capture of Kharkov the Soviet counteroffensive ended. In a three-week offensive the Soviet forces had advanced some 140 kilometers toward the south and southwest and had prepared the ground for the follow-up offensive to the Dnieper River. The counteroffensive broke the backbone of the German Army, which lost the initiative and was forced to turn to the strategic defense along the entire Soviet-German front, from the Barents Sea to the Black Sea.

Soviet Order of Battle

Western Army Group (left wing) (as of
    July 12, 1943)
First echelon
  Fifteenth Combined Arms Army
    First echelon
      6 rifle divisions
      1 tank brigade
    Army reserve
      1 rifle division
  Eleventh Guards Army
    First echelon
      7 rifle divisions
      3 tank brigades
    Second echelon
      4 rifle divisions
      2 tank corps
      1 tank brigade
    Army reserve
      1 rifle division
Second echelon
  1 tank corps

Bryansk Army Group (as of July 12,
    1943)
First echelon
  Sixty-first Combined Arms Army
    First echelon
      6 rifle divisions
      1 tank brigade
    Second echelon
      2 rifle divisions
      1 tank corps
  Third Combined Arms Army
    First echelon
      5 rifle divisions
    Second echelon
      1 rifle division
  Sixty-third Combined Arms Army
    First echelon
      4 rifle divisions
    Second echelon
      3 rifle divisions
      1 tank corps
  Army group reserve
    1 rifle corps

Central Army Group (as of July 15,
    1943)
First echelon
  Forty-eighth Combined Arms Army
    First echelon
      3 rifle divisions
    Second echelon
      2 rifle divisions
  Thirteenth Combined Arms Army
    First echelon
      9 rifle divisions
      1 tank brigade
    Second echelon
      3 rifle divisions

Seventieth Combined Arms Army
  First echelon
    7 rifle divisions
  Second echelon
    1 rifle division
    1 tank corps
Sixty-fifth Combined Arms Army
  First echelon
    6 rifle divisions
    1 rifle brigade
  Second echelon
    2 rifle divisions
Sixtieth Combined Arms Army
  First echelon
    4 rifle divisions
    1 rifle brigade
    1 tank brigade
  Second echelon
    1 rifle division
Second echelon
  1 tank army
Army group reserve
  1 tank corps
  1 rifle division

Voronezh Army Group (as of August 3,
    1943)
First echelon
  Thirty-eighth Combined Arms Army
    First echelon
      5 rifle divisions
  Fortieth Combined Arms Army
    First echelon
      4 rifle divisions
    Second echelon
      1 tank corps
  Twenty-seventh Combined Arms Army
    First echelon
      4 rifle divisions
      1 tank brigade
    Second echelon
      2 rifle divisions
      2 tank corps
  Sixth Guards Army
    First echelon
      4 rifle divisions
    Second echelon
      2 rifle divisions
  Fifth Guards Army
    First echelon
      5 rifle divisions
    Second echelon
      1 rifle division
    Army reserve
      1 rifle division
Second echelon
  2 tank armies
Army group reserve
  1 tank corps
  3 tank brigades

Soviet Order of Battle—(continued)

Steppe Army Group (as of August 3, 1943)
First echelon
  Fifty-third Combined Arms Army
    First echelon
      3 rifle divisions
    Second echelon
      4 rifle divisions
      1 mechanized corps

Sixty-ninth Combined Arms Army
  First echelon
    7 rifle divisions
    1 tank brigade
Seventh Guards Army
  First echelon
    7 rifle divisions
    2 tank brigades
  Second echelon
    1 rifle division

Table 1

Composition of Soviet Army Groups

Formations and Units	Army Groups, July 10, 1943				Army Groups, August 1, 1943		
	Western[1]	Bryansk	Central	Total	Voronezh	Steppe	Total
Armies							
Combined arms	2	3	5	10	5	3	8
Tank	—	—	1	1	2	—	2
Air	1	1	1	3	1	1	2
Corps							
Rifle	4	3	11	18	10	5	15
Tank	3	2	4[2]	9	8[3]	—	8
Mechanized	—	—	—	—	2	1[4]	3
Artillery	1	2	1	4	1	—	1
AA defense area	—	—	—	—	1	—	1
Divisions							
Rifle	19	24	39	82	28	22	50
Artillery	3	5	3	11	1	1	2
MRL	—	2	1	3	1	—	1
AAA	3	3	5	11	5	3	8
Fortified areas	—	—	3	3	—	—	—
AA defense areas	—	—	1	1	—	—	—
Independent brigades							
Rifle	—	—	2	2	—	—	—
Assault	—	1	—	1	1	2	3
Tank	5	1	2	8	4	3	7
Artillery	—	1	1	2	3	1	4
Tank destroyer	—	1	3	4	4	1	5
MRL	2	1	—	3	—	—	—
Mortar	—	1	1	2	—	—	—

[1] Left wing only: Fiftieth Combined Arms and Eleventh Guards armies.   *(cont.)*

[2] Includes IX and XIX independent tank corps.

[3] Includes IV, V Guards; II and X independent tank corps.

[4] I Independent Mechanized Corps.

Table 1—(continued)
Composition of Soviet Army Groups

Formations and Units	Army Groups, July 10, 1943				Army Groups, August 1, 1943		
	Western[1]	Bryansk	Central	Total	Voronezh	Steppe	Total
Independent regiments							
Tank	3	9	15	27	6	10	16
Assault gun	2	4	4	10	8	2	10
Artillery	25	4	3	32	6	3	9
Mortar	4	3	10	17	18	4	22
Tank destroyer	2	4	8	14	35	10	45
MRL	6	6	10	22	9	5	14
AAA	7	3	10	20	4	2	6
Independent battalions							
Artillery	—	—	1	1	—	1	1
AAA	2	1	4	7	—	—	—
Armored train	2	7	3	12	—	2	2

During the combat operations the following additional formations were committed:
Western Army Group: Eleventh Combined Arms Army, Fourth Tank Army, and II Guards Cavalry Corps
Bryansk Army Group: Third Guards Army
Voronezh Army Group: Fourth Guards and Forty-seventh Combined Arms armies, III Guards Tank Corps, and III Guards Mechanized Corps
Steppe Army Group: Fifty-seventh Combined Arms Army.

The average personnel strength of rifle divisions was:
Western Army Group: 7,120 men
Bryansk Army Group: 7,920 men
Central Army Group: 6,810 men
Voronezh Army Group: 7,180 men
Steppe Army Group: 6,070 men

[1] Left wing only: Fiftieth Combined Arms and Eleventh Guards armies.

Table 2

Soviet Army Group Strengths

| | July 10, 1943 | | | | | | | | August 10, 1943 | | | | | |
| | Western[1] | | Bryansk | | Central | | Total of 3 | | Voronezh | | Steppe | | Total of 2 | |
	Total	Combat	Total	Combat	Total	Combat	Total	Combat	Total	Combat	Total	Combat	Total	Combat
Men	211,458	189,043	433,616	298,068	640,975	440,383	1,286,049	927,494	693,554	458,167	287,034	198,034	980,588	656,201
Rifles	114,660	71,300	248,952	165,801	366,709	238,100	730,321	475,201	287,551	192,263	147,811	95,129	435,362	287,392
Submachine guns	38,033	37,100	77,313	72,044	120,059	110,538	235,405	219,682	122,502	108,569	55,946	43,247	178,448	151,816
Machine guns														
Light	4,940	4,320	12,605	11,162	14,603	12,126	32,148	27,608	14,334	13,561	7,825	6,363	22,159	19,924
Heavy	1,911	1,813	2,993	2,824	5,249	4,363	10,153	9,000	3,860	2,391	2,023	1,592	5,883	3,983
Super heavy	322	315	499	407	845	761	1,666	1,483	1,032	611	423	223	1,455	834
TOTAL	7,173	6,448	16,097	14,393	20,697	17,250	43,967	38,091	19,226	16,563	10,271	8,178	29,497	24,741
AT rifles	4,713	4,610	8,592	8,025	13,948	11,731	27,253	24,366	11,413	10,381	4,123	4,076	15,536	14,457
AT guns (45 and 57mm)	715	709	1,339	1,259	1,894	1,881	3,948	3,849	1,491	1,473	854	823	2,345	2,296
Field guns 76mm	736	688	1,481	1,325	2,057	2,056	4,274	4,069	1,481	1,351	1,025	943	2,506	2,294
107mm and larger	934	906	1,250	1,230	1,023	1,009	3,207[2]	3,145	788	682	428	411	1,216	1,093
TOTAL	2,385	2,303	4,070	3,814	4,974	4,946	11,429	11,063	3,760	3,506	2,307	2,177	6,067	5,683
Mortars														
120mm	705	701	1,425	1,357	1,621	1,580	3,751	3,638	1,455	1,428	664	639	2,119	2,067
82mm	1,199	1,190	2,147	1,973	3,549	3,395	6,895	6,558	2,953	2,849	1,488	1,414	4,441	4,263
TOTAL	1,904	1,891	3,572	3,330	5,170	4,975	10,646	10,196	4,408	4,277	2,152	2,053	6,560	6,330

1 Left wing only: Fiftieth Combined Arms and Eleventh Guards armies.
2 Without MRL of the Sixtieth and Sixty-fifth combined arms armies.

(cont.)

Table 2—(continued)
Soviet Army Group Strengths

| | July 10, 1943 | | | | | | | | August 10, 1943 | | | | | |
| | Western[1] | | Bryansk | | Central | | Total of 3 | | Voronezh | | Steppe | | Total of 2 | |
	Total	Combat	Total	Combat	Total	Combat	Total	Combat	Total	Combat	Total	Combat	Total	Combat
AA guns 76 and 85mm	48	48	80	79	135	134	263	261	161	161	68	68	229	229
25 and 37mm	263	261	243	234	413	370	919	865	399	399	354	225	753	624
TOTAL	311	309	323	313	548	504	1,182	1,126	560	560	422	293	982	853
MRL BM-8 and 13	136	136	160	160	200	200[2]	496	496	269	269	66	66	335	335
M-30	576	576	1,582	1,582	468	468[2]	2,626	2,626	432	432	—	—	432	432
Tanks	287	277	952	661	1,429	1,248	2,668	2,186	1,859	1,845	454	448	2,313	2,293
Assault guns	27	27	135	133	63	63	225	223	113	112	13	13	126	125
TOTAL	314	304	1,087	794	1,492	1,311	2,893	2,409	1,972	1,957	467	461	2,439	2,418
Vehicles	8,932	7,044	19,745	11,536	17,748	14,490	46,425	33,070	25,942	14,744	13,907	7,507	39,849	22,251

[1] Left wing only: Fiftieth Combined Arms and Eleventh Guards armies.

Table 3

Planned vs. Actual Scope of Operations
July–August 1943

Army Groups	Width of Front (km)			Advance (km)		Duration (days)		Daily Average Advance Rate (km)			
	Attack Zone	Breakthrough Sector						Planned		Actual	
		Planned	Actual	Planned	Actual	Planned	Actual	Rifle	Mobile	Rifle	Mobile
Western (Left wing)	70	20	20.0	80	80	3–4	19	10–15	20–25	4–5	8–10
Bryansk	158	30	30.0	100–120	150	4–5	37	10–15	20–25	4–5	7–9
Central	150	36	30.0	70	120	6	22	10–12	15–20	4–6	8–10
Voronezh	160	20	20.0	150	140	10–12	21	10–15	15–20	6–7	10–15
Steppe	90	11	8.5	100	100	10–12	21	8–10	10–15	4–5	10–12

Table 4

Soviet Air Forces
July 10 and August 1, 1943

	Army Groups, July 10, 1943				Army Groups, August 1, 1943		
	Western[1]	Bryansk[2]	Central[3]	Total	Voronezh[4]	Steppe[5]	Total
Air Corps							
Fighter	2	1	1	4	2	3	5
Ground attack	1	1	—	2	1	1	2
Bomber	1	—	1	2	1	1	2
Mixed	1	—	1	2	—	—	—
TOTAL	5	2	3	10	4	5	9
Air divisions							
Fighter	6	4	5	15	4	7	11
Ground Attack	5	3	2	10	3	3	6
Bomber	3	1	4	8	1	2	3
Night bomber	1	2	—	3	1	—	1
TOTAL	15	10	11	36	9	12	21
Combat aircraft (operational)							
Fighter[6]	565	265	311	1,141	315	240	555
Ground attack	459	269	119	847	254	181	435
Day bomber	84	111	197	392	86	126	212
Night bomber	191	326	71	588	73	—	73
Reconnaissance	23	24	8	55	20	16	36
TOTAL	1,322	995	706	3,023	748	563	1,311
Long range aviation (bombers)	—	—	—	300	—	—	200

[1] First Air Army.

[2] Fifteenth Air Army.

[3] Sixteenth Air Army.

[4] Second Air Army.

[5] Fifth Air Army

[6] Does not include IX Fighter Air Corps and 36th and 101st fighter divisions of the Air Defense of the Country.

Table 5
German Forces on Orel and Belgorod-Kharkov Axes

Formations	Corps			Divisions				Width of Front (km)	
	Army	Panzer	Total	Infantry	Panzer	Motorized	Total	Total	Per Division
Orel Axis (July 10, 1943)									
Second Panzer Army	3	—	3	13	3	1	17	240	14.1
Ninth Army	2	3	5	14	5	1	20	220	11.0
Second Army	2	—	2	8	—	—	8	200	25.0
TOTAL	7	3	10	35	8	2	45*	660	14.7
Belgorod-Kharkov Axis (August 1, 1943)									
Fourth Panzer Army	2	1	3	8	4	—	12	85	7.1
Task Force Kempf	2	—	2	6	—	—	6	80	13.3
TOTAL	4	1	5	14	4	—	18	165	9.2

* In the reserve of Army Group Center there were also nine infantry and one panzer divisions.

Table 6

Comparison of Soviet and German Forces at Start of Counteroffensive

	Orel Operation (July 12, 1943)			Belgorod-Kharkov Operation (Aug 3, 1943)		
	Soviet Forces[1]	German Forces[2]	Ratio S/G	Soviet Forces[3]	German Forces[4]	Ratio S/G
Men						
Total	1,286,000	600,000	2.1:1	980,500	300,000	3.3:1
In combat units	927,500	492,300	1.9:1	656,200	200,000	3.3:1
Guns and mortars[5]	21,000+	7,000+	3.0:1	12,000+	3,000	4.0:1
Tanks and assault guns	2,400	1,200	2.0:1	2,400	600	4.0:1
Aircraft	3,000+	1,100[6]	2.7:1	1,300	1,000[7]	1.3:1

[1] Fiftieth and Eleventh Guards armies, Western Army Group; Bryansk and Central army groups.

[2] Second Panzer Army, Second and Ninth armies of Army Group Center.

[3] Voronezh and Steppe army groups.

[4] Fourth Panzer Army and Task Force Kempf.

[5] Excludes MRLs, AA guns, and 50mm mortars.

[6] Includes 350 fighter aircraft, 560 bombers, and 200 reconnaissance aircraft.

[7] Includes 326 fighter aircraft, 457 bombers, 29 night bombers, and 188 reconnaissance aircraft.

Table 7
Operational Density of Soviet Forces[1]

Army Groups	Width of Front (km)		Kilometers/Division		Guns and Mortars[2]/ Kilometer		Tank and Assault guns/ Kilometer	
	Attack Zone	Breakthrough Sector	Attack Zone	Breakthrough Sector	Attack Zone	Breakthrough Sector	Attack Zone	Breakthrough Sector
Western (Left wing)	70	20	3.7	1.4	60.1	183.6	8.8	30.7
Bryansk	158	30	8.0	1.9	40.3	173.7	4.9	18.6
Central	150	36	5.4	1.6	42.0	104.9	8.0	40.0
Voronezh	160	20	5.0	1.9	53.9	215.8	13.5	70.0
Steppe	90	11	4.0	1.3	57.5	230.0	5.5	42.0

[1] Western (left wing) and Bryansk army groups as of July 12, Central Army Group as of July 15, and Voronezh and Steppe army groups as of August 3, 1943.

[2] Excludes MRLs, AAA, and 50mm mortars.

The Race to the Dnieper

August–September 1943

The German failure at Kursk and the successful Soviet counteroffensive presaged a new Russian drive that brought the Red Army to the Dnieper River.

The German Army High Command (OKH) hoped that after the long and bloody engagements around the Kursk salient the Soviets would not have the strength to continue the offensive westward, and that the Wehrmacht would have enough time to regroup, bring up reserves, and block any further Russian advance. But OKH miscalculated. The Soviet forces were stronger than Hitler and OKH had imagined they could be.

Early in August 1943, the Soviet Supreme Command decided to launch a major offensive against the German forces deployed in the eastern Ukraine and southern Russia, roughly between the Kharkov area in the north and the Azov Sea in the south. The Red Army was to liberate Ukrainian territories east of the Dnieper River, then assault across the Dnieper without halting, and capture a strategic bridgehead on the west bank of the river.

Committed to the operation were five army groups—Central, Voronezh, Steppe, Southwestern, and Southern (from north to south). The main effort would be concentrated toward Kiev in the sector of the Voronezh Army Group. The Southwestern and Southern army groups, before reaching the Dnieper, were to capture the important industrial Donets Basin, which was strongly defended by the German Sixth Field and First Panzer armies of Army Group South.

The combined strength of the five Soviet army groups was 2,633,000 men. They had over 51,000 guns and mortars, more than 2,400 tanks and assault guns, and nearly 2,900 aircraft.

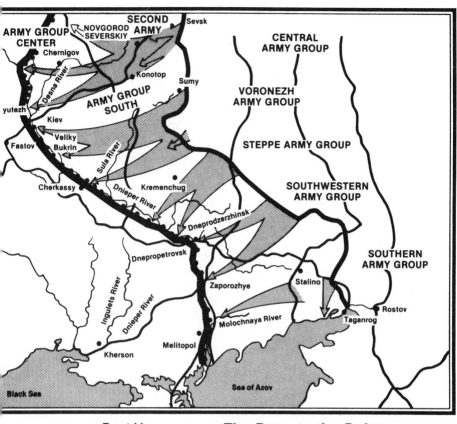

Front Line August 26, 1943

Front Line End of September 1943

The Race to the Dnieper
August - September 1943

The Germans, who knew that sooner or later the Soviets would turn to a decisive offensive, decided to hold their ground, dig in, and cling to their positions. On August 11, OKH ordered the construction of several deeply echeloned, strongly fortified zones, chiefly along large rivers, of which the most important was the Dnieper, a formidable barrier for attacking troops.

German forces facing the Red Army attack were composed of the Second Field Army of Army Group Center, under Field Marshal von Kluge, and the First and Fourth panzer armies and Sixth and Eighth field armies of Army Group South, commanded by Field Marshal von Manstein. These forces numbered about 1,240,000 men, 12,600 guns and mortars, 2,100 tanks and assault guns, and some 2,000 aircraft, giving the Red Army a numerical superiority over the Wehrmacht of 2.1:1 in men, 4.0:1 in artillery, 1.1:1 in tanks and assault guns, and 1.4:1 in aircraft. However, since they had the initiative, the Soviets could and did increase these ratios in critical sectors.

The Soviet offensive commenced in the second half of August 1943. The Central Army Group, under General Rokossovskiy, launched its operations on the morning of August 26 against the well-prepared defensive positions of General Maximilian von Weichs's Second Field Army. The main effort was concentrated on the Chernigov axis. Especially heavy fighting developed on the right flank of the army group, for the town of Sevsk, which had been transformed by the Germans into a strong center of resistance. The town was taken on the evening of August 27, enabling the Soviets to continue their push.

South and southwest of Sevsk, Rokossovskiy also encountered stubborn resistance. During the first six days of the offensive his troops advanced 60 kilometers, taking Rylsk and Glukhov. As the German resistance weakened, Rokossovskiy committed his Second Tank Army, which advanced rapidly westward and crossed the Desna River near Novgorod Severskiy on September 3, threatening the flanks of both Army Group Center and Army Group South. General Chernyakhovskiy's Sixtieth Army took Konotop on September 6, and three days later the important railroad junction at Bakhmach.

Chernigov was captured on September 21, and the same day the Thirtieth Army reached the Dnieper. Soon afterward it established the first bridgehead in the Nivki-Masheva area.

Between August 26 and September 22, the Central Army Group advanced from 250 to 350 kilometers and reached the Dnieper on a 258-kilometer front. By the end of September the army group had established seven bridgeheads on the western bank, the largest of which was 40 kilometers wide and 33 kilometers deep. These bridgeheads created favorable conditions for a further drive to the west.

To the left (south) of the Central Army Group was the Voronezh Army Group, commanded by General Vatutin, deployed between Sumy and Akhtyrka. The main effort of the group was directed in the area between Kiev and Cherkassy.

The group jumped off on August 25, 1943. The Soviet advance was slowed by the fierce resistance of the German Fourth Panzer Army. By the end of August the army group had advanced only 30 kilometers. Sumy was taken on September 2 and Romny and Priluki several days later. Despite the fact that Army Group South was in serious danger of being enveloped from the north, Manstein did not receive permission from Hitler to pull back behind the Dnieper until September 15.

As soon as the German forces started to retreat along the entire front, Vatutin decided to advance on the broadest possible frontage and to continue his pursuit with an assault crossing of the Dnieper. He committed seven of his nine armies for this operation. On September 22, advance mobile elements of the army group arrived at the Dnieper. The first two bridgeheads were established on the same day, one by the Fortieth Army near Rzhischev, and the other by the Third Guards Tank Army in the Veliky Bukrin–Zarubentsy area.

Crossings by other armies followed, and by the end of September the Voronezh Army Group had seized nine bridgeheads on the western bank of the Dnieper, north and south of Kiev. In November, two of the bridgeheads, near Lyutezh and Veliky Bukrin, were to play major roles in the liberation of Kiev, the capital of the Soviet Ukraine.

During the period between August 25 and September 22, the Voronezh Army Group advanced nearly 300 kilometers and took positions along the Dnieper River on a 180-kilometer front.

To the south of the Voronezh Army Group, the Steppe Army Group, commanded by General Konev, was ordered to launch an offensive against well-established positions of the German Eighth Field Army, directing its main effort toward Poltava and Kremenchug.

Deployed on a 120-kilometer front, the army group attacked on August 26 and, after heavy fighting, broke through the German defenses. On August 29 the Soviets took Lyubotin, an important strongpoint on the way to the Dnieper. Four days later, the Merefa fortified area fell into Russian hands. The backbone of the German defense was broken.

On September 24, after advancing nearly 210 kilometers, the Seventh Guards Army reached the Dnieper, and on the same day it captured a large bridgehead (25 kilometers wide and 9 kilometers deep) on the west bank between Dneprokamenki and Domotkan. By the end of September, all of the armies of the Steppe Army Group had reached the Dnieper on a 130-kilometer front; they had seized four additional bridgeheads.

The Southwestern Army Group under General R. Ya. Malinovskiy, deployed between the Steppe Army Group in the north and the Southern Army Group in the south, had launched the first attack of the offensive on August 13. In close cooperation with the Southern Army Group, it was to liberate the Donets Basin and then continue to the Dnieper River north of Zaporozhye.

In heavy fighting the army group broke through the defensive positions of the First Panzer Army. The advance was slow. The Germans offered formidable resistance. On September 6 the Soviets finally captured Kramatorsk and Konstantinovka. Pushing the First Panzer Army back still further, Malinkovskiy took Krasnoarmeyskoye, threatening the rear of the German Sixth Army.

On September 21, elements of the Southwestern Army Group seized Sinelnikovo, an important railroad center east of the Dnieper. Four days later, forward units of the advancing forces reached the Dnieper and immediately started to cross it.

During the next three days the Southwestern Army Group established two small bridgeheads on the western bank, one by the Forty-sixth Army near Dneprodzerzhinsk, and the other by the Sixth Army south of Dnepropetrovsk. Then the army group took up defensive positions along 150 kilometers of the east bank of the Dnieper, between Dnieprodzerzhinsk and Zaporozhye.

On the southern flank of the Soviet offensive, the Southern Army Group under General F. I. Tolbukhin attacked on August 18 in two directions. One group pressed south toward Taganrog and the Sea of Azov, and the other southwest toward the Donets Basin. The area was defended by elements of the German First Panzer and Sixth Field armies.

The breakthrough at the Mius River made the German defense untenable. Following the fall of Taganrog on August 30, the Sixth Field Army was forced to retreat westward. On September 8, Stalino, the capital of the Donets Basin, was taken.

However, German resistance stiffened. Facing the danger of having German troops in the Crimea cut off from the mainland, Manstein committed heavy reinforcements and halted Tolbukhin's offensive along the Molochnaya River, making it impossible for the Russians to reach the lower Dnieper as planned.

In the battle for the Dnieper the Soviets scored a decisive victory. The Central, Voronezh, Steppe, and Southwestern army groups had advanced between 175 and 300 kilometers. They had reached the Dnieper on a 700-kilometer front, captured 23 bridgeheads, and laid solid foundations for future offensive operations.

German Army Group South was fortunate enough and skillful enough to withdraw most of its troops and redeploy them on the other side of the Dnieper. However, Manstein could hold only the inside bend of the Dnieper at Krivoy Rog and Nikopol, where there were rich manganese deposits that Hitler considered indispensable to the German war efforts.

Table 1

Composition of Soviet Forces
September 1, 1943

Elements	Central	Voronezh	Steppe	Southwestern	Southern	Total
				Army Groups		
Armies						
Combined arms	4	8	4	6	5	27
Tank	1	1	1	—	—	3
Air	1	1	1	1	1	5
Corps						
Rifle	11	14	11	11	10	57
Cavalry	—	—	—	1	1	2
Tank	3	7	2	1	1	14
Mechanized	1	2	2	1	2	8
Divisions						
Rifle	38	47	30	41	38	194
Cavalry	—	—	—	3	3	6
Fortified areas	3	—	—	—	3	6
Brigades (ind)						
Rifle	2	—	—	—	—	2
Motorized	—	—	—	1	—	1
Tank and assault gun	3	1	5	3	4	16
Artillery						
Corps	1	1	—	—	—	2
Divisions	3	2	1	3	1	10
AA divisions	5	6	5	3	3	22
MRL divisions	1	1	—	—	—	2
Brigades (ind)	1	3	1	—	—	5
Mortar brigades (ind)	1	1	—	1	1	4
MRL brigades (ind)	—	—	—	1	1	2
TD artillery brigades (ind)	4	5	3	2	3	17
Air corps	3	3	4	2	3	15
Air divisions	12	9	9	9	10	49
Engineer brigades	5	6	3	6	5	25

Table 2
Composition of Soviet Forces
October 1, 1943

	Army Groups					
	Central	Voronezh	Steppe	Southwestern	Southern	Total
Armies						
Combined arms	5	6	6	5	5	27
Tank	—	1	—	—	—	1
Air	1	1	1	1	1	5
Corps						
Rifle	14	10	13	10	11	58
Cavalry	1	1	—	—	2	4
Tank	1	6	—	1	3	11
Mechanized	1	2	1	1	2	7
Divisions						
Rifle	46	35	42	29	35	187
Cavalry	3	3	—	—	6	12
Fortified areas	3	—	—	—	3	6
Brigades (ind)						
Rifle	2	—	—	—	—	2
Airborne	—	3	—	—	3	6
Motorized	—	—	—	1	—	1
Tank and assault gun	3	2	5	2	5	17
Artillery						
Corps	1	1	—	—	—	2
Divisions	3	2	2	2	2	11
AA divisions	5	6	6	3	3	23
MRL divisions	1	1	—	—	—	2
Brigades (ind)	1	3	1	—	—	5
Mortar brigades (ind)	1	1	—	1	1	4
MRL brigades (ind)	—	—	—	1	1	2
TD artillery brigades (ind)	8	5	2	3	5	23
Air corps	3	3	3	3	2	14
Air divisions	12	9	8	9	10	48
Engineer brigades	5	7	5	7	5	29

Table 3

Composition of Soviet Forces
November 1, 1943

	Army Groups					
	Central	Voronezh	Steppe	Southwestern	Southern	Total
Armies						
Combined arms	7	5	7	4	6	29
Tank	—	1	1	—	—	2
Air	1	1	1	1	1	5
Corps						
Rifle	15	13	17	8	14	67
Cavalry	2	1	—	—	2	5
Tank	2	5	3	1	1	12
Mechanized	—	1	4	—	2	7
Divisions						
Rifle	57	45	54	25	45	226
Cavalry	6	3	—	—	6	15
Fortified areas	3	—	—	—	3	6
Brigades (ind)						
Rifle	1	1	—	—	—	2
Airborne	—	1	1	—	3	5
Motorized	—	—	—	—	1	1
Tank and assault gun	1	4	4	2	5	16
Artillery						
Corps	1	1	—	—	—	2
Divisions	2	3	2	1	3	11
AA divisions	7	7	8	3	3	28
MRL divisions	1	1	—	—	1	3
Brigades (ind)	2	3	1	—	—	6
Mortar brigades (ind)	1	1	—	1	1	4
MRL brigades (ind)	—	—	—	—	1	1
TD artillery brigades (ind)	7	6	3	3	5	24
Air corps	3	3	4	3	2	15
Air divisions	13	10	10	9	10	52
Engineer brigades	9	8	6	6	5	34

Table 4

Composition of German Forces
September 1–November 1, 1943

	Army Group Center	Army Group South				
	Second Army	Fourth Panzer Army	Eighth Army	First Panzer Army	Sixth Army	Total
September 1						
Corps						
Army	—	3	2	1	3	9
Panzer	1	2	2	2	—	7
Corps groups	1	—	—	—	—	1
Divisions						
Infantry	10	9	12	8	12	51
Panzer	3	2	6	1	3	15
Motorized	—	1	—	1	—	2
October 1						
Corps						
Army	2	3	1	3	2	11
Panzer	2	—	4	2	—	8
Divisions						
Infantry	13	12	14	17	13	69
Panzer	3	3	7	4	2	19
Motorized	—	—	2	2	—	4
Cavalry	—	—	—	1	—	1
Security	2	2	—	—	—	4
November 1						
Corps						
Army	2	3	1	3	3	12
Panzer	2	1	2	2	—	7
Corps groups	1	—	—	2	—	3
Divisions						
Infantry	14	18	11	17	17	77
Panzer	4	5	2	6	2	19
Motorized	—	1	1	2	—	4
Cavalry	—	—	—	1	—	1

Table 5

Scope of Operation from Jump-Off Area to Dnieper River

Army Groups	Duration	Jump-Off Attack Sector (km)	Advance (km)		Width of Dnieper River Front (km)
			Total	Km/day	
Central	Aug 26–Sep 22	160	250–330	8.2–10.2	258
Voronezh	Aug 25–Sep 22	300	250–300	10.1–13.5	182
Steppe	Aug 26–Sep 24	120	190–210	6.3– 7.0	130
South-western	Aug 26–Sep 25	260	175	5.6	150
Southern	Aug 26–Sep 30	220	250[1]	7.0	160[2]
Total	—	1,060	—	—	720[3]

[1] To the Molochnaya River.

[2] Front along the Molochnaya River.

[3] Does not include the Molochnaya River front.

Table 6

Soviet Bridgeheads on West Bank of the Dnieper
September 30, 1943

Army and Crossing Date	Number of Bridgeheads	Bridgehead Locations	Bridgehead Size (km)	
			Width	Depth
Central Army Group				
Sixty-first	3	SW of Radul	2	1
September 24–29		E of Glushets	6	1–2
		N of Nivki	18	1–7
Thirteenth	1	Nivki, Masheva,	40 max	33 max
September 22–26		Teremtsy		
Sixtieth	3	Strakholese, Rotichi	15	4–10
September 22–29		S of Sukholuchiye,	12	1–2
		Yasnogorodka		
		E of Dymer	8	3–4
Voronezh Army Group				
Thirty-eighth	2	W of Svaromye	2 max	1 max
September 27–29		Lyutezh,	8 max	0.5–1
		Novopetrovtsy		
Fortieth	2	S of Stayki, Rzhischev	10–11	2–3
September 22–29		SE of Rzhischev	8	3
Third Guards Tank	2	Vel. Bukrin, Zarubentsy	11 max	5 max
September 22–29		Grigorovka	4.5	2–3
Forty-seventh	2	N of Kanev	2 max	1
September 27-29		S of Kanev	1 max	0.5
Fifty-second	1	N of Ross River	1–1.5	0.5–1
September 27-29		estuary		
Steppe Army Group				
Thirty-seventh	2	W of Koleberda	6	2–5
September 28–30		NW of Mishurin Rog	18	2–6
Seventh Guards	1	Dneprovokamenki to	25 max	6–9
September 24–30		Domotkan		
Fifty-seventh	2	N of Verkhne Dneprovska	5 max	2–3
September 30		NW of Romankovo	6	3
Southwestern Army Group				
Sixth	2	Zvonetskoye	2	1
September 25–28		S of Voyskovoye	5	3 max

Table 7

Table 7

Voronezh Army Group Units and Equipment in the Bridgehead
October 1–7, 1943

Armies	Rifle Regiments	Rifle and Motorized Rifle Bns	AT Guns	Field Guns	Mortars	Tanks/ Assault Guns	MRLs
October 1							
Thirty-eighth	4	3	27	16	—	—	—
Fortieth	24	—	185	286	415	52/8	5
Twenty-seventh	11	—	25	40	94	—	—
Forty-seventh	12	—	128	94	223	5/0	—
Fifty-second	6	—	—	—	—	—	—
Third Guards Tank	—	19	49	39	93	62/14	—
TOTAL	57	22	414	475	825	119/22	5
October 3							
Thirty-eighth	11	3	35	22	35	—	5
Fortieth	19	2	190	316	397	52/8	5
Twenty-seventh	12	—	88	92	149	—	—
Forty-seventh	12	—	148	110	238	8/0	—
Third Guards Tank	—	19	127	62	234	430/84	4
TOTAL	54	24	588	602	1,053	490/92	14
October 7							
Thirteenth[1]	—	—	—	—	—	—	—
Sixtieth[2]	—	—	—	—	—	—	—
Thirty-eighth	11	3	35	36	35	—	5
Fortieth	19	2	190	316	397	52/8	5
Twenty-seventh	15	—	88	92	149	—	—
Third Guards Tank	—	19	127	62	234	430/84	—
TOTAL[3]	45	24	440	506	815	482/92	10

[1] The entire army.

[2] The entire army except 121st Rifle Division, 248th Rifle Brigade, and one regiment.

[3] Excluding Thirteenth and Sixtieth armies.

Table 8

Means of Crossing of Voronezh Army Group
October 16, 1943

	Voronezh Army Group Armies					
Units and Equipment	Thirteenth	Sixtieth	Thirty-eighth	Fortieth	Twenty-seventh and Third Guards Tank	Forty-seventh
Engineer units						
Pontoon bridge bdes	—	—	—	1	1	—
Pontoon bridge bns	2	2	2	2	2	1
Sapper engineer bdes	—	—	—	1	—	—
Sapper engineer assault bdes	—	—	—	—	1	—
Motorized engineer bns	—	—	1	—	1	—
Engineer bns	—	—	—	—	—	3
Engineer obstacle bns	—	—	—	1	—	—
Crossing equipment						
Type N2P	2	2	1.0	2.0	4.5	1
Type DMP	1	1	2.5	2.0	3.0	1
Type NLP	—	—	—	1.5	2.0	2
Type V	—	1	1.0	—	—	—
Cutter BMK-70	—	—	2.0	5.0	13.0	3
Hydrogliders	—	—	1.0	2.0	5.0	1
Bridges						
Single stringer						
Number	1	1	1	1	1	—
Length (meters)	190	284	250	300	620	—
Load capacity (tons)	30	30	30	30	30	—
Combined						
Number	1	2	—	—	—	1
Length (meters)	190	n/a	—	—	—	470
Load capacity (tons)	30	n/a	—	—	—	12
Floating						
Number	1	2	1	1	1	—
Length (meters)	190	n/a	n/a	n/a	500	—
Load capacity (tons)	16	n/a	16	n/a	9	—
Ferry boats						
5 ton	3	—	—	2	5	6
8 ton	—	—	3	—	—	—
12 ton	—	2	—	3	7	—
30 ton	—	4	4	1	1	2
60 ton	—	—	—	—	1	—
Landing ferries	—	3	—	2	—	—

The Melitopol Operation

September 26–November 5, 1943

The Melitopol operation, which was carried out by the Soviet Southern Army Group (renamed 4th Ukrainian Army Group on October 20) under General F. I. Tolbukhin, was aimed at defeating the Germans still occupying the southeastern part of the Ukraine east of the Dnieper River. The Russian plan called for breaking through the powerful German defenses along the Molochnaya River, encircling and destroying the German forces in the Melitopol area, reaching the lower Dnieper, and cutting off the German troops in the Crimea from the mainland. Tolbukhin's forces consisted of five combined arms armies, one air army, and numerous independent formations and units, with some 500,000 men, nearly 800 tanks and assault guns, 6,000 artillery pieces and mortars, and over 1,100 aircraft.

German forces in the area of the forthcoming Soviet attack were composed of elements of the reestablished Sixth Field Army of Manstein's Army Group South. They were deployed in well-prepared defensive positions ranging from 10 to 20 kilometers in depth. The key defensive stronghold was the city of Melitopol. At the start of the offensive the Sixth Field Army had over 200,000 men, some 1,500 guns and mortars, and nearly 300 tanks and assault guns, and was supported by 700 combat aircraft.

The ratio of forces was in the Soviets' favor: 2.5:1 in men, 4.0:1 in artillery, 2.7:1 in tanks and assault guns, and 1.6:1 in aircraft.

The offensive was launched along the entire 111 kilometers of the army group front on September 26, preceded by an hour-long artillery and air preparation. The main effort was made on the right flank, north of Melitopol on the Mikhaylov axis, by forces of the Fifth Strike Army and the Second and Forty-fourth Guards armies. The secondary attack was delivered by the Twenty-eighth Combined Arms Army south of Melitopol. The Fifty-first Combined Arms Army was in the second echelon.

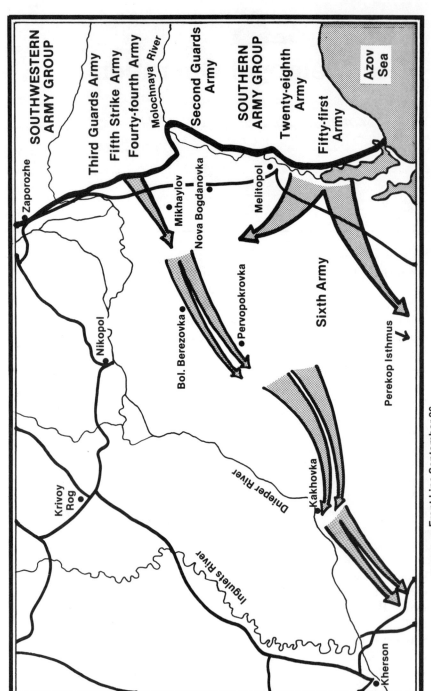

The Melitopol Operation
September 26 - November 5, 1943

——— Front Line September 26

German resistance was fierce, limiting Soviet progress to a few hundred meters per day at the best. Manstein sought to hold the defensive positions on the Molochnaya River at all costs, for this was the last advantageous line covering the approaches to the Crimea. Units of the German Sixth Field Army, kept up to strength with reinforcements, counterattacked frequently, with infantry and tanks maneuvering very effectively.

On October 9 the Soviet Twenty-eighth Army pierced the German defenses south of Melitopol, established a bridgehead on the western bank of the Molochnaya River, and reached the outskirts of the city. This Soviet achievement on the secondary axis changed the operational plan. General Tolbukhin decided to exploit the success. He transferred his reserves—the Fifty-first Army and the XIX Tank and IV Guards Cavalry corps—to the Twenty-eighth Army sector.

For ten days, starting October 13, the Fifty-first Army fought bitterly for Melitopol, which it finally captured on October 23. By that time, forces of the army group's right wing, reinforced by the Third Guards Army from the 3rd Ukrainian Army Group, had broken through the German defenses north of Melitopol. On the morning of October 24 the XIX Tank Corps was committed to combat, and after a day of bitter fighting the Soviet tanks broke through the German second defense zone southwest of Melitopol. On the evening of October 25, the IV Guards Cavalry Corps was thrown into the breach on the Veseloye axis. Its mission was to raid German rear areas and cut off the main communication arteries north of Melitopol. The German High Command, facing the danger of encirclement, ordered the Sixth Field Army to withdraw westward toward the Dnieper. In the morning of October 27 the Red Army went into pursuit along the entire front.

Overcoming the resistance of the German rear guards, the Southern (4th Ukrainian) Army Group fought its way to the lower reaches of the Dnieper and to the Perekop Isthmus, south of the Turkish Wall. This cut off the German Seventeenth Field Army in the Crimea from all land contacts with the German forces on the mainland. The Germans were now cleared from the left bank of the Dnieper except for a small bridgehead at Kherson and a larger one in the Nikopol area.

Soviet Order of Battle
September 26, 1943

Southern Army Group
First echelon
  Fifth Strike Army
  Forty-fourth Combined Arms Army
  Second Guards Army
  Twenty-eighth Combined Arms Army
Second echelon
  Fifty-first Combined Arms Army
Mobile groups

Cavalry-Mechanized Group "Uragan"
  V Guards Cavalry Corps
  XX Tanks Corps
Cavalry-Mechanized Group "Burya"
  IV Guards Cavalry Corps
  IV Guards Mechanized Corps
Army group reserve
  XI Tank Corps
  XIX Tank Corps

Table 1

Soviet Strengths
September 26, 1943

	Fifth Strike Army	Forty-fourth Army*	Second Guards Army	Twenty-eighth Army*	Fifty-first Army*	Army Group Units	Eighth Air Army	Total	National Air Defense Forces	Grand Total
Personnel										
Total	71,351	81,237	67,147	59,547	57,609	130,427	34,957	502,275	22,449	524,724
Combat units	48,534	64,782	52,166	40,779	36,902	74,646	34,957	352,766	22,449	375,215
Rifles and carbines	32,611	30,868	23,892	19,132	21,011	51,406	12,555	191,475	11,233	202,708
Submachine guns	13,075	15,380	11,334	4,422	10,412	17,977	1,131	73,731	1,378	75,109
Light and heavy machine guns	1,834	1,549	1,296	1,168	1,238	2,676	441	10,202	577	10,779
AT rifles	991	1,274	678	761	684	1,280	56	5,724	87	5,811
Field guns (76mm and larger)	488	502	349	354	315	470	—	2,478	—	2,478
AA guns (37mm and 85mm)	67	33	71	26	41	155	88	481	263	744
Mortars (82mm and larger)	560	572	575	267	277	555	—	2,806	36	2,842
MRLs										
BM-13	—	—	—	—	—	270	—	270	—	270
M30	—	—	—	—	—	210	—	210	—	210
Tanks (operational)	27	46	16	7	3	568	—	667	—	667
Assault guns (operational)	—	10	9	—	—	92	—	111	—	111
Cars and trucks	2,483	2,743	3,323	1,878	2,031	10,089	3,634	26,181	1,212	27,393
Tractors	26	79	18	34	45	228	197	627	85	712
Horses	7,703	6,120	6,580	4,500	5,782	31,135	179	61,999	122	62,121

* Combined Arms Army.

Table 2

Composition of Soviet Forces
September 26, 1943

	Southern Army Group							National Air Defense Forces	Grand Total
	Fifth Strike Army	Forty-fourth Army[1]	Second Guards Army	Twenty-eighth Army[1]	Fifty-first Army[1]	Army Group Units	Total		
Corps[2]									
Rifle	3	2	3	1	2	—	11	—	11
Tank	—	—	—	—	—	3	3	—	3
Mechanized	—	—	1	—	—	1	2	—	2
Cavalry	—	—	—	—	—	2	2	—	2
Air defense areas	—	—	—	—	—	—	—	1	1
Divisions									
Rifle	9	6	8	6	6	—	35	—	35
Cavalry	—	—	—	—	—	6	6	—	6
Artillery[2]	1	—	1	—	—	—	2	—	2
AAA	1	1	1	—	—	—	3	—	3
Brigades									
Assault	—	—	—	—	1	—	1	—	1
Artillery	3	1	4	—	—	3	11	—	11
Tank destroyer	1	1	1	—	—	2	5	—	5
Mortar	1	—	1	—	—	—	2	—	2
MRL	—	—	—	—	—	1	1	—	1
Tank	2	1	2	—	—	11	16	—	16
Mechanized	—	—	3	—	—	3	6	—	6
Motorized rifle	—	—	—	—	—	3	3	—	3
Independent airborne	—	—	—	—	—	3	3	—	3
Fortified areas	—	—	—	3	—	—	3	—	3
Independent regiments									
Artillery	1	5	1	2	1	—	10	—	10
Tank destroyer	1	2	3	2	1	8	17	—	17
Mortar	1	1	1	1	1	3	8	—	8
MRL	—	—	—	—	—	11	11	—	11
AAA	1	1	1	1	2	7	13	5	18
AA machine gun	—	—	—	—	—	—	—	1	1
Tank	—	1	1	—	—	1	3	—	3
Assault gun	—	—	2	—	—	7	9	—	9
Motorcycle	—	—	—	—	—	1	1	—	1
Independent battalions									
Mortar	—	—	1	—	—	4	5	—	5
Tank	—	—	1	1	—	—	2	—	2
Tank destroyer	—	—	1	—	—	5	6	—	6
AAA	—	—	—	—	—	—	—	12	12
AA machine gun	—	—	—	—	—	—	—	2	2
Armored train	1	1	—	—	2	1	5	—	5
Motorcycle	—	—	1	—	—	4	5	—	5

[1] Combined Arms Army.

[2] Command and Staff only.

NOTE: In the course of the operation, the Southern Army Group was reinforced by: 4th MRL Division (October 3); LXVII Rifle Corps (4 rifle divisions) (October 14); Third Guards Army (6 rifle divisions and 1 breakthrough artillery division) (October 18); and XXIII Tank Corps (October 20).

Table 3

Composition and Strength of the Soviet Air Force
September 26, 1943

	Eighth Air Army	Long Range Aviation	National Air Defense Forces	Total
Air corps*				
Fighter	1	—	1	2
Ground attack	1	—	—	1
Long range bomber	—	1	—	1
Air divisions				
Fighter	5	—	1	6
Ground attack	3	—	—	3
Bomber	1	—	—	1
Night bomber	1	—	—	1
Long range bomber	—	2	—	2
Independent air regiments				
Fighter	—	—	7	7
Reconnaissance	1	—	—	1
Aircraft				
Fighter (YAK 1, 7, 9, Cobra, Spitfire)	405	6	150	561
Ground attack (IL-2)	237	—	—	237
Bombers (PO-2, A-20-B, PE-2)	147	149	—	296
Reconnaissance (PE-2)	16	—	—	16
TOTAL AIRCRAFT	805	155	150	1,110

* Command and Staff only.

Table 4

Soviet and German Strength Ratio
September 26, 1943

	Soviet	German	Ratio
Personnel			
Total	524,724	c. 210,000	2.5:1
In combat units	375,215	c. 150,000	2.5:1
Artillery and mortars (75mm and larger)	5,320*	c. 1,500	3.5:1
Tanks and assault guns	778	c. 300	2.6:1
Combat aircraft	1,110	700	1.6:1

* Excluding MRLs and AAA.

Table 5

Operational Density of the Southern Army Group
September 26, 1943

Armies	Frontage (km)		Divisions			Artillery[1]		Tanks and Assault Guns	
	Total	Breakthrough Sector	Total	Breakthrough Sector		Breakthrough Sector		Breakthrough Sector	
				Total	Km/Div	Total	Per Km	Total	Per Km
Main attack sector									
Fifth Strike	23	7	9	4	1.7	687	98	27	3.9
Forty-fourth Combined Arms	7	7	6	6	1.2	1,053	150	56	8.0
Second Guards	31	8	8	5	1.6	840	105	25	3.0
TOTALS MAIN ATTACK	61	22	23	15	—	2,580	—	108	—
Secondary attack sector									
Twenty-eighth Combined Arms	50	8	6	5	1.6	577	72	7	0.9
OVERALL TOTAL	111[2]	30	29	20	—	3,157	—	115	—

[1] 76mm and larger. Excluding MRLs and AAA.
[2] Excluding 52km front along the eastern bank of Lake Molochnoye and along the northern bank of the Azov Sea where no offense was planned.

Table 6

Supply Status of the Soviet Forces
September 26, 1943

Type of Materiel	Second Guards Army	Fifth Strike Army	Twenty-eighth Army*	Forty-fourth Army*	Fifty-first Army*	Army Group Depots
Units of fire						
Small arms ammunition	4.77	5.30	8.20	5.70	5.50	1.20
Field artillery rounds	6.65	4.89	6.22	5.40	6.60	1.52
Mortar rounds	1.90	3.05	2.20	3.40	3.20	0.83
AAA rounds	1.69	3.60	4.00	5.20	2.50	1.62
Hand grenades	1.80	2.80	1.50	1.70	2.30	0.60
AT grenades	1.54	2.30	1.60	0.80	4.90	0.54
POL refuels						
Gasoline, B-70	0.40	4.90	1.30	9.50	4.50	0.30
Car gasoline	0.30	0.40	1.20	0.70	0.60	0.10
Diesel fuel	3.30	3.80	1.70	2.60	1.90	2.80
Food and forage in daily rations						
Flour and barley	15.10	6.80	16.40	43.10	63.70	8.40
Meat products	17.90	20.90	11.20	17.50	30.90	2.10
Canned fish	5.40	0.80	3.10	1.90	2.00	1.50
Sugar	5.00	6.00	2.80	3.10	7.10	3.00
Fodder	17.20	18.00	15.80	35.00	13.00	34.60

* Combined Arms Army.

Table 7

Operational Deployment of Army Group and Armies
September 26, 1943

Army Group				Armies		Number of Divisions				Reserves	
First Echelon	Second Echelon	Mobile Groups	Reserves	Armies	Mobile Groups	Total	First Echelon	Second Echelon	Reserve	Tank	Anti-tank
Fifth Strike Army	Fifty-first Army*	Cavalry-Mech Grp "Uragan"	XI Tank Corps	Fifth Strike Army	—	9	8	—	1	140th Tank Bde	426th TD Rgt 6th TD Bde
Forty-fourth Army*	—	—	XIX Tank Corps	Forty-fourth Army*	—	6	3	2	1	—	530th TD Rgt
Second Guards Army	—	Cavalry-Mech Grp "Burya"	—	Second Guards Army	II Gds Mech Corps	8	7	—	1	—	8th TD Bde, 113th TD Rgt
Twenty-eighth Army*	—	—	—	Twenty-eighth Army*	—	6 (3 fort. areas)	3	2	1	512th Ind Tank Bde	512th and 1250th TD rgts

* Combined Arms Army.

Table 8

Rates of Advance of Soviet Forces
September 26–November 5, 1943

	Third[1] Guards Army	Fifth Strike Army	Forty- fourth Army[2]	Sec- ond Guards Army	Twenty- eighth Army[2]	Fifty- first Army[2]	Mechanized Cavalry Groups[3]
Phase One: Breakthrough of Tactical Defense Zone							
September 26–October 26, 1943							
Depth of advance (km)	5.0	12.0	18.0	17.0	17.0	42.0	—
Days in combat	6	31	31	31	30	14	—
Average km/day	0.8	0.4	0.6	0.5	0.6	3.0	—
Phase Two: Pursuit							
October 27–November 5, 1943							
Advance (km)	65.0	130.0	—[4]	303.0	95.0	130.0	250.0
Days in combat	5	6	—	10	6	6	7
Average km/day	13.0	21.7	—	30.3	15.8	21.7	35.7
September 26–November 5, 1943							
Total advance (km)	70.0	142.0	18.0	320.0	112.0	172.0	250.0
Days in combat	11	37	31	41	36	20	7
Average km/day	6.4	3.8	0.6	7.8	3.1	8.6	35.7

[1] Transferred to the Southern Army Group on October 18.

[2] Combined arms armies.

[3] Uragan and Burya.

[4] Transferred to the army group second echelon on October 27.

The Korsun-Shevchenkovskiy Operation

January 24–February 17, 1944

A t the end of 1943 Field Marshal Manstein's Army Group South, unable to stop the Soviet offensive in the Ukraine, was forced to withdraw westward. The situation of the army group had rapidly deteriorated, and there was danger that Manstein's forces would become separated from those of Army Group Center to the north.

On January 14, the 1st Ukrainian Army Group, commanded by General Vatutin, after an advance of 80 to 200 kilometers in three weeks, halted its offensive southwest of Kiev. The army group's left wing enveloped German forces which were still entrenched on the western bank of the Dnieper River in the vicinity of Kanev.

To the south, the 2d Ukrainian Army Group under General Konev, which had been on the offensive since January 5, captured Kirovograd and enveloped the south flank of the same German force, subsequently known as the Korsun-Shevchenkovskiy group. The result of these two envelopments was to leave a large salient bulging into the Russian line, with the 1st Ukrainian Army Group facing it in the north and the 2d Ukrainian Army Group in the south. This presented an opportunity for encirclement and the liquidation of nearly 80,000 German troops.

The Soviet Supreme Command considered the liquidation of the Korsun-Shevchenkovskiy bulge to be extremely important. German forces deployed in the bulge formed a wedge between the 1st and the 2d Ukrainian army groups, pinning down their flanks and endangering future operations. In addition, the Dnieper River was useless as a transportation artery as long as Germans were sitting on one of its banks. Generals Vatutin and Konev were therefore ordered to encircle and destroy the Korsun-Shevchenkovskiy group immediately. The two army groups were to advance in converging directions and link up at Zvenigorodka.

The German Army High Command (OKH) also fully realized both the vulnerability and the importance of the Korsun-Shevchenkovskiy bulge, for it could be used as a springboard for future German operations aimed at reestablishing the front line along the western bank of the Dnieper. The bulge was defended by elements of the First Panzer Army's right wing and by the left wing of the Eighth Field Army—a total of eight infantry divisions, one panzer division, one motorized brigade, and several independent panzer and assault gun battalions.

For the operation, the Soviets committed five combined arms armies (27 rifle and 1 cavalry divisions), two tank armies (four tank corps and one mechanized corps), and one cavalry corps. The ratio of forces was in the

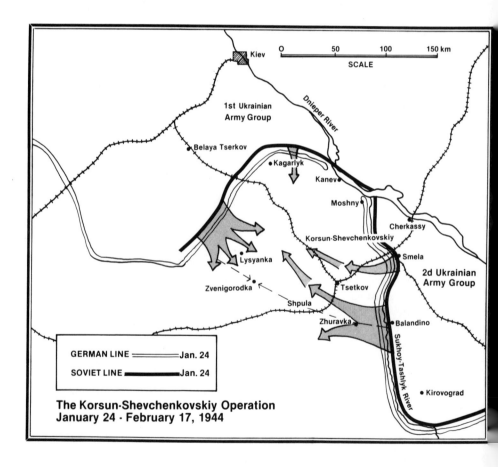

The Korsun-Shevchenkovskiy Operation
January 24 - February 17, 1944

Russians' favor—3:1 in men, 3.2:1 in artillery, and 1.9:1 in tanks and assault guns. The ratio in aircraft was 1:1.

On January 24, at 6:30 in the morning, the assault task force of the 2d Ukrainian Army Group, composed of the Fourth Guards Army and the Fifty-third Army, opened the offensive. By the end of the day Soviet forces had broken through German defenses on a 25-kilometer front and advanced over 15 kilometers. Konev moved his tank army into the breach, and it successfully exploited the breakthrough.

On January 26, after a 35-minute artillery preparation, an attack by the 1st Ukrainian Army Group's Twenty-seventh Combined Arms Army and Sixth Tank Army was launched. Soviet troops penetrated the German positions and, despite stubborn resistance, advanced rapidly toward Zvenigorodka, where several days later they met advance elements of Pavel Rotmistrov's Fifth Guards Tank Army of the 2d Ukrainian Army Group.

On February 3 the encirclement of the German group in the pocket was complete. The Soviets formed two rings—the inner made up of infantry units, to squeeze the Germans in the pocket; and the outer made up of tank armies, ready to repel the awaited German counterattack to relieve the encircled troops.

On February 8 the Soviet Command called on the Germans to surrender, offering humane and honorable terms. The call was rejected by the commander of the surrounded group, General W. Stemmermann. The Soviet troops continued the attack, and by February 10 the whole of the pocket was within range of Soviet artillery.

Meanwhile, Manstein was making an all-out effort to relieve the encircled forces. The first attempt, made by the III Panzer Corps, started on February 4. After five days the German forces came to a standstill in a sea of mud and blood. The XLVIII Panzer Corps took up the attack, but it, too, could advance no more than 10 to 20 kilometers. The III Panzer Corps, after regrouping, made one more effort; and on February 12 it reached Lysyanka, about 12 kilometers from the encircled forces. The Stavka, in a desperate effort to prevent the rescue, committed the Second Tank Army from its reserve. Soviet resistance stiffened, and the counterattacking relief force was stopped.

As the Germans were trying to reach the pocket, the surrounded forces attempted to break out of the ring, attacking fiercely toward the panzer divisions pushing to their rescue. But every attempt cost them many casualties. The determined Soviet forces drew the noose around the pocket tighter and tighter. Only a few German units and formations kept their organizational structure. Most of the troops became masses of stragglers under the command of whatever officers were available, or turned into endless columns of prisoners marching forward to the Red Army rear.

When it became clear that outside help could not be expected, General Stemmermann decided to make one more attempt to break out of the encirclement. Matters came to a head during the night of February 16/17. The remnants of the battered German divisions massed near the village of Shanderovka and, during a heavy blizzard, struck toward Lysyanka, breaking through the Soviet line on a frontage of about five kilometers.

Despite Soviet efforts to prevent the escape, some of the encircled troops came out of the pocket and, on February 17, joined with the III Panzer Corps near Lysyanka. However, all sick and wounded were left behind, and all heavy arms and equipment were abandoned.

The Soviets claim that the Germans lost 55,000 dead and wounded and 18,000 prisoners in the Korsun-Shevchenkovskiy pocket. They give no figures for their own losses.

Table 1

Composition of Ground Forces of 1st and 2d Ukrainian Army Groups

	January 24, 1944			February 3, 1944						
	Army Group			Internal Encirclement Front			External Encirclement Front			2d Ukrainian Army Group Reserves
				Army Group			Army Group			
	1st	2d	Total	1st	2d	Total	1st	2d	Total	
Armies*										
Combined arms	2	3	5	1	2	3	1	1	2	—
Tank	1	1	2	—	—	—	1	1	2	—
Corps										
Rifle	2	7	9	—	4	4	2	4	6	—
Cavalry	—	1	1	—	1	1	—	—	—	—
Tank	1	3	4	—	—	—	2	3	5	—
Mechanized	1	—	1	—	—	—	1	—	1	—
Divisions										
Rifle	7	17	24	3	7	10	5	14	19	1
Airborne	—	3	3	1	2	3	1	2	3	—
Cavalry	—	3	3	—	3	3	—	—	—	—
Artillery (break-through)	—	1	1	—	—	—	—	1	1	—
AAA	1	4	5	—	2	2	1	2	3	—
Independent brigades										
Tank	—	1	1	—	1	1	—	—	—	—
Howitzer	—	2	2	—	2	2	—	—	—	
Gun artillery	1	—	1	—	—	—	1	—	1	—
Light artillery	—	1	1	—	—	—	—	2	2	—
TD artillery	—	3	3	—	—	—	2	2	4	2
MRL	2	2	4	—	—	—	2	2	4	—
Fortified areas	2	—	2	2	—	2	—	—	—	—
Independent regiments										
Tank	—	3	3	—	2	2	—	1	1	—
Assault gun	3	—	3	4	—	4	4	—	4	—
Howitzer	4	1	5	—	—	—	2	—	2	—
Gun artillery	—	3	3	—	2	2	—	1	1	—
TD artillery	2	5	7	—	5	5	3	1	4	—
Mortar	7	4	11	2	3	5	3	1	4	—
MRL	3	6	9	1	3	4	4	2	6	—
AAA	1	1	2	1	1	2	—	—	—	—

* The Fortieth Combined Arms Army (1st Ukrainian Army Group) and the Forty-third Combined Arms Army (2d Ukrainian Army Group) were understrength. On February 5, the Second Tank Army (two tank corps, six tank brigades) was committed in the 1st Ukrainian Army Group sector.

Table 2

Soviet Air Forces Attached to the 1st and 2d Ukrainian Army Groups
January 24, 1944

	Second Air Army* 1st Ukrainian Army Group	Fifth Air Army 2d Ukrainian Army Group	Total
Air Corps	1	4	5
Bomber	—	1	1
Ground attack	—	1	1
Fighter	1	2	3
Air divisions	4	10	14
Bomber	1	3	4
Ground attack	1	2	3
Fighter	2	5	7
Air regiments	13	32	45
Bomber	4	9	13
Ground attack	3	7	10
Fighter	6	15	21
Reconnaissance	—	1	1
Aircraft			
Total	243	754	997
Operational	199	573	772
Bomber			
Total	120	239	359
Operational	120	189	309
Ground attack			
Total	18	120	138
Operational	10	100	110
Fighter			
Total	105	372	477
Operational	69	264	333
Reconnaissance			
Total	—	23	23
Operational	—	20	20

* Only part of the army took part in the operation. After February 3 one additional ground attack corps (two ground attack divisions), one fighter corps (two fighter divisions), two independent ground attack divisions, and one independent fighter division of the 2d Air Army also were assigned to support the ground forces.

Table 3

Operational Deployment in the Main Effort Zone of the 1st and 2d Ukrainian Army Groups January 24, 1944

Army Groups	Operational Deployment		Echelons	
	Army Groups	Armies	Corps	Divisions
1st Ukrainian	Two combined arms armies in one echelon; the mobile group—one tank army.	Twenty-seventh Combined Arms Army in one echelon, three rifle divs and one fortified area. In reserve—one fortified area.	—	two
		Fortieth Combined Arms Army in one echelon, two rifle corps (four rifle divisions).	one	two
		Sixth Tank Army in two echelons. First echelon: one mechanized corps; second echelon: one tank corps.	two	—
2d Ukrainian	Three combined arms armies in one echelon; the mobile group—one tank army. Army group's reserve—one cavalry corps.	Fifty-second Combined Arms Army in one echelon, two rifle corps (three rifle div)	one	two
		Fourth Guards Army in one echelon, two rifle corps (four rifle and one airborne div). In reserve—one rifle division.	one	two
		Fifty-third Combined Arms Army in one echelon, three rifle corps (eight rifle and one airborne div). In reserve—one rifle division.	one	two
		Fifth Guards Tank Army in two echelons: in the first echelon two tank corps; in the second echelon one tank corps echeloned to the right. In reserve—one tank brigade.	two	—

Table 4
Soviet Personnel and Materiel
January 24, 1944

	1st Ukrainian Army Group					2d Ukrainian Army Group							Grand Total
	Twenty-seventh Army[1]	Fortieth Army[1]	Sixth Tank Army	Second Air Army	Total	Fifty-second Army[1]	Fourth Guards Army	Fifty-third Army[1]	Fifth Guards Tank Army	Fifth Air Army	Army Group Reserve[2]	Total	
Men	28,348	33,726	24,423	2,709	89,206	15,886	45,653	54,043	22,301	7,618	20,258	165,759	254,965
Rifles	14,206	16,088	9,772	482	40,548	7,930	20,285	25,323	6,990	1,500	9,832	71,860	112,408
Submachine guns	3,474	6,728	7,819	30	18,051	2,974	9,257	11,230	5,338	347	5,017	34,163	52,214
Machine guns	1,458	1,068	755	—	3,281	748	1,317	1,304	450	—	672	4,491	7,772
AT rifles	658	841	478	—	1,977	314	1,084	1,006	256	—	371	3,031	5,008
Guns (45mm and larger)	468	445	96	—	1,009	167	581	611	122	—	187	1,668	2,677
Mortars (50mm)	112	66	—	—	178	24	42	16	—	—	7	89	267
Mortars (82mm and larger)	307	372	83	—	762	184	460	467	189	—	160	1,460	2,222
AA guns	—	32	34	—	66	64	62	58	102	—	49	335	401
MRLs (BM-8 and BM-13)	24	39	—	—	63	—	44	20	27	—	12	103	166
Chassis (frame) M-30	36	270	—	—	306	—	—	282	—	—	—	282	588
Tanks	—	—	168	—	168	—	27	21	178	—	57	283	451
Assault guns	—	—	22	—	22	—	2	—	19	—	19	40	62
Armored cars	—	—	39	—	39	—	14	3	6	—	—	23	62
Trucks	466	1,218	1,273	29	2,986	502	2,358	2,011	1,297	112	791	7,071	10,057
Tractors	—	18	1	—	19	2	220	150	6	—	—	378	397
Radio receivers/transmitters	341	169	190	—	700	121	502	778	254	—	126	1,781	2,481
Horses	4,956	5,096	—	—	10,052	2,958	5,927	7,737	—	—	14,113	30,735	40,787

[1] Combined arms armies.

[2] Includes the V Guards Cavalry Corps, 2d Tank Destroyer Artillery Regiment, and 804th AA Artillery Regiment.

Table 5

Intensity of Soviet and German Air Activities
January–February 1944

Air Armies	Soviet Sorties				Number of Air Battles	German Sorties			
	Fighters	Ground Attack	Bombers	Total		Fighter	Bombers	Transport	Total
Second Air Army (1st Ukrainian Army Group)	1,824	1,713	2,544*	6,081	106	1,078	2,500	992	4,570
Fifth Air Army (2d Ukrainian Army Group)	1,478	1,318	416	3,212	117	428	800	200	1,428
TOTAL	3,302	3,031	2,960	9,293	223	1,506	3,300	1,192	5,998

* During the period February 3–16 the Soviet Air Force, in 882 sorties, delivered to the troops deployed at the outer encirclement 65 tons of ammunition, 620 shells for rocket launchers, and 49 tons of fuel.

Table 6

Soviet-German Force Ratio
January 24, 1944

	Soviet Forces	German Forces*	Ratio Soviet/German
	24 rifle divs 3 airborne divs 2 tank corps	8 inf divs 1 corps task force	
Personnel strength	244,638	80,000	3.1:1
Guns and mortars	5,166	1,640	3.2:1
Tanks and assault guns	513	270	1.9:1
Aircraft	997	1,000	1:1

* Average strength of a German infantry division was 8,500 men. Corps Task Force "B" consisted of the remnants of the German 112th, 332d, and 255th infantry divisions and was equal in strength to an infantry division.

The Crimea Operation

April 8–May 12, 1944

The successful offensive of the Red Army in the Ukraine west of the Dnieper River in the winter and spring of 1944 created favorable conditions for the liberation of the Crimea. Early in April, as the Russian forces came close to Odessa and entered Moldavia, German forces in the Crimea became totally isolated. Their position was untenable.

Deployed in the Crimea was the German Seventeenth Army under General Erwin Jaenecke (replaced on April 24 by General Karl Allmendinger), composed of the V Corps and the XXXIX Mountain Corps, a total of twelve divisions (five German and seven Romanian), two assault gun brigades, and numerous support units. The XXXIX Mountain Corps held the northern part of the peninsula, including the Perekop Isthmus. The V Corps was deployed close to Kerch, where it contained a small Soviet bridgehead, and along the southeastern shore of the Black Sea.

Soviet forces assigned for the offensive were the 4th Ukrainian Army Group under General Tolbukhin, General Yeremenko's Independent Maritime Army (on April 18 renamed Maritime Army, put under the command of General K. S. Melnik, and attached to the 4th Ukrainian Army Group), the Black Sea Fleet under Admiral F. S. Oktyabrskiy, and the Azov Naval Flotilla, commanded by Admiral S. G. Gorshkov.

The ratio of forces in the Soviets' favor was 2.4:1 in men, 1.7:1 in artillery, 2.6:1 in tanks and assault guns, and 8.4:1 in aircraft.

The Soviet Supreme Command assigned the decisive role in the operation to the 4th Ukrainian Army Group, composed of the Second Guards and Fifty-first Combined Arms armies. The main effort of the army group was to be made by the Fifty-first Army from the bridgehead on the southern bank of the

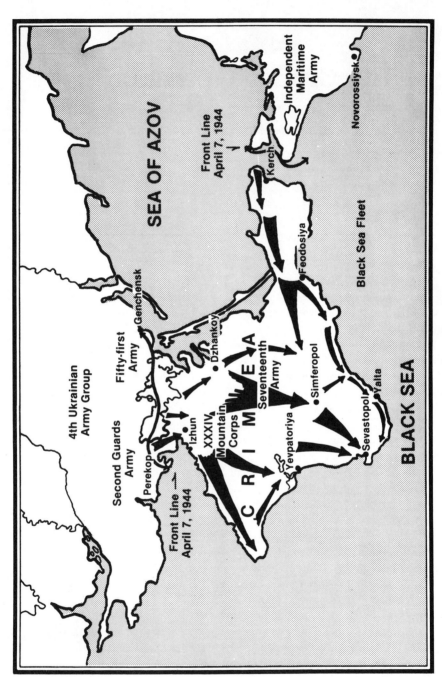

The Crimea Operation
April-May 1944

Sivash, directed toward the rear of the German positions at the Perekop Isthmus and at Dzhankoy. Then the army would continue along two axes, one toward Simferopol and the other toward the Kerch Peninsula.

A secondary thrust would be made by the Second Guards Army across the Perekop Isthmus toward Yevpatoriya and then toward Sevastopol.

The Independent Maritime Army would break through the German defenses north of Kerch, and its right flank and center would advance to Simferopol and then Sevastopol. The left flank would drive along the southern coast of the Crimean Peninsula to Feodosiya, Yalta, and Sevastopol.

The offensive of the 4th Ukrainian Army Group started on April 8, 1944, after a five-day artillery and air bombardment to soften German fortifications on the narrow Perekop Isthmus. During the first two days of operations, the Second Guards Army, despite stubborn German resistance, broke through the first defense zone, which was defended by the XXXIX Mountain Corps. It was halted in front of the second zone near Ishun, which barred the approaches to the open Crimea steppes.

The Fifty-first Army was more successful, attacking on the army group's left flank. On April 10, that army crashed through German fortifications, crossed the narrow defiles, and reached open country. The XIX Tank Corps, committed to combat on April 11, took the important town and railroad center of Dzhankoy and, together with forward mobile elements of the Fifty-first Army, streamed toward the center of the peninsula and its capital, Simferopol.

Meanwhile, the right flank of the army turned toward the rear of the German Ishun defense zone, forcing the XXXIX Mountain Corps to retreat along the entire front. This was what Tolbukhin had waited for. He ordered an immediate pursuit—the Second Guards Army along the west coast toward Yevpatoriya, and the Fifty-first Army in the general direction of Simferopol. The two armies were to meet at Sevastopol.

The capture of Dzhankoy and the rapid advance of the Fifty-first Army threatened the withdrawal routes of the V Corps from the Kerch Peninsula. Especially threatening was the possibility that the Red Army might close the Feodosiya Narrows, bottling up the main forces of the corps near Kerch. The corps commander ordered an immediate withdrawal. Some of the forces were ferried by sea to Sevastopol, and the rest retreated speedily toward Yalta, with Yeremenko's troops at their heels.

German troops, conscious of their isolation and the vulnerability of their situation, continued to retreat without any serious resistance. Since there were only a few trucks available, the German and Romanian divisions moved on foot, closely pursued by Russian tanks and motorized infantry. On April 13, the 4th Ukrainian Army Group captured Simferopol, and on the same day the Independent Maritime Army took Feodosiya. Two days later Yalta fell to the Soviets.

By then German defenses had fallen apart, and what was left of the Seventeenth Army was trying to reach safety in Sevastopol, where the disorganized remnants of the divisions took up defensive positions.

On April 15 forward elements of Tolbukhin's and Yeremenko's forces reached the outer ring of Sevastopol defenses, where the Germans had built strong fortifications. Especially powerfully defended was a group of hills, including Sakharnaya Golovka and Sapun Hill, which rose above the British War Cemetery. These hills were generally considered virtually impenetrable. Behind these fortifications was a garrison of about 72,000 men, with more than 1,500 artillery pieces, about 50 assault guns, and several dozen combat aircraft.

The final assault on the city was launched toward Northern Bay on May 5 by the Second Guards Army. On May 7 the Fifty-first and Maritime armies attacked in the south. The attack was carried out under very difficult conditions, with the Soviet troops forced to climb precipitous slopes under heavy fire. The fighting was particularly heavy at Sapun Hill, which was the key to the German defenses. With its fall, the German resistance was broken. On May 9 Sevastopol was taken.

The remnants of German forces fled to Cape Khersones, where they were either killed or taken prisoner. Many of those who tried to escape by ship were drowned when the ships were sunk by the very active Soviet Air Force, which dominated the skies.

The Crimea operation was concluded on May 12, thirty-five days after it commenced. The Germans lost about 100,000 men, including 62,000 prisoners, and all of their combat equipment. Of the 95,000 who were evacuated, almost half drowned when the ships were sunk.

These disastrous German losses could have been avoided had it not been for Hitler's personal intrusions, prohibiting, and then delaying, withdrawal and evacuation until it was too late.

Table 1

Composition of Soviet Forces
April 8, 1944

	4th Ukrainian Army Group				Independent Maritime Army	National Air Defense Forces	Total
	Second Guards Army	Fifty-first Combined Arms Army	Army Group Units	Total			
Corps*							
Rifle	3	3	—	6	4	—	10
Tank	—	—	1	1	—	—	1
Divisions							
Rifle	8	10	—	18	12	—	30
Artillery*	1	1	—	2	—	—	2
MRL*	—	—	1	1	—	—	1
AAA	1	3	—	4	1	—	5
Brigades							
Naval infantry	—	—	—	—	2	—	2
Artillery	4	5	—	9	1	—	10
Tank destroyer	1	3	—	4	1	—	5
Mortar	1	1	—	2	1	—	3
MRL	—	—	3	3	1	—	4
Tank	—	1	4	5	1	—	6
Motorized rifle	—	—	1	1	—	—	1
Engineer	1	2	2	5	1	—	6
Fortified areas	1	1	—	2	—	—	2
Independent regiments							
Artillery	3	5	—	8	5	—	13
Tank destroyer	2	2	1	5	2	—	7
Mortar	2	1	1	4	2	—	6
MRL	—	—	6	6	4	—	10
AAA	2	1	3	6	5	4	15
Tank	—	1	—	1	3	—	4
Assault gun	1	—	2	3	1	—	4
Motorcycle	—	—	1	1	—	—	1
Independent battalions							
Artillery	2	—	—	2	—	—	2
Tank	1	—	—	1	—	—	1
Motorcycle	—	—	1	1	—	—	1
MRL	—	—	—	—	3	—	3
AAA	—	—	—	—	8	6	14

* Command and Staff only.

Table 2

Soviet-German Force Ratio
April 8, 1944

	Soviet 4th Ukrainian Army Group Independent Maritime Army National Air Defense Forces	German Seventeenth Army	Ratio
Men[1]	471,202	over 195,000	2.4:1
Guns and mortars[2]	5,982	c. 3,600	1.7:1
Tanks and assault guns	566	215[3]	2.6:1
Combat aircraft	1,250[4]	148[5]	8.4:1

[1] Including rear services.

[2] Excluding MRL, AAA, and 50mm mortars.

[3] Mostly assault guns.

[4] Excluding long range aircraft, Black Sea Fleet aircraft, and National Air Defense forces.

[5] Based at Crimea airfields only.

Table 3

Personnel and Materiel
April 8, 1944

	4th Ukrainian Army Group				Independent Maritime Army	National Air Defense Forces	Total
	Second Guards Army	Fifty-first Combined Arms Army	Army Group Units	Total			
Men	86,527	150,899	89,784	327,210	135,562	8,430	471,202
Combat troops only	71,912	96,125	21,741	189,778	92,367	8,430	290,575
Infantry weapons							
Rifles and carbines	43,540	53,613	28,704	125,857	49,884	1,372	177,113
Submachine guns	15,640	23,555	8,008	47,203	22,614	—	69,817
Light and heavy machine guns	3,257	3,785	722	7,764	2,857	1	10,622
AT rifles	1,585	2,079	420	4,084	1,383	—	5,467
Artillery							
Field guns	1,043	1,415	45	2,503	961	—	3,464
AA guns	81	186	69	336	257	266	859
82mm mortars and larger	750	862	82	1,694	824	—	2,518
MRLs (BM-13, BM-8)	—	—	161	161	121	—	282
Chassis for MRL M-20, M-30 and M-31	—	—	455	455	278	—	733
Armor							
Tanks	33	89	174	296	212	—	508
Assault guns	7	—	44	51	7	—	58
Transport							
Cars and trucks	3,067	3,784	6,729	13,580	7,661	504	21,745
Tractors/prime movers	546	1,202	271	2,019	892	49	2,960
Horses	11,859	12,678	5,381	29,918	33,160	17	63,095

Table 4

Composition and Strength of the Soviet Air Force
April 8, 1944

	Fourth Air Army	Eighth Air Army	Black Sea Fleet Air Force	Long Range Air Force	National Air Defense Forces	Total
Air corps*						
Fighter	—	1	—	—	—	1
Ground attack	—	1	—	—	—	1
Long range	—	—	—	4	—	4
Air divisions						
Fighter	2	3	1	—	1	7
Ground attack	2	3	1	—	—	6
Bomber	—	1	1	—	—	2
Night bomber	1	1	—	—	—	2
Torpedo	—	—	1	—	—	1
Long range	—	—	—	8	—	8
Operational aircraft						
Fighter	231	348	239	—	85	903
Ground attack	128	215	74	—	—	417
Bomber	143	147	49	504	—	843
Reconnaissance	21	17	16	—	—	54
Torpedo attack	—	—	28	—	—	28
TOTAL	523	727	406	504	85	2,245

* Command and Staff only.

Table 5

Partisan Personnel Strength
April 8, 1944

	Southern Group	Northern Group	Eastern Group	Total
Men	2,218	774	687	3,679
Rifles	1,511	520	530	2,561
Submachine guns	329	373	171	873
Heavy machine guns	1	5	2	8
Light machine guns	89	38	21	148
AT rifles	3	23	3	29
50mm mortars	15	1	2	18
82mm mortars	—	4	—	4
Pistols/revolvers	183	106	60	349

Table 6

Soviet and German Naval Strength
April 8, 1944

Type of Ship	Soviet Black Sea Fleet	German Fleet
Battleships	1	—
Cruisers	4	—
Destroyers	6	3
Destroyer escorts	—	3
Patrol craft	2	—
Minesweepers	8	5
PT boats	47	40
Attack cutters	—	34
Patrol cutters	80	—
Launchers	—	c.180
Armored Cutters	34	—
Submarines	26	14*
Gunboats	3	10
Landing craft	—	60

* Includes 6 German, 3 Romanian, and 5 Italian submarines.

Table 7

Soviet and German Force Ratios Along the Advance Axes
April 8, 1944

	Northern Crimea Sector			Kerch Peninsula Sector		
	Soviets[1]	Germans[2]	Ratio	Soviets[3]	Germans[4]	Ratio
Men[5]	189,778	80,000	2.4:1	92,367	60,000	1.5:1
Guns/mortars[6]	4,197	1,430	2.9:1	1,785	1,150	1.6:1
Tanks/assault guns	347	c.125	2.8:1	219	c.90	2.4:1

[1] The 4th Ukrainian Army Group: Second Guards and Fifty-first Combined Arms armies (18 rifle divisions, one tank corps).

[2] Seventeenth Army: XLIX Mountain Infantry Corps (5 infantry divisions, 1 cavalry division, support elements).

[3] Independent Maritime Army (12 rifle divisions and support elements).

[4] Seventeenth Army: V Army Corps (4 infantry divisions, 1 cavalry division, support elements).

[5] Combat troops only.

[6] Excluding MRLs, AAA, 50mm mortars.

Table 8

Operational Density of Soviet Forces
April 8, 1944

Armies	Total Front		Breakthrough Sector	
	Total	Per Km	Total	Per Km
Second Guards				
Width (km)	14	—	8	—
Divisions	8	1.8	8	1.0
Guns/mortars	1,792	128.0	1,200	150.0
Tanks/assault guns	42	3.0	40	5.0
Fifty-first Combined Arms				
Width (km)	14	—	10	—
Divisions	10	1.4	10	1.1
Guns/mortars	2,268	162.0	2,590	185.0
Tanks/assault guns	84	6.0	90	9.0
Independent Maritime				
Width (km)	17	—	6	—
Divisions	12	1.4	5	1.2
Guns/mortars	1,785	105.0	972	162.0
Tanks/assault guns	225	15.0	216	36.0

Table 9

Statistical Summary
April 8–May 12, 1944

	4th Ukrainian Army Group	Independent Maritime Army
Initial strengths		
Men	327,210	135,562
Guns/mortars[1]	4,197	1,785
Tanks and assault guns	347	219
Combat aircraft[2]	[2]	[2]
Duration of the operation	35 days	32 days
Width of the advance sector on April 8	28 kms	17 kms
Total distance advanced	c.200 kms	c.260 kms
Average daily advance	5–6 kms	7–8 kms

[1] Excluding MRLs, AAA, and 50mm mortars.

[2] The total number of aircraft taking part in the operation was 2,245.

Table 10

Soviet Personnel and Materiel in Assault on Sevastopol
May 1, 1944

	Second Guards Army	Fifty-first Combined Arms Army	Independent Maritime Army	Army Group Units	Total	National Air Defense Forces	Total
Men	82,662	84,810	124,948	88,780	381,200	16,407	397,607
Combat troops only	66,716	66,990	79,836	26,617	240,159	16,407	256,566
Artillery							
Field guns	1,166	979	923	215	3,283	—	3,283
AA guns	81	127	232	120	560	120	680
Mortars (82mm							
and larger)	689	575	887	107	2,258	—	2,258
MRLs	—	—	300	300	—	—	300
Tanks/assault guns							
Tanks	15	45	118	124	302	—	302
Assault guns	4	—	7	27	38	—	38
Transport							
Cars and trucks	3,447	2,787	7,007	7,239	20,480	134	20,614
Tractors/prime							
movers	242	862	1,154	451	2,709	23	2,732
Horses	14,560	12,461	16,727	5,014	48,762	63	48,825

Table 11

Soviet and German Force Ratio in Assault on Sevastopol
May 1, 1944

Personnel and Materiel	Soviet[1]	German[2]	Force Ratio
Men	242,159[3]	72,000	3.4:1
Guns and mortars	5,541[4]	2,000	2.8:1
Tanks/assault guns	340	50	6.8:1
Combat aircraft	567	c.100	5.7:1

[1] Second Guards, Fifty-first Combined Arms, and Independent Maritime armies.

[2] Seventeenth Army.

[3] Combat troops only.

[4] Excluding MRLs, AAA, and 50mm mortars.

The Byelorussian Offensive

June–July 1944

In the spring of 1944 the Red Army carried out several spectacular operations in the Ukraine, pushed the German forces to the Romanian border, and by April found itself within 75 kilometers of the Bug River, across which the Wehrmacht had launched the Barbarossa campaign three years earlier.

To the north, Army Group Center under Field Marshal Ernst Busch (replaced by Field Marshal Walter Model on June 29) held a salient deep to the east in Byelorussia. The 1,100-kilometer front line of this salient stretched from Lake Neshcherdo in the north, east to Vitebsk-Orsha-Mogilev-Bobruisk, and along the Pripyet River to the vicinity of Kovel in the south. Busch's forces were composed of the Second, Fourth, and Ninth field armies and the Third Panzer Army, and were supported by the Sixth and parts of the First and Fourth air fleets. In addition to Army Group Center, German forces opposing the Soviet thrust in Byelorussia included the Sixteenth Army of Army Group North on the left and the Fourth Panzer Army of Army Group Northern Ukraine on the right. The 63 German divisions and 3 brigades totaled some 800,000 combat troops (1,200,000 with rear services), about 9,500 guns and mortars, 900 tanks and assault guns, and 1,350 aircraft.

Army Group Center, in addition to presenting a threat to the northern flank of the Soviet forces in the Ukraine, was a link between Army Group Northern Ukraine and Army Group North in the Baltic states. The loss of Byelorussia in the central sector of the Soviet-German front would open the door to East Prussia and Poland, create a huge gap in German defenses, and endanger the German forces in the Ukraine, southeastern Poland, and the Baltic states.

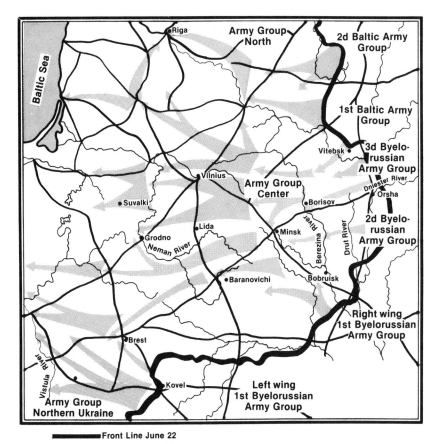

Front Line June 22

**The Byelorussian Offensive
June-July 1944**

To Soviet strategists the salient presented an inviting opportunity to envelop a portion of the German Army, with the additional possibility of striking
a decisively critical blow that would open Germany to invasion.

For this Byelorussian offensive (code-named "Operation Bagration") the
Soviet Supreme Command committed the 1st Baltic and the 3d, 2d, and 1st
Byelorussian army groups. These forces totaled nearly 1,450,000 combat
troops (2,400,000 including rear services), nearly 32,000 guns and mortars,
5,200 tanks and assault guns, and over 5,000 aircraft. The ratio of forces was
overwhelmingly in the Russians' favor: 2:1 in men, 3.3:1 in artillery, 5.8:1 in
tanks and assault guns, and 3.9:1 in aircraft.

The plan of the operation was a simple one. It envisaged six widely
dispersed main assault thrusts aimed at splitting the German forces, weaken-
ing their resistance, and creating a gap in their defenses through which mobile

tanks and mechanized troops would be committed. The German forces would be encircled in several pockets and destroyed.

The operation was to start in the north with a converging attack on the German LIII Army Corps in the strategically important, well-defended Vitebsk area. The adjoining wings of the 1st Baltic and 3d Byelorussian army groups were to encircle and destroy the German defenders.

In the south, the right wing of the 1st Byelorussian Army Group was to encircle and eliminate elements of the German Ninth Army defending Bobruisk. In the center, the left wing of the 3d Byelorussian Army Group and the 2d Byelorussian Army Group were to launch two frontal attacks, one against Orsha, the other toward Mogilev.

In the next phase, the 3d and 1st Byelorussian army groups would converge on Minsk and encircle the German Fourth Field Army. The 2d Byelorussian Army Group would continue to press its frontal attack westward.

An important role in the operation was to be played by a force of 300,000 partisans. They would cut German communications, harass the retreating troops, blow up bridges, and do whatever else they could to disrupt and confuse the Germans.

The offensive was launched on June 23, with the troops of the 1st Baltic Army Group under General I. K. Bagramyan moving from northwest of Vitebsk toward Lepel, with the right wing of General Ivan Chernyakhovskiy's 3d Byelorussian Army Group deployed southeast of Vitebsk and advancing toward Bogushev, and with the rest of the army group moving toward Orsha.

On June 24 Bagramyan crossed the Western Dvina River near Beshenkovichi and established several bridgeheads on its western bank. On June 25 the Forty-third Army of the 1st Baltic Army Group and the Thirty-ninth Army of the 3d Byelorussian Army Group linked up west of Vitebsk, and the German LIII Army Corps found itself in a pocket. During the next two days the corps tried unsuccessfully to fight its way out of encirclement. On June 27 it was overrun, and its 35,000 men either surrendered or were killed.

The German forces defending the approach to Orsha offered stubborn resistance, and initially the Soviets made little progress. Only after the main roads from Orsha to Borisov and other points to the west were cut did the Germans start to withdraw. Orsha was taken on June 27. One day later mobile formations of the 3d Byelorussian Army Group approached the Berezina River near Borisov along a 60-kilometer front and crossed it. The Soviets advanced some 150 kilometers to the west, and the entire German defense system between the Western Dvina and the Dnieper collapsed.

On the left (southern) flank of the Soviet forces, the 1st Byelorussian Army Group, commanded by General Rokossovskiy, moved into action on June 24, attacking toward Bobruisk. While the Third Army, advancing in the Ozerane-Kostyshevo sector, achieved little success in the face of fierce resistance, the offensive was highly successful in the southern sector in the zones of the Sixty-fifth and Twenty-eighth armies. There, on the first day the Russians broke through the German defenses on a 30-kilometer front and advanced up to 20 kilometers. The next day mechanized and cavalry units were committed into the breach and pushed forward to the Ptich River west of Glussk, forcing the Germans to retreat to the north and northwest.

On June 26 Rokossovskiy threw all his forces into a swift advance on Bobruisk. The IX Tank Corps penetrated deep into the German rear, captured Staritsa and cut the Mogilev-Bobruisk highway, and on June 27 straddled all the highways and river crossings northeast of Bobruisk. The infantry units accelerated their advance and enveloped Bobruisk from the northwest, blocking the planned retirement routes of the German divisions. By June 28 most of the German forces in the Bobruisk area were encircled and had either surrendered or been killed. In Bobruisk itself the fighting continued until June 29. Only a few of the 10,000-man garrison were able to break out, and they were soon surrounded and taken prisoner. In the entire Bobruisk area the Ninth Army lost some 70,000 men killed or captured.

While the 3d and 1st Byelorussian army groups were fighting on the flanks, in the center the 2d Byelorussian Army Group (commanded by General G. F. Zakharov) attacked the German Fourth Field Army, which quickly retreated westward under overwhelming pressure. On June 26 Zakharov crossed the Dnieper and two days later took Mogilev. The army group continued to roll forward, reaching the area between the Drut and Dnieper rivers on June 27. General Gotthard Heinrici's Fourth German Field Army, in danger of being cut off by Soviet tanks, was fleeing toward Minsk.

The commitment of the few German reserves had little impact on the Soviet advance. Suffering from a serious shortage of gasoline, the German mechanized and motorized troops could not maneuver freely. Rail transport was almost totally incapacitated by Soviet air strikes and partisan activities.

Mogilev, which Hitler had viewed as the strongest part of the German defense, was taken on July 1, and the Soviet onslaught continued almost unopposed. Units of the 3d and 1st Byelorussian army groups, in a pincer move from north and south, linked up near Minsk and encircled a 110,000-man-strong German force of the Fourth and Ninth field armies. Only a few thousand were able to escape. By July 7 the rest were either killed or taken prisoner. Minsk was taken on July 3.

This closed the first round of the Byelorussian offensive. The Soviet forces had advanced nearly 280 kilometers westward and created a gigantic breach—400 kilometers wide—in the German front. OKH lacked reserves to close the gap. The only fighting forces remaining in Army Group Center were the Second Field Army to the south in the Pripyet Marshes, and the remnants of the Third Panzer Army in the north. The overall German casualties were about 300,000 men killed, wounded, and captured.

On orders of the Soviet Supreme Command the momentous Russian offensive continued without a pause. During July, forces of the 1st Baltic Army Group liberated a large part of Lithuania and entered Latvia. The 3d Byelorussian Army Group captured Vilnius, and in close cooperation with the 2d Byelorussian Army Group reached the German borders in East Prussia. The 1st Byelorussian Army Group took Baranovichi and Brest and crossed the Bug River, where it was finally halted.

To the south, the left wing of the 1st Byelorussian Army Group attacked westward in mid July, took Lublin on July 23, and two days later reached the Vistula River at Deblin. On July 27 the town of Pulawy was captured, and Rokossovskiy established a bridgehead on the western bank of the Vistula. Next Soviet tanks struck northward along the right bank of the river and took Praga, a suburb of Warsaw.

On August 1 Polish patriots in Warsaw rose against the Germans. They undoubtedly expected that the Soviet forces just across the Vistula would seize the opportunity to attack the hard-pressed Germans. But the Soviets gave no help to the Polish insurgents. After nearly two months of desperate battle the remnants of the Polish Home Army (Armia Krajowa) surrendered to the Germans. The city was totally destroyed.

Following the uprising in Warsaw, there were no major combat activities on the central front until mid-January 1945, when the 1st Byelorussian and 1st Ukrainian army groups commenced their Vistula-Oder offensive.

Soviet Order of Battle
June–July 1944

1st Baltic Army Group (one echelon)
  Sixth Guards Army (two echelons)
  Forty-third Combined Arms Army (one echelon)
    Army reserve (one rifle division)
    Reserve (one rifle division)
  Mobile group
    I Tank Corps
3d Byelorussian Army Group (one echelon)
  Thirty-ninth Combined Arms Army (two echelons)
  Fifth Combined Arms Army (one echelon)
  Eleventh Guards Army (one echelon)
    Army reserve (one rifle division)
  Thirty-first Combined Arms Army (one echelon)
    Army reserve (one rifle division)
  Mobile groups
    Fifth Guards Tank Army
    Cavalry-mechanized groups
      III Guards Mechanized Corps
      III Guards Cavalry Corps

2d Byelorussian Army Group (one echelon)
  Fiftieth Army (one echelon)
  Forty-ninth Army (one echelon)
  Thirty-third Army (one echelon)
1st Byelorussian Army Group (right wing only; one echelon)
  Third Combined Arms Army (two echelons)
    Mobile group
      IX Tank Corps
  Forty-eighth Combined Arms Army (one echelon)
  Sixty-fifth Combined Arms Army (one echelon)
    Mobile group
      I Guards Tank Corps
  Twenty-eighth Combined Arms Army (one echelon)
    Cavalry—mechanized groups
      I Mechanized Corps
      IV Guards Cavalry Corps

Table 1

Composition of Soviet Army Groups
June 20, 1944

Formations and Independent Units	Army Groups					
	1st Baltic	3d Byelo-russian	2d Byelo-russian	1st Byelo-russian (right wing)	Total	1st Byelo-russian (left wing)*
Armies						
Combined arms	3	4	3	4	14	5
Tank	—	1	—	—	1	1
Air	1	1	1	1	4	1
Corps						
Rifle	8	11	7	13	39	11
Cavalry	—	1	—	1	2	2
Tank and mech	1	4	—	3	8	4
Divisions						
Rifle	24	33	22	39	118	36
Cavalry	—	3	—	3	6	6
Artillery	2	4	—	4	10	3
AAA	3	5	2	4	14	4
MRL	1	1	—	1	3	1
Brigades						
Rifle	1	—	—	1	2	—
Tank, mech, and assault gun	5	5	4	1	15	4
Artillery	3	5	6	7	21	11
TD arty	2	3	4	4	13	6
Mortar	1	—	1	1	3	3
MRL	—	—	1	—	1	—
Engineer	7	10	5	8	30	8
Regiments						
Artillery	7	10	13	4	34	4
TD arty	3	4	3	7	17	6
AAA	6	7	10	4	27	5
Mortar	4	4	4	6	18	5
MRL	5	7	5	11	28	7
Fortified areas	1	1	1	4	7	—

* July 17, 1944.

Table 2

Composition of German Forces
June 22, 1944

Formations	Divisions											Brigades		
	Inf	Tank	Mot	Lt Inf	Luftwaffe Field Div	Cav	Security (Guard)	Field-Training	Ski Jaeger	Reserve	Total	Inf	Cav	Total
Army Group Center														
Third Panzer Army	8	—	—	—	2	—	1	—	—	—	11	—	—	—
Fourth Army	8	—	2	—	—	—	1	—	—	—	11	—	—	—
Ninth Army	10	—	—	—	—	—	—	—	—	—	10	—	—	—
Second Army	5	1	—	—	—	1	1	—	—	3	11	1	2	3[1]
Reserve[2]	3	—	1	1	—	—	3	1	—	—	9	—	—	—
TOTAL	34	1	3	1	2	1	6	1	—	3	52	1	2	3[1]
Sixteenth Army	4	—	—	—	—	—	1	1	—	—	5	1	—	—
Fourth Panzer Army	4	1	—	—	—	—	—	—	1	—	6	—	—	—
GRAND TOTAL	42	2	3	1	2	1	7	1	1	3	63	1	2	3[1]

[1] Equivalent to 1.5 divisions.

[2] Included in the Reserve was the 60th Motorized Division, subordinated directly to OKH (Army High Command).

Table 3

Men and Equipment of Soviet Army Groups
June 20, 1944

Men and Equip-ment	Army Groups					1st Byelorussian Army Group (left wing) (July 17, 1944)
	1st Baltic	3d Byelo-russian	2d Byelo-russian	1st Byelorussian (right wing)	Total[1]	
Men[2]	227,000	389,500	202,900	434,900	1,254,300	416,000
Machine guns	8,432	13,214	5,750	16,035	43,431	n/a
Tanks	561	1,169	102	883	2,715	1,126
Assault guns	126	641	174	414	1,355	622
AT guns (45–57mm)	778	1,175	833	1,444	4,230	1,107
Field guns (76mm and larger)	2,133	2,893	1,768	3,769	10,563	3,640
Mortars (82mm and 120mm)	2,213	3,552	1,957	3,792	11,514	3,985
MRLs	604	689	264	749	2,306	710
AAA guns	420	792	329	762	2,303	512
Aircraft	902	1,864	528	2,033	5,327	1,465
Trucks	19,537	16,208	7,727	17,177	60,649	19,550

[1] Combat personnel only.

[2] Including rear services and reinforcements that arrived in the course of the operation, the total strength equaled 2,500,000 men, over 45,000 guns and mortars, over 6,000 tanks and assault guns, and about 7,000 aircraft.

Table 4

Operational Density of Soviet Troops
June 22, 1944

	Entire Front			Breakthrough Sector		
Army Groups	Frontage (km)	Divisions	Km/Div	Frontage (km)	Divisions	Km/Div
1st Baltic	160	24	6.7	25	16	1.6
3d Byelorussian	140	33	4.2	30	25	1.2
2d Byelorussian	160	22	7.3	12	10	1.2
1st Byelorussian (right wing)	230	39	5.9	29	22	1.3
TOTAL	690	118	5.8	96	73	1.3
Sixty-first Combined Arms Army[1] 1st Byelorussian Army Group	320[2]	6	53.3	—	—	—
Left wing 1st Byelorussian Army Group (July 17, 1944)	120	36	3.3	20	20	1.0

[1] Deployed in the center between the right and left wings of the 1st Byelorussian Army Group.
[2] Includes Pripyet Marshes.

Table 5

Composition and Strength of Soviet Air Armies
June 20, 1944

	Air Armies					
Formations and Aircraft	Third (1st Baltic)	First (3d Byelo-russian)	Fourth (2d Byelo-russian)	Sixteenth (1st Byelo-russian)*	Total	Long Range Air Force
Air divisions						
Fighter	3	8	2	8	21	—
Ground attack	3	4	2	5	14	—
Bomber	—	4	—	4	8	16
Night bomber	1	2	1	2	6	—
TOTAL	7	18	5	19	49	16
Aircraft						
Fighters	403	767	196	952	2,318	—
Ground attack	368	547	193	636	1,744	—
Bombers	—	392	—	263	655	1,007
Night bombers	79	81	121	150	431	—
Reconnaissance	52	77	18	32	179	—
TOTAL	902	1,864	528	2,033	5,327	1,007

* Right wing.

Table 6

Deployment and Operational Density of German Forces
June 20, 1944

Armies	First Line Div	First Line Bde	Second Line Div	Second Line Bde	Total Div	Total Bde	Army Group Reserve[1]	Grand Total	Frontage (km)	Km/Div
Sixteenth (right-wing formations)	3	—	2	—	5	—	—	5.0	80	16.0
Third Panzer	10	—	1	—	11	—	2	13.0	160	12.3
Fourth	10	—	1	—	11	—	4	15.0	245	16.3
Ninth	10	—	—	—	10	—	3	13.0	250	19.2
Second	8	2	3	1	11	3	—	12.5[2]	325	26.0
Fourth Panzer (left-wing formations)	5	—	1	—	6	—	—	6.0	60	10.0
TOTAL	46	2	8	1	54	3	9	64.5	1,120	17.4

[1] Divisions assigned to the army group reserve and divisions directly subordinate to the OKH were deployed in the sectors of their probable commitment.

[2] Two brigades equivalent to one division.

Table 7
Soviet Reinforcements
June–July 1944

Reinforcements to Army Groups	Combined Arms				Tank and Mechanized					Artillery										AA Arty			Eng	Air Force	
	Rifle Corps	Rifle Div	Cav Corps	Cav Div	Tank Corps	Mech Corps	Tank Bde	Ind Tank Rgt	Ind Assault Rgt	Corps	Div	Bde	Rgt	Mortar Rgt	TD Bde	TD Rgt	MRL Div	MRL Bde	MRL Rgt	Div	Rgt	Heavy Arty Bn	Bde	Corps	Div
Before operation																									
1st Baltic Ind formations	1	2	—	—	1	—	—	2	3	—	1	—	—	—	1	—	1	—	2	1	—	—	1	1	3
3d Byelorussian																									
Eleventh Guards Army (arrived May 28)	3	9	—	—	—	—	—	—	—	—	—	1	3	1	1	1	—	—	—	—	1	—	—	—	—
Fifth Guards Tank Army (arrived June 23)	—	—	—	—	2	—	—	1	5	—	—	—	—	—	—	—	—	—	—	—	—	—	—	—	—
Ind formations and units	—	—	1	3	1	1	—	6	11	1	2	2	—	—	—	1	—	—	—	—	—	5	1	4	10
TOTAL	3	9	1	3	3	1	—	7	16	1	2	3	3	1	1	1	—	—	—	—	1	5	1	4	10
2d Byelorussian Ind formations	2	5	—	—	—	—	—	—	—	—	—	2	—	—	2	—	—	1	—	1	—	—	—	—	—

(cont.)

Table 7—(continued)

1st Byelorussian																									
Twenty-eighth Army* (arrived May 29)	3	9	—	—	—	—	—	—	—	—	1	—	1	1	—	—	1	—	—	3	—	1	—	—	—
Eighth Guards Army (arrived June 15)	3	9	—	—	—	—	1	1	—	1	1	1	—	1	1	—	—	1	—	1	—	1	—	1	—
Second Tank Army (arrived June 15)	—	—	3	1	1	—	—	1	1	—	—	1	—	1	—	—	—	1	—	—	—	—	—	1	—
First Polish Army	—	4	—	—	1	—	—	4	—	—	1	1	1	—	1	1	—	1	—	1	2	—	1	—	5
Ind formations	—	—	3	8	—	—	2	6	—	—	1	—	—	—	1	—	—	—	2	—	7	2	—	1	—	10
TOTAL	6	22	3	9	2	1	2	11	2	3	4	2	1	3	4	1	1	4	2	5	9	3	2	3	5	10
TOTAL	12	38	4	10	2	1	4	17	3	4	5	3	1	2	7	1	1	4	2	8	18	4	4	7	10	23
During operation																									
1st Baltic																									
Fifty-first Army* (arrived July 1)	3	9	—	—	—	—	—	1	—	1	1	1	—	1	1	—	—	—	—	—	—	—	—	—	—
Second Guards Army	3	9	—	—	—	—	—	1	—	1	1	—	—	—	—	—	—	3	—	1	3	2	1	—	—
TOTAL	6	18	—	—	—	—	—	2	—	2	2	1	—	1	1	—	—	3	—	1	3	2	1	—	—
GRAND TOTAL	18	56	4	12	10	2	1	18	31	3	1	4	19	7	5	7	4	1	3	1	6	2	7	4	10	23

* Combined Arms Army.

161

Table 8

Frontage and Density of Artillery,[1] Tanks, and Assault Guns
June–July 1944

Army Groups	Frontage			Guns and Mortars[2]					Tanks and Assault Guns				
	Total Kms	Breakthrough Sector		Entire Front		Breakthrough Sector			Entire Front		Breakthrough Sector		
		/Km	% of Total	Total	/Km	Number	% of Total	/Km	Total	/Km	Number	% of Total	/Km
1st Baltic	160	25	15.6	4,950	31	3,768	76.1	151	687	4.3	535	77.8	21.4
3d Byelorussian	140	33	23.6	7,134	51	5,764	80.8	175	1,810	12.9	1,466	80.9	44.4
2d Byelorussian	160	12	7.5	3,989	30	2,168	54.3	181	276	1.7	227	82.2	18.9
1st Byelorussian (right wing only)	230	29	12.6	8,310	36	5,929	71.3	204	1,297	5.6	1,297	100.0	44.7
TOTAL	690	99	14.3	24,383	36	17,629	72.3	178	4,070	5.9	3,525	86.6	35.6
1st Byelorussian (left wing as of July 15, 1944)	120	20	16.7	8,335	70	7,126	85.5	356	1,748	14.5	1,663	95.1	83.2

[1] Excludes antitank and AA artillery.
[2] Includes multiple rocket launchers.

Table 9

Average Daily Rate of Advance
June–August 1944

Army Groups	June 23–28 (6 days)		June 29–July 4 (6 days)		July 5–16 (12 days)		July 17–31 (15 days)		August 1–28 (28 days)		Total (67 days)	
	Total Km	Km/Day	Total Km	Km/Day	Total Km	Km/Day	Total Km	Km/Day	Total Km	Km/Day	Total Km	Km/Day
1st Baltic	80	13.3	120	20.0	120	10.0	190	12.7	30	1.1	540	8.1
3d Byelorussian	130	21.7	130	21.7	190	15.8	60	4.0	40	1.4	550	8.2
2d Byelorussian	80	13.3	110	18.3	200	16.6	90	6.0	90	3.2	570	8.5
1st Byelorussian*	110	18.3	100	16.7	170	14.2	110	7.3	100	3.6	590	8.8

* Right wing only. The left wing of the 1st Byelorussian Army Group attacked on July 18 and in 11 days advanced 230 kilometers, an average of 20.9 kilometers per day.

Table 10

Rates of Advance of Mobile Groups[1]
June–July 1944

Operation	Army Group	Formations	Dates	Number of Days	Distance Advanced (km)	Rate of Advance (km/day)
Bogushev-Orsha	3d Byelorussian	Fifth Guards Tank Army	June 26–28	3	125	41
		Mixed Cavalry–Mechanized Group	June 24–28	4[2]	140	35
Bobruisk	1st Byelorussian	I Guards Tank Corps	June 24–27	3[2]	70–80	23.3–26.6
		Mixed Cavalry–Mechanized Group	June 25–28	4	110–120	27.5–30.0
Minsk	3d Byelorussian	Fifth Guards Tank Army	June 29–July 4	6	120–130	20.0–21.7
		II Guards Tank Corps[3]	July 1–4	4	100–110	25.0–27.5
	1st Byelorussian	Mixed Cavalry–Mechanized Group	June 29–July 4	6	100–130	16.7–21.7
		I Guards Tank Corps	June 29–July 3	5	100–110	20.0–22.0
Vilnius	3d Byelorussian	Fifth Guards Tank Army	July 5–8	4	120–130	30.0–32.5
		III Guards Mechanized Corps	July 5–7	3	70–80	23.3–26.7
Lublin-Brest	1st Byelorussian	Second Tank Army	July 22–25	4	150–160	37.5–40.0
Ponevezh-Siauliau	1st Baltic	III Guards Mechanized Corps	July 26–27	2	70–80	35.0–40.0
Mitavsk	1st Baltic	III Guards Mechanized Corps[4]	July 28–29	2	70–80	35.0–40.0

[1] Tank, mechanized, or cavalry-mechanized.
[2] Days in combat only.
[3] The II Guards Tank Corps in two days advanced over 70 kilometers.
[4] The 2d Mechanized Brigace and the III Guards Mechanized Corps advanced over 70 kilometers in one day.

Table 11

German Formations Defeated or Destroyed*
June–August 1944

Months/Armies	Divisions									Brigades				Total Div Equivalent
	Inf	Panzer	Mot	Lt Inf	Luftwaffe Field	Training	Security (Guard)	Cav	Total	Inf	Panzer	Mot	Total	
June														
Third Panzer	6	—	—	—	2	—	—	—	8	—	—	—	—	8.0
Fourth	6	—	1	—	—	—	—	—	7	—	—	—	—	7.0
Ninth	9	1	—	—	—	—	—	—	10	—	—	—	—	10.0
Total	21	1	1	—	2	—	—	—	25	—	—	—	—	25.0
July														
Sixteenth	6	—	—	—	—	—	1	—	7	—	—	—	—	7.0
Third Panzer	1	—	—	—	—	1	1	—	3	1	—	—	1	3.5
Fourth	2	1	2	—	—	—	—	—	5	—	—	—	—	5.0
Ninth	4	—	—	—	—	1	2	—	7	—	—	—	—	7.0
Second	1	—	—	—	—	—	—	1	2	1	—	—	1	2.5
Fourth Panzer	3	—	—	1	—	—	—	—	4	—	—	—	—	4.0
Total	17	1	2	1	—	2	4	1	28	2	—	—	2	29.0
August														
Sixteenth	1	—	—	—	—	—	—	—	1	—	—	—	—	1.0
Fourth	1	—	—	—	—	—	—	—	1	—	—	—	—	1.0
Second	1	—	—	—	—	—	—	—	1	—	1	—	1	1.5
Total	3	—	—	—	—	—	—	—	3	—	1	—	1	3.5
TOTAL DEFEATED	41	2	3	1	2	2	4	1	56	2	1	—	3	57.5
TOTAL DESTROYED	9	1	—	—	2	1	2	—	15	2	—	—	2	16.0

* Divisions that were reorganized and defeated or destroyed again are counted twice.

Table 12

German Reinforcements
June–August 1944

Periods					Divisions					
	Inf	Panzer	Mot	Lt Inf	Luftwaffe Field	Training	Reserve	Total	Bde	Ind Rgt*
June 23–28	1	1	—	—	—	—	—	2	—	3
June 29–July 4	4	1	—	—	—	—	—	5	—	1
July 5–16	8	2	—	1	1	1	—	13	4	15
July 17–31	9	4	1	1	—	—	1	16	2	8
August 1–29	7	2	1	—	—	—	—	10	1	—
TOTAL	29	10	2	2	1	1	1	46	7	27

* Includes police, SS regiments, and independent grenadier regiments.

The Lvov-Sandomierz Offensive

July 1944

E xploiting the German defeat in Byelorussia in June–July 1944, the Soviet High Command ordered an offensive in the Ukraine against the Northern Ukraine Army Group. The objective was to liberate the western regions of the Ukraine as well as southern Poland. The operation was to be carried out by the 1st Ukrainian Army Group, commanded by Marshal Ivan Konev.

On the eve of the attack Konev's army group was deployed along a 440-kilometer front, running west of Kovel, Luck, Ternopol, and Kolomya (in the south). It was composed of seven combined arms armies, three tank armies, and one air army, a total of 80 rifle and cavalry divisions, 10 tank and mechanized corps, 850,000 combat troops (1,200,000 with rear services), some 14,000 artillery pieces and mortars, nearly 2,200 tanks and assault guns, and 3,000 aircraft.

The German Northern Ukraine Army Group, under General Josef Harpe, faced this formidable force. Although three panzer and three infantry divisions had been transferred to Army Group Center in Byelorussia, Harpe's force was still quite strong. It included the Fourth Army, the First Panzer Army, and the First Hungarian Army, with 600,000 combat troops (900,000 with rear services), 6,300 guns and mortars, 900 tanks and assault guns, and 700 aircraft. The Hungarian Army was grouped with the First Panzer Army to form Task Force Raus.

The Soviet plan called for two main blows, one on the right flank toward Rava Ruska, and the other in the center toward Lvov. A secondary blow was to be delivered in the south on the left flank toward Stanislav. The objective was to divide the German forces and then destroy them piecemeal. In the first

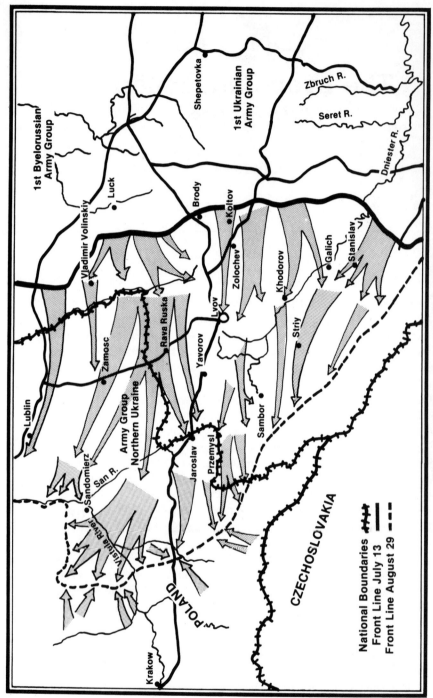

The Lvov-Sandomierz Offensive
July - August 1944

1st Byelorussian Army Group

1st Ukrainian Army Group

Zbruch R.

Seret R.

Dniester R.

Shepetovka

Luck

Vladimir Volinskiy

Brody

Koltov

Zolochev

Galich

Stanislav

Khodorov

Lvov

Rava Ruska

Yavorov

Striy

Zamosc

Army Group Northern Ukraine

Sambor

Lublin

Jaroslav

Przemysl

Sandomierz

San R.

Vistula River

CZECHOSLOVAKIA

POLAND

Krakow

National Boundaries
Front Line July 13
Front Line August 29

phase of the operation the Soviet forces were to reach the line Hrubieshuv-Tomashuv-Yavoruv-Galich. Then they would continue toward the San and Vistula rivers and the Carpathian Mountains.

The offensive was launched on July 13 on the right flank, with an attack toward Rava Ruska by the Third Guards and Thirteenth armies, the First Guards Tank Army, and General Baranov's cavalry-mechanized group. Deployed in the center, the Sixteenth and Thirty-eighth armies, the Third and Fourth Guards tank armies, and General S. V. Sokolov's cavalry-mechanized group attacked on July 14 in the direction of Lvov. In the south, the First Guards Army and the Eighteenth Army moved on Berezhany and Stanislav on July 21.

The advance on the Rava Ruska axis was very successful. Despite resolute resistance, Soviet armies broke through well-prepared German defenses. In the first two days they advanced up to 20 kilometers. On July 16 mobile troops of General M. Y. Katukhov's First Guards Tank Army and Baranov's cavalry-mechanized group pushed through the breach and soon advanced rapidly toward Jaroslav, leaving a small force to envelop the German XIII Corps in the Brody area from the north.

On the Lvov axis the Germans also offered fierce resistance. Initially the attack did not bring the expected results. On July 15, strong counterattacks by the XLVIII Panzer Corps and other panzer and infantry elements south of Zolochev halted the Soviet movement. Konev succeeded only in opening a corridor (the Koltov Corridor) 4 to 6 kilometers wide and 18 kilometers long. Through it on July 16 he committed the Third Guards Tank Army and, on the following day, the Fourth Guards Tank Army. Despite stubborn resistance, Soviet tanks punched their way through the corridor and reached the open area beyond.

By the evening of July 18, the right wing and the center of the 1st Ukrainian Army Group broke through the German defenses in a 200-kilometer-wide sector, advanced from 50 to 80 kilometers, and in the Brody area encircled eight German divisions, a force of nearly 50,000 men.

The Germans made desperate efforts to relieve the pressure on the surrounded corps at Brody and to hold Lvov, which was the headquarters of Army Group Northern Ukraine. Orders were given to the XIII Corps to break out to the south and join the XLVIII Panzer Corps, which was coming north to its rescue. But both corps made very slow progress, and finally the operation failed. The Russian attacks on the pocket were persistent and their perimeter was tight. The defenders split into many small groups and tried desperately to get out, but only a small number succeeded. The rest either were wiped out or surrendered.

While the right flank of the Soviet army group moved ahead and on July 23 crossed the San River near Jaroslav, the Germans put all their reserves into action on the Lvov axis and frustrated the attempts of the Third and Fourth Guards tank armies to capture the city. When it became obvious that Lvov could not be taken quickly, Konev decided to envelop the city by a deep flanking maneuver from south and north, with a simultaneous attack from the east.

The Third Guards Tank Army, after a 120-kilometer march, reached Yavorov on July 24 and enveloped Lvov from the north. Then one part of the army moved toward Lvov, while the other turned westward toward Przemysl and the San River.

Meanwhile, the Fourth Guards Tank Army approached the southern suburbs of Lvov on July 22. At the same time the Sixteenth Army closed in from the east.

To avoid encirclement, the Germans began to withdraw southwest toward Sambor, leaving behind very strong rear guards. Fierce fighting for Lvov continued for several days. Finally, on July 27, Soviet troops occupied the city. On the same day the army group's left wing captured Stanislav and continued toward Striy.

This ended the first phase of the offensive. Soviet forces had reached the line Vilkolaz-Nisko-Dubetsko-Przemysl north of Sambor-Khodorov-Kalush. The Germans were retreating in two directions: the remnants of General W. Nehring's Fourth Panzer Army toward the Vistula, and Task Force Raus toward the Carpathian Mountains. During the fifteen days of the offensive the 1st Ukrainian Army Group had defeated Army Group Northern Ukraine, liberated the western regions of the Ukraine, advanced more than 200 kilometers in a 400-kilometer sector, and entered southern Poland.

On July 27, following new directives from the Stavka, Konev transferred his main effort to the right wing, where he deployed the First and Third guards tank armies and advanced rapidly to the Vistula. Advanced elements of the Third Guards and Thirteenth armies and of the First and Third guards tank armies reached the Vistula near Baranuv and Sandomierz on July 29. They immediately began crossing and established two bridgeheads on the western bank of the river.

The defending German forces were ordered to hold the Vistula line at all costs. Early in August several reinforcing divisions arrived from Germany and Hungary. The Fourth Panzer Army and the Seventeenth Field Army launched a series of counterattacks against the Soviet bridgeheads west of the Vistula in efforts to destroy the Russian troops that had crossed. Heavy and bloody fighting continued through August, but in spite of German efforts the Soviets not only repelled all the attacks but enlarged the Sandomierz bridgehead to a width of over 65 kilometers and a depth of 50 kilometers.

While fighting for the Sandomierz bridgehead continued, Konev's center and the left wing moved toward Dembica and the Carpathian Mountains.

There, the Germans offered very strong resistance and halted the Soviet advance. On July 30 the Soviet Supreme Command organized a new army group, the 4th Ukrainian Army Group, which took over the two left-wing armies of the 1st Ukrainian Army Group.

At the end of August the front stabilized. It was relatively calm until January, when Konev launched his drive toward the Oder River and Berlin.

Soviet Order of Battle
July 13, 1944

1st Ukrainian Army Group
  First echelon
    First Guards Army
    Third Guards Army
    Thirteenth Combined Arms Army
    Eighteenth Combined Arms Army
    Thirty-eighth Combined Arms Army
    Sixtieth Combined Arms Army
  Second echelon
    Fifth Guards Army

Mobile groups
  First Guards Tank Army
  Third Guards Tank Army
  Fourth Tank Army
  Cavalry-Mechanized Group No. 1
  Cavalry-Mechanized Group No. 2
Army group reserve
  XLVII Rifle Corps

Table 1

Composition of the 1st Ukrainian Army Group
July 13, 1944

Formations and Units	Number
Armies	
Combined arms	7
Tank	3
Air[1]	1
Corps	
Rifle	25
Cavalry	2
Tank	7
Mechanized	3
Fighter aviation	3
Ground attack aviation	3
Bomber	2
Mixed aviation (fighter, ground attack, bomber)	1
Artillery	1
Divisions	
Rifle	74
Cavalry	6
Breakthrough artillery	4
MRL	1
AAA	10
Fighter aviation	12
Ground attack aviation	9
Bomber	6
Night bomber	1
Brigades	
Independent tank and assault gun	4
Heavy gun artillery	7
TD	8
Independent mortar	3
Independent MRL	1
Engineer	16
Regiments	
Independent tank and assault gun[2]	8
Independent howitzer	4
Independent TD	39
Independent MRL	10
Independent mortar	16
Independent AAA	21

[1] Eighth Air Army Hqs. arrived on July 16. Until August 2 the Eighth Air Army was under operational command of the Second Air Army.

[2] Excludes tank and assault regiments in tank and mechanized corps.

Table 2

1st Ukrainian Army Group: Men and Weapons Strengths July 13, 1944

Formations	Combat Troops	Guns and Mortars (76mm and larger)	AT Guns	AAA Guns	MRLs
Armies					
First Guards	102,151[1]	1,669	327	152	28
Third Guards	106,925	2,207	422	114	192
Fifth Guards	65,578	879	153	61	—
Thirteenth Combined Arms	76,077	1,696	267	111	24
Eighteenth Combined Arms	72,556	1,351	236	19	209
Thirty-eighth Combined Arms	90,728	1,657	308	88	24
Sixtieth Combined Arms	96,719	1,841	353	72	340
First Guards Tank	29,301	383	54	116	40
Third Guards Tank	36,527	570	50	80	72
Fourth Tank	29,774	402	41	128	40
Second Air	41,768[2]	—	—	—	—
Groups					
Cavalry-Mechanized Group No. 1 (I Guards Cavalry Corps and XXV Tank Corps)	28,699	366	74	50	8
Cavalry-Mechanized Group No. 2 (VI Guards Cavalry Corps and XXXI Tank Corps)	28,969	376	48	55	20
Units directly under army group	41,783[3]	428	99	176	59
TOTAL	847,555[4]	13,825	2,432	1,222	1,056[5]

[1] Includes the IV Guards Tank Corps.

[2] Includes ground support troops.

[3] Includes the XL Rifle Corps, the Army Group's Reserve.

[4] With rear services, 1,200,000 effectives.

[5] Includes 546 M-30 MRLs.

Table 3

1st Ukrainian Army Group: Tanks and Assault Guns
July 13, 1944

Formations/Armies	Tanks					Assault Guns				
	IS–122	KV	T–34	T–80[1]	Foreign	ISU–152	SU–122	SU–85	SU–76	Total
Direct infantry support group										
Third Guards	—	1	71	12	—	2	7	8	—	101
Thirteenth Combined Arms	—	—	21	7	14	—	21	—	—	63
Sixtieth Combined Arms	21	—	38	1	—	16	—	—	24	100
Thirty-eighth Combined Arms	—	3	37	—	—	21	—	—	24	85
First Guards	3	—	79	1	—	6	—	6	5	100
Eighteenth Combined Arms	—	1	—	—	—	—	—	—	32	33
TOTAL	24	5	246	21	14	45	28	14	85	482
Mobile force										
First Guards Tank	15	—	277	—	9	21	—	24	—	346
Third Guards Tank	42	—	299	6	—	—	—	32	75	454
Fourth Tank	21	—	327	—	9	21	—	9	—	387
Cavalry-Mechanized Group No. 1	—	—	133	47	50	1	3	20	49	303
Cavalry-Mechanized Group No. 2	—	—	129	2	21	15	—	3	43	213
TOTAL	78	—	1,165	55	89	58	3	88	167	1,703
Army group reserve	21	—	—	—	—	—	—	—	—	21
TOTAL ARMY GROUP	123	5	1,411	76	103	103	31	102	252	2,206[2]

[1] Includes T-60 and T-70 tanks also.

[2] 1,598 tanks and 381 assault guns were combat-ready. Not included are 57mm guns mounted on gun trucks of the 16th and 19th artillery brigades.

Table 4

Composition and Strength of the Soviet Second Air Army July 13, 1944

Formations	Fighter			Ground Attack			Bomber			Reconnaissance			Totals	
	Type	Total	Combat Ready	Type	Total	Combat Ready	Type	Total	Combat Ready	Type	Total	Combat Ready	Total	Combat Ready
V Fighter Aviation Corps 8th Guards Fighter Div 256th Fighter Div	La– 5 Yak–1 Yak–3 Yak–7 Yak–9	228	207	—	—	—	—	—	—	—	—	—	228	207
VII Fighter Aviation Corps 9th Guards Fighter Div 205th Fighter Div 304th Fighter Div	All types	204	200	—	—	—	—	—	—	—	—	—	204	200
X Fighter Aviation Corps 10th Guards Fighter Div 235th Fighter Div	La– 5	292	261	—	—	—	—	—	—	—	—	—	292	261
6th Guards Fighter Div	Yak–1 Yak–9	120	115	—	—	—	—	—	—	—	—	—	120	115
I Guards Mixed Aviation Corps 5th Guards Ground Attack Div 6th Guards Ground Attack Div 11th Guards Fighter Div	La– 5 Yak–1 Yak–9	134	127	Il–2	244	236	—	—	—	—	—	—	378	363
I Guards Ground Attack Aviation Corps 8th Guards Ground Attack Div 9th Guards Ground Attack Div 12th Guards Fighter Div	Yak–1	145	136	Il–2	209	206	—	—	—	—	—	—	354	342

(cont.)

Table 4—(continued)

Unit	Fighters (type)			Il-2			Bombers (type)			Reconnaissance (type)			Total	
V Ground Attack Aviation Corps	Yak-1, Yak-9	121	100	Il-2	244	235	—	—	—	—	—	—	365	335
4th Guards Ground Attack Div														
264th Ground Attack Div														
331st Fighter Div														
VIII Ground Attack Aviation Corps	Yak-1, Yak-7, Yak-9	121	113	Il-2	202	197	—	—	—	—	—	—	323	310
224th Ground Attack Div														
227th Ground Attack Div														
236th Fighter Div														
10th Guards Ground Attack Div	Yak-1, Yak-7	54	54	Il-2	144	142	—	—	—	—	—	—	198	196
II Guards Bomber Aviation Corps	—	—	—	—	—	—	Pe-2	290	271	—	—	—	290	271
1st Guards Bomber Div														
8th Guards Bomber Div														
244th Bomber Div														
IV Bomber Aviation Corps	—	—	—	—	—	—	Pe-2	282	272	—	—	—	282	272
202d Bomber Div														
219th Bomber Div														
321st Bomber Div														
208th Night Bomber Div	—	—	—	—	—	—	Po-2	105	104	—	—	—	105	104
98th Ind Guards Reconnaissance Rgt	—	—	—	—	—	—	—	—	—	Pe-2	43	34	43	34
50th Ind Reconnaissance Rgt	—	—	—	—	—	—	—	—	—	Pe-2	25	20	25	20
118th Ind Reconnaissance Rgt	—	—	—	—	—	—	—	—	—	Il-2, Yak-7, Yak-9	34	22	34	22
TOTALS	La-5, Yak-1, Yak-3, Yak-7	1,419	1,313	Il-2	1,043	1,016	Po-2 and Pe-2	677	647	Pe-2, Il-2, Yak-7, Yak-9	102	76	3,241	3,052

Table 5

German Forces Facing the 1st Ukrainian Army Group
July 13, 1944

Armies	Frontage (km)	Corps Groups	Inf, Lt Inf, Sec Div	Panzer Div	Motorized Div	Inf Bde	Total Div	Total Bde	Operational Density Km/Div[1]
Fourth Panzer	115	1[2]	10	2	—	—	14	—	8.2
First Panzer	215	—	13	2	1	—	16	—	13.4
First Hungarian Field	110	—	9	1	—	2	10	2	10.0
TOTAL	440	1	32	5	1	2	40	2	10.7

[1] Two brigades equal one division.
[2] Corps Group "C" composed of two divisions.

Table 6
Soviet and German Force Ratio
July 13, 1944

Men and Equipment	1st Ukrainian Army Group	German Forces	Ratios
Personnel (combat only)	843,000	600,000	1.4:1
Guns and mortars	13,825	6,300	2.2:1
Tanks and assault guns	1,979[1]	900	2.2:1
Combat aircraft	3,052[2]	700	4.4:1

[1] Operational only.

[2] Operational only.

Table 7
1st Ukrainian Army Group
Force Densities in the Breakthrough Sectors
July 13, 1944

Army	Breakthrough Sector (km)	Rifle Divisions Total	Rifle Divisions Km/div	Artillery/ Mortars Total	Artillery/ Mortars Per Km	Tanks/Assault Guns Total	Tanks/Assault Guns Per Km
Third Guards	8	9	0.9	2,098	262.3	101	12.6
Thirteenth Combined Arms	4	5	0.8	1,159	289.8	63	15.8
Sixtieth Combined Arms	8	8	1.0	1,965	245.6	100	12.5
Thirty-eighth Combined Arms	6	8	0.8	1,809	301.5	85	14.2
TOTAL	26	30	0.9	7,031	270.4	349	13.4

Note: Width of Army Group front: 440 kilometers.
Total breakthrough sector: 26 kilometers.
Percentage of total width: 6%.

Table 8

Operational Deployment of First Echelon Armies, 1st Ukrainian Army Group July 13, 1944

Armies	Total Front Width (km)	Total Front Div	Breakthrough Sector Width (km)	First Echelon Div	Second Echelon Div	Reserve	Total Div
Third Guards	65	12	8	8	—	1	9
Thirteenth Combined Arms	82	9	4	4	—	1	5
Sixtieth Combined Arms	30	10	8	5	2	1	8
Thirty-eighth Combined Arms	40	10	6	7	—	1	8
First Guards	118	12	—	—	5*	—	5
Eighteenth Combined Arms	105	9	—	—	—	—	—
TOTAL	440	62	26	24	7	4	35

* The Assault Group (five rifle divisions and the IV Guards Tank Corps) of the First Guards Army was to exploit the successful breakthrough of the Thirty-eighth Army and advance toward Yezerna and Galich.

Table 9

Reinforcements Sent to the 1st Ukrainian Army Group
July 13–August 29, 1944

Formations and Units	Rifle Corps	Rifle Divs	Arty Divs	AAA Divs	Arty Bdes	TD Arty Bdes	Air Armies	Aviation Corps	Aviation Divs	MRL Bdes	MRL Rgts
Fifth Guards Army	3	9	—	—	—	—	—	—	—	—	—
Headquarters, Eighth Air Army	—	—	—	—	—	—	1	—	—	—	—
I Guards Ground Attack Aviation Corps	—	—	—	—	—	—	—	1	3	—	—
II Guards Bomber Aviation Corps	—	—	—	—	—	—	—	1	3	—	—
VII Fighter Aviation Corps	—	—	—	—	—	—	—	1	3	—	—
I Guards Mixed Aviation Corps	—	—	—	—	—	—	—	1	3	—	—
6th Guards and 236th Fighter Aviation divs	—	—	—	—	—	—	—	—	2	—	—
13th Artillery Div	—	—	1	—	—	—	—	—	—	—	—
36th, 68th, 69th AAA divisions	—	—	—	3	—	—	—	—	—	—	—
26th and 37th tank destroyer arty bdes	—	—	—	—	—	2	—	—	—	—	—
155th Heavy Artillery Bde	—	—	—	—	1	—	—	—	—	—	—
1st MRL Bde	—	—	—	—	—	—	—	—	—	1	—
8th, 21st, 23d MRL rgts	—	—	—	—	—	—	—	—	—	—	3
TOTAL	3	9	1	3	1	2	1	4	14	1	3

Table 10

Reinforcements Sent to German Forces
July 13–August 29, 1944

	Divisions						Total Division Equivalent
Periods	Infantry, Light Infantry, Security	Motorized	Ski	Panzer	Total	Brigades	
July 13–27	3	1	—	1	5	—	5
July 29–August 28	9	—	1	2	12	4	14
TOTAL	12	1	1	3	17	4	19

Table 11

Soviet Second Air Army Sorties
July 13–August 29, 1944

Periods	Total Sorties	Fighter	Ground Attack	Bomber*	Reconnaissance
July 13–28	30,366	15,858	9,579	$\frac{4,805}{1,282}$	124
July 29–August 29	18,359	10,247	4,029	$\frac{3,564}{3,076}$	519
TOTAL	48,725	26,105	13,608	$\frac{8,369}{4,358}$	643

* Numerator shows total number of sorties. Denominator shows night sorties only.

Table 12

Average Daily Rates of Advance of the 1st Ukrainian Army Group (km) July 13–August 29, 1944

	Depth of Adv (km)	Combined Arms Armies							Tank Armies			Cav-Mech Groups	
		Third Guards	Thirteenth	Sixtieth	Thirty-eighth	First Guards[1]	Eighteenth	Fifth Guards	First Guards	Third Guards	Fourth	No. 1	No. 2
Phase one (July 13–27)													
Breakthrough (July 13–18)	45–50	7–8	10	7–8	2–3	—	—	—	—	—	—	—	—
Exploitation (July 19–27)		—	—	—	—	—	—	—	40–45	30	20	30	—
Pursuit (July 19–27)	210–220	17–18	21–22	8–9	9–10	10–11	c. 12	—	30–35[2]/50–60	20–25[2]/60	14–15	30–35[2]/50	22[3]
Phase two (July 29–August 29)													
Advance toward the Vistula and capture of bridge-heads (July 29–August 3)	34–40	5–6	10–11	12–13[4]	12–13	2.2	2.3	—	—	10–11	12–13	13–14	—	—
Consolidation and expansion (August 4–29)	40	1	1	1.2	1	—	—	8–9[5]	1–2	1–2	1–2	—	—

[1] First Guards and Eighteenth Combined Arms armies transferred to the 4th Ukrainian Army Group as of August 5, 1944.
[2] Denominator shows maximum daily rate of advance (km).
[3] From July 23, 1944.
[4] From July 29–August 10, 1944.
[5] August 4–10, 1944.

The Yassy-Kishinev Operation

August 20–29, 1944

In the summer of 1944 the Soviet Supreme Command decided that the military and political situation was ripe for a decisive strike in the southern sector of the front in Moldavia. The offensive was scheduled to start in August.

Poised for the offensive on a 590-kilometer front from Chernovtsy in the west to the Black Sea in the east were the 2d and 3d Ukrainian army groups, composed of almost 1,250,000 men, 1,890 tanks and assault guns, 16,000 artillery pieces and mortars, and over 2,000 aircraft.

The 2d Ukrainian Army Group, under General Malinovskiy, deployed on a 330-kilometer front along a line stretching from Chernovtsy to the southeast and then north to Orgeyev, was to break through the German defenses north of Yassy; take Bacau, Vaslui, and Husi; capture the crossings on the Prut River near Husi; and, in close cooperation with the 3d Ukrainian Army Group, encircle and destroy the German-Romanian forces concentrated in the Yassy-Kishinev area.

On the left, the 3d Ukrainian Army Group, commanded by General Tolbukhin and deployed on a 260-kilometer front along the Dniester River from Orgeyev to the Black Sea, was to break the German defenses south of Bendery, strike toward Opachi and Husi, take Leovo and Tarutino, and join with the 2d Ukrainian Army Group to close the encirclement ring from the southeast. A secondary effort was directed against the Third Romanian Army southwest of Odessa toward Ismail.

Since the 2d and 3d Ukrainian army groups were to breach the defenses at two points some 200 kilometers apart, the coordination of their effort was meticulously planned, and great importance was given to high rates of advance to prevent the Germans from escaping the encirclement.

The Yassy-Kishinev Operation
August 20 - 29, 1944

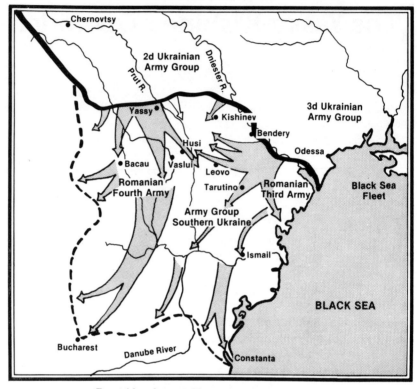

Front Line August 20 ━━━━━━

Front Line August 29 ━ ━ ━ ━ ━ ━ ━

Facing the Soviet forces was the German Army Group Southern Ukraine under General Hans Friessner, consisting of the German Sixth and Eighth armies and the Romanian Third and Fourth armies, 47 divisions altogether, including 3 panzer divisions and 5 infantry brigades. The army group was over 800,000 men strong (360,000 were Germans and the rest Romanians) and had 7,600 artillery pieces and mortars, 400 tanks and assault guns, and 800 aircraft. The ratio was in the Soviet favor—1.5:1 in men, 2.1:1 in artillery, 4.7:1 in armor, and 2.7:1 in aircraft.

The battle readiness of Friessner's formations was far from satisfactory. The most serious deficiencies were in tanks and aircraft. Although the Germans had 280 assault guns, there were only 60 tanks in German units, with 60 more in Romanian units. The loyalty of the Romanian allies, furthermore, was questionable. Mutual distrust and hostility prevailed. By August some elements of the Romanian Army were already in secret contact with the Red Army.

On the morning of August 20, a powerful and devastating artillery and air preparation signaled the start of the offensive. In the course of the first two days both Soviet army groups penetrated the entire tactical defense zone on a wide front, and in their assault sectors mechanized units moved into open areas behind the German-Romanian defensive lines.

In the 2d Ukrainian Army Group sector, during the first two days, the Twenty-seventh and Fifty-second armies broke through the German defenses to a depth of 25 kilometers. The Sixth Tank Army, which was committed to the battle late on August 20, advanced some 40 kilometers.

Similar success was registered by the 3d Ukrainian Army Group. Toward the end of August 21, the Thirty-seventh and Forty-sixth armies, attacking on the axis of the main effort, advanced over 30 kilometers, while the IV Guards Mechanized Corps went nearly 50 kilometers.

Attempting to halt the Soviet advance, the Germans counterattacked frequently and fought fiercely for each position. Nevertheless, they were unable to stop the offensive. In two days the German defenses were crushed, and the situation of the entire German army group became extremely precarious. The Romanian Third Army was cut off from the German Sixth Army. General Friessner had committed all of his reserves and could no longer influence developments.

On the evening of August 21, Malinovskiy and Tolbukhin were ordered to complete the encirclement of the German Sixth Army in the Kishinev salient and of the IV Army Corps of the Eighth Army west of the Prut River, as soon as possible.

Realizing that the main forces of Army Group Southern Ukraine were faced with imminent encirclement, on August 22 OKH ordered the German Sixth and Romanian Third armies to withdraw behind the Prut. But it was already too late.

On August 22, tank and motorized units of the 2d Ukrainian Army Group advanced some 30 kilometers. Those of the 3d Ukrainian Army Group advanced over 50 kilometers to a point within 40 kilometers of the Prut crossings, while the main forces of the Sixth Army were still 90 kilometers away. Then, early on August 24, forward elements of the two army groups linked up at the towns of Husi and Leovo, closing the encirclement. Six corps headquarters, twenty divisions, and several independent units were caught in the great pocket between the Dniester and the Prut. Only the headquarters of the Sixth Army was able to slip out of the pocket in time. The Romanian Third Army, its flanks deeply enveloped, surrendered on August 23.

Meanwhile, in Bucharest on the same day, as a result of a political upheaval in Romania, King Michael arrested the pro-German prime minister and strongman Ion Antonescu, proclaimed the formation of a new government, and announced the end of the war. He ordered that Romanian troops cease hostilities and gave the Germans two weeks to leave the country. Enraged, Hitler ordered that Bucharest be bombed. This gave the new Romanian government an excuse to declare war on Germany, which it did on August 25.

These new developments made Friessner's task even more difficult. With Romanians turned from friends to enemies, it became impossible to extricate the Sixth Army and the IV Army Corps from the pocket, and they were left abandoned in a hopeless situation.

Fierce fighting developed during the mopping-up operations against the surrounded German forces. During August 25 and 26, the ring on the eastern bank of the Prut River was gradually tightened. A Soviet ultimatum to surrender was rejected. The encircled troops had hardly any centralized system of command, and most of the units were retreating in a disorganized way. Only the XXIX Corps, along with the 13th Panzer Division and 10th Panzer Grenadier Division of the Sixth Army, succeeded in crossing to the western bank of the Prut, where for two days they fought stubbornly against the Soviet Fifty-second Army. The Soviets were too widely dispersed to be able to prevent a breakout. The Germans slipped through and retreated toward Hungary via the Carpathians, with six Red Army divisions in hot pursuit.

Those German units that remained in the pocket continued to fight until August 29. Only a handful were able to make it back to German territory after weeks of wandering. The Russians claimed 106,000 prisoners and 150,000 German dead. Again, Red Army losses were not reported.

Soviet Order of Battle
August 20, 1944

2d Ukrainian Army Group
First echelon
  Fortieth Combined Arms Army (one echelon)
  Seventh Guards Army (one echelon, one rifle division in reserve)
  Twenty-seventh Combined Arms Army (two echelons)
  Fifty-second Combined Arms Army (two echelons)
  Fourth Guards Army (one echelon, one rifle division in reserve)
Second echelon
  Fifty-third Combined Arms Army
Mobile groups
  Sixth Tank Army
  XVIII Tank Corps
Cavalry-tank groups
  XXIII Tank Corps
  V Guards Cavalry Corps

Reserve
  LVII Rifle Corps
  XXVII Guards Rifle Corps
3d Ukrainian Army Group
First echelon
  Fifth Strike Army (one echelon, one rifle division in reserve)
  Fifty-seventh Combined Arms Army (three echelons, one rifle corps each)
  Thirty-seventh Combined Arms Army (two echelons)
  Forty-sixth Combined Arms Army (one echelon, two rifle divisions in reserve)
Mobile group
  IV Guards Corps
  VII Mechanized Corps
Reserve
  X Guards Rifle Corps

Table 1

Composition of Soviet Forces
August 20, 1944

Formations and Units	2d Ukrainian Army Group	3d Ukrainian Army Group	Total
Armies			
Combined arms	6	4	10
Tank	1	—	1
Air	1	1	2
Corps			
Rifle	16	12	28
Cavalry	1	—	1
Tank and mechanized	4	2	6
Air	2	1	3
Divisions			
Rifle and airborne	51*	37	88
Cavalry	3	—	3
Artillery	3	2	5
MRL	1	—	1
AAA	7	4	11
Air	8	7	15
Fortified areas	2	1	3
Brigades (independent)			
Naval infantry	—	2	2
Tank, mechanized and assault gun	2	2	4
Artillery	2	—	2
TD artillery	8	4	12
Mortar	—	1	1
MRL	—	1	1
Engineer	11	8	19
Regiments (independent)			
Tank and assault gun	6	8	14
Artillery	—	3	3
TD artillery	11	7	18
Mortar	9	—	9
MRL	10	9	19
AA	11	10	21
Engineer	2	2	4

* Excludes one Romanian volunteer rifle division and one Yugoslavian infantry brigade.

Table 2

Effective Strength of Soviet Forces
August 20, 1944

Men and Equipment[1]	2d Ukrainian Army Group	3d Ukrainian Army Group	Total
Men	537,858	348,633	886,491[2]
Tanks	954	474	1,428
Assault guns	329	117	446
AT guns (45 and 57mm)	1,406	901	2,307
Field guns (76mm and larger)	3,744	2,993	6,737
Mortars (82–120mm)	4,904	3,210	8,114
MRLs	637	256	893
AA guns	589	667[3]	1,256
Aircraft[4]	882	966	1,848
Vehicles	15,476	1,305[5]	16,781

[1] Excludes rear elements of armies and army groups, Romanian volunteer division, and the Yugoslav infantry brigade.

[2] 1,250,000 men with rear element of armies, army groups, Romanian volunteer division, and the Yugoslav infantry brigade.

[3] Includes XII AA Defense Corps of National Air Defense Forces (PVO Strany).

[4] Excludes reconnaissance, transport, medical, and communications aircraft.

[5] Incomplete data.

Table 3

Composition and Density of German and Romanian Forces
August 20, 1944

Southern Ukraine Army Group Armies	Width of Front (km)		Divisions					Infantry Brigades
	Total	per Division[1]	Infantry[2]	Cavalry	Panzer	Motorized	Total	
Fourth Romanian	260	c.18.0	—	—	—	—	—	—
German	—	—	4	—	1	—	5	—
Romanian	—	—	8	—	1	—	9	3
Eighth German	60	8.0	—	—	—	—	—	—
German	—	—	2	—	—	—	2	—
Romanian	—	—	4	1	—	—	5	1
Sixth German	180	10.6	—	—	—	—	—	—
German	—	—	15	—	1	—	16	—
Romanian	—	—	1	—	—	—	1	—
Third Romanian	100	13.3	—	—	—	—	—	—
German	—	—	1	—	—	—	1	—
Romanian	—	—	5	1	—	—	6	1
Army group reserve	—	—	—	—	—	—	—	—
German	—	—	—	—	—	1	1	—
Romanian	—	—	—	1	—	—	1	—
TOTAL	600	12.1	—	—	—	—	—	—
German	—	—	22	—	2	1	25	—
Romanian	—	—	18	3	1	—	22	5
TOTALS	—	—	40	3	3	1	47	5

[1] Assuming that two brigades equal one division.

[2] Includes light and mountain infantry.

Table 4

Operational Density of Soviet Forces
August 20, 1944

Army Groups	Front			Breakthrough Sector (Main Effort)		
	Width (km)	Divisions	Km/Div	Width (km)	Divisions	Km/Div
2d Ukrainian	330	51	6.5	16	25	0.64
3d Ukrainian	260	37	7.0	18	24	0.75

Table 5

Average Density of Weapons
August 20, 1944

	Army Group	
	2d Ukrainian	3d Ukrainian
Width of front		
Total	330	260
Breakthrough sector	16	18
Percent of total	4.5	7.0
Number of guns* and mortars		
Total	8,648	6.203
In breakthrough sector	3,852	4,076
Percent	45	65
Guns and mortars/km		
Entire front	26	24
In breakthrough sector	240	c.230
Tanks and assault guns		
Total	1,283	591
In breakthrough sector	899	455
Percent	70	77
Tanks and assault guns/km		
Entire front	3.9	2.3
In breakthrough sector	56	25

* Excludes 45 and 57mm AT guns, AA guns, and MRLs.

Table 6

Ratio of Forces
August 20, 1944

	Soviet Forces	German and Romanian Forces	Ratio
Men (includes rear services)	1,250,000	800,000[1]	1.5:1
Guns and mortars	16,000	7,600	2.1:1
Tanks and assault guns	1,870	404	4.6:1
Combat aircraft	2,200[2]	810	2.7:1

[1] Approximately 360,000 Germans.

[2] Includes the air arm of the Black Sea Fleet.

Table 7
Daily Average Advance (km)
August 20–29, 1944

	August 20–24		August 25–29		August 20–29	
Army Group	Advance (km)	Daily Average (km)	Advance (km)	Daily Average (km)	Advance (km)	Daily Average (km)
2d Ukrainian	135	27.0	190	38.0	325	32.5
3d Ukrainian	135	27.0	165	33.0	300	25.0

Table 8
Ammunition and Fuel Availability
August 20, 1944

	Ammunition (units of fire)		Fuel (refueling units)			Daily Rations (days)
Army Group	Small Arms	Artillery	Aviation	Automobile	Diesel	
2d Ukrainian	2.0	4.2	8.4	2.7	9.0	20–24
3d Ukrainian	2.5	6.6	7.4	2.6	7.5	8–10

Table 9
Ammunition Consumption (Units of Fire)

Types of Ammunition	2d Ukrainian Army Group		3d Ukrainian Army Group	
	Planned	Used	Planned	Used
76mm (regimental artillery)	3.5	0.7	3.4	0.9
76mm (divisional artillery)	1.8	0.7	2.5	0.9
122mm	3.6	1.7	3.3	1.6
152mm	3.5	2.4	4.2	1.6
203mm	4.2	1.5	2.6	1.1
45mm antitank	2.1	0.3	2.9	0.3
Mines				
82mm	3.0	0.7	4.0	1.0
120mm	4.2	1.0	4.6	1.1

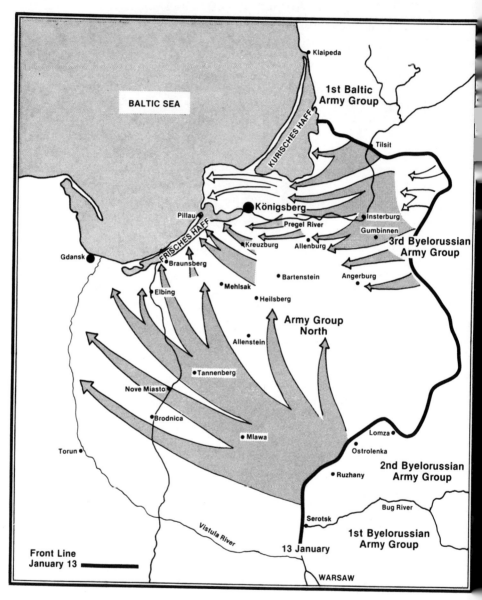

The Battle for East Prussia, January-April 1945

The Battle for East Prussia

January–April 1945

In January 1945, after regrouping and bringing up reserves, the Red Army was ready to launch an offensive against East Prussia, considered by Moscow to be the cradle of German militarism. It had also been one of the springboards for the invasion of the Soviet Union in the summer of 1941. The plan of campaign called for cutting off the German troops in East Prussia from those in Pomerania and East Poland, pushing them toward the Baltic Sea, and destroying them piecemeal.

The offensive was to be carried out by the 3d and 2d Byelorussian army groups and the Forty-third Army of the 1st Baltic Army Group, the First and Fourth air armies, and elements of the Baltic Fleet. These forces included fourteen combined arms armies, one tank army, two air armies, and several independent tank, mechanized, and artillery corps, numbering 1,220,000 men (1,660,000 including support elements), 25,000 artillery pieces and mortars, 3,800 tanks and assault guns, and over 3,000 aircraft.

Defending East Prussia and northern Poland was German Army Group Center under General Hans Reinhardt,* deployed along a 500-kilometer front from the estuary of the Neman (Nieman) River in the northeast to the junction of the Bug and Vistula rivers in the southwest. The army group was composed of the Third Panzer Army and Fourth and Second field armies, a total of 34

---

* In the course of the battle, on January 26, German Army Group North, cut off in the Baltic states, was renamed Army Group Kurland, and Army Group Center was designated Army Group North and put under General Lothar Rendulic. Army Group A, on the Oder, became the new Army Group Center. Between Army Group North and Army Group Center was deployed the newly organized Army Group Vistula.

infantry, 3 panzer, and 4 motorized divisions, numbering 780,000 men (including 200,000 members of the Volkssturm), 8,200 guns and mortars, and 700 tanks and assault guns. The ground forces were supported by the Sixth Air Fleet with 775 aircraft.

The ratios of forces in the Soviets' favor were 2.1:1 in men, 3.5:1 in artillery, 5.5:1 in tanks and assault guns, and 4:1 in aircraft. In the breakthrough sectors the ratios were even more advantageous to the Soviets.

According to the directives issued by the Stavka, the 3d Byelorussian Army Group under General Ivan Chernyakhovskiy was to launch its attack from the east and northeast, destroy German forces in the Tilsit and Insterburg areas, and continue toward Königsberg along both banks of the Pregel River.

Attacking from the south, the 2d Byelorussian Army Group, commanded by Marshal Rokossovskiy, would annihilate German forces in the Mlawa area and press toward Nove Miasto and Marienburg.

The Forty-third Army of the 1st Baltic Army Group would advance along the left bank of the Neman River and cooperate with the 3d Byelorussian Army Group in taking Tilsit.

Chernyakhovskiy's assault units moved out on the morning of January 13 after a two-hour artillery preparation. A planned air bombardment was canceled because of heavy fog. Overcoming strong resistance from the Third Panzer Army, Soviet forces broke through the German first defense zone and advanced 15 kilometers during the first two days. Slowly and stubbornly, the Soviet army group continued its advance and pushed steadily deeper into the German defenses, inflicting heavy casualties. Taking advantage of the breakthrough achieved by the Thirty-ninth Army south of Tilsit in the sector defended by the IX Army Corps, Chernyakhovskiy committed his second echelon and reached the Inster River on January 18. One day later Soviet troops captured Tilsit, and on January 21 they took Gumbinnen. Heavy fighting developed at the approaches to Insterburg. The city fell on January 22, and the Red Army pressed toward Königsberg.

Toward the end of the month, the army group, after overcoming the powerful fortifications of the Heilsberg defense area, advanced rapidly toward Königsberg, bypassed the city on both north and south, cut it off from its only port, Pillau, and seized part of the Samland Peninsula. It seemed likely that Königsberg would fall any day. But the Grossdeutschland Panzer Grenadier Division and the Hermann Göring Panzer Division counterattacked and relieved the city.

Meanwhile, on January 14, the 2d Byelorussian Army Group, after a 90-minute artillery preparation, launched its main attack from the Ruzhany and Serotsk bridgeheads toward Mlawa and Torun. The German Second Field Army, battered by tank and rifle formations, gave up Mlawa on January 19 and retreated northwest and north toward the Baltic Sea. Tannenberg, the site of Hindenberg's historic victory over the Russians in World War I, was taken on January 21, by an enveloping maneuver of General M. Sakhno's tank corps. Allenstein, the second largest city in East Prussia, surrendered to General N. Oslikovskiy's cavalry group one day later. In a swift advance, on the evening of January 23 the XXIX Tank Corps, under General K. I. Malakhov, passed through Elbing, a city still living a peaceful life deep in the German rear, and reached the Frisches Haff Bay on the Baltic shore. This sealed the fate of the German forces in East Prussia, which were now cut off from Pomerania.

To the east, in the center of East Prussia, the German Fourth Field Army commanded by General Friederich Hossbach, with its flanks threatened, abandoned the Masurian Lakes fortifications and, under pressure from the Soviet Fiftieth Army, retreated toward the Baltic Sea.

The Red Army, by gaining the Baltic coast in the west, the center, and the east, had split the German forces in East Prussia into three groups. Four German divisions were fighting desperately in the narrow Samland Peninsula, five were in the city and fortress of Königsberg, and about twenty, with their backs to the sea, were putting up fierce resistance southwest of Königsberg.

Early in February, after taking Torun and reaching the Vistula on a wide front, Rokossovskiy was ordered to advance into eastern Pomerania, leaving the mopping-up of the surrounded German forces in East Prussia to Chernyakhovskiy.

On February 18 General Chernyakhovskiy was mortally wounded near Mehlsak. He died several days later. His command was taken over by Marshal A. M. Vasilevskiy.

Fierce fighting continued. The Germans resisted desperately, counterattacking repeatedly. The main Soviet attack was directed against Heiligenbeil, the center of a well-prepared defense zone close to the Frisches Haff. The German Fourth Army fought bitterly but was forced back by overwhelming pressure. By March 20 the army held only a small beachhead on the narrow Balga Peninsula. At the end of the month the remnants of the German forces were overrun, and Königsberg was surrounded.

Königsberg was assaulted on April 6 with a powerful artillery barrage and air strikes. The garrison commander, General Otto Lasch, surrendered on April 9.

The capture of Königsberg enabled Vasilevskiy to destroy the German troops in the Samland Peninsula. The final attack began on April 13. The 70,000-man German force of some eight infantry divisions and one panzer division retreated quickly under Soviet pressure toward the Frischhausen Pillau Peninsula. But only 20,000 reached Pillau, where they organized hasty defenses. On April 25, after six days of heavy fighting, Pillau fell, ending the 105 days of the East Prussian campaign.

Soviet Order of Battle
January 10, 1945

3d Byelorussian Army Group
  First echelon
    Thirty-ninth Combined Arms Army
    Fifth Combined Arms Army
    Twenty-eighth Combined Arms Army
    Second Guards Army
    Thirty-first Combined Arms Army
  Second echelon
    Eleventh Guards Army
  Mobile group
    II Guards Tank Corps
  Army group reserves
    I Tank Corps

2d Byelorussian Army Group
  First echelon
    Fiftieth Combined Arms Army
    Forty-ninth Combined Arms Army
    Forty-eighth Combined Arms Army
    Third Combined Arms Army
    Second Strike Army
    Sixty-fifth Combined Arms Army
    Seventieth Combined Arms Army
  Mobile groups
    Fifth Guards Tank Army
    III Guards Cavalry Corps

Table 1

Composition of Soviet Forces
January 10, 1945

Independent Units	3d Byelo-russian Army Group	2d Byelo-russian Army Group	Forty-third Army (1st Baltic Army Group)	Total
Armies				
Combined arms	6	7	1	14
Tank	—	1	—	1
Air	1	1	—	2
Corps				
Rifle	18	19	5	42
Cavalry	—	1	—	1
Tank and mechanized	2	6[1]	—	8
Divisions				
Rifle	54	63	13	130
Cavalry	—	3	—	3
Fortified areas	1	3	—	4
Ind tank and mech bdes	6	4	1	11
Ind tank and assault gun rgts	27[2]	30[3]	3	60
Artillery				
Divisions	4	6	—	10
AA divisions	5	6	1	12
Ind MRL divisions	1	1	—	2
Ind brigades	6	9	3[4]	18
TD brigades	9	9	—	18
Ind MRL brigades	—	2	—	2
Ind mortar brigades	2	1	—	3
Ind regiments	9	10	—	19
Ind TD regiments	7	8	1	16
Ind AA regiments	9	15	1	25
Ind mortar regiments	6	9	2	17
Ind MRL regiments	8	11	1	20
Engineer brigades	11	14	1	26

[1] III Guards Tank Corps did not participate in the operation.

[2] Includes 17 assault gun regiments, 2 engineer-tank regiments (with blades to clear mines), and 1 flamethrower tank regiment.

[3] Includes 23 assault gun regiments, 1 engineer-tank regiment, and 1 flamethrower regiment.

[4] 2 brigades were attached to the 20th and 21st artillery divisions. They were deployed in other armies of the 1st Baltic Army Group.

Table 2

Soviet Personnel Strengths, Weapons, and Equipment[1]
January 10, 1945

Men and Equipment	3d Byelo-russian Army Group	2d Byelo-russian Army Group	Forty-third Army (1st Baltic Army Group)	Total
Men	483,978	671,016	67,662	1,222,656[2]
Tanks	836	1,178	21	2,035
Assault guns	762	1,017	45	1,824
AT guns (45–57mm)	1,611	2,088	286	3,985
Field guns (76mm and larger)	4,213	5,793	778	10,784
Mortars (82–120mm)	4,490	5,411	756	10,657
MRLs	567	970	26	1,563
AA guns	704	1,026	114	1,844
Vehicles	23,069	32,864	3,948	59,881

[1] Excludes rear elements of army groups.

[2] Including rear service elements, January 1, 1945 strength—1,669,105 (2d Byelorussian Army Group, 881,500 men; 3d Byelorussian Army Group, 708,600 men, and Forty-third Army, 79,005 men).

Table 3

Operational Density of Soviet Forces
January 10, 1945

Army Groups and Armies	Entire Front Width (km)	Rifle Divs and Fortified Areas	Km/ Div	Breakthrough Sector Width (km)	Rifle Divs	Km/ Div
3d Byelorussian	170	54 + 1FA[1]	3.1	24	21[2]	1.1
2d Byelorussian	285	63 + 3FA	4.3	28	35[3]	0.8
Forty-third	95	13	7.3	—	—	—
TOTAL/AVERAGE	550	130 + 4FA	4.1	52	56	0.9

[1] FA = Fortified area.

[2] 18 divisions in first line.

[3] 27 divisions in first line.

Table 4

Soviet Operational Aircraft
January 10, 1945

Type	First Air Army, 3d Byelorussian Army Group	Fourth Air Army, 2d Byelorussian Army Group	Total
Fighters	605	652	1,257
Ground attack	449	566	1,015
Bombers	237	195	432
Night bombers	106	121	227
Reconnaissance	107	59	166
TOTAL	1,504	1,593	3,097

Table 5

Composition and Operational Density of German Forces[1]
January 10, 1945

Army Group Center[2]	Divisions					Front Line (km)	Km/ Div
	Inf	Panzer	Motorized	Lt Inf	Total		
Third Panzer Army	11	1	—	—	12	135	11.2
Fourth Army	11	1	2	1	15	280	18.7
Second Army	9	1	—	1	11	135	12.3
Reserves	1	—	2	—	3	—	—
TOTAL/AVERAGE	32	3	4	2	41	550	13.4

[1] Twelve additional divisions (including two panzer) and one engineer brigade were committed during the operation.

[2] On January 26 the name was changed to Army Group North.

Table 6

**Soviet Army Groups Buildup
Before January 10, 1945**

Armies	Rifle Formations			Tank and Mechanized Formations					Air Force		Eng Bde
	Corps	Div	Fortified Areas	Corps	Bde	Tank Rgt	Assault Gun Rgt	Motorcycle Rgt	Corps	Div	
3d Byelorussian Army Group											
Twenty-eighth[1]	3	9	—	—	—	—	—	—	—	—	1
Second Guards[2]	3	9	—	—	—	—	2	—	—	—	1
Ind elements	—	—	—	—	—	2	—	—	—	6	—
TOTAL	6	18	—	—	—	2	2	—	—	6	2
2d Byelorussian Army Group											
Second Strike[3]	3	9	—	—	—	—	1	—	—	—	1
Sixty-fifth[4]	4	12	—	—	—	—	—	—	—	—	1
Seventieth[4]	2	5	—	—	1	—	2	—	—	—	1
Fifth Tank[5]	—	—	—	2	1	1	1	1	—	—	1
Ind elements	1	9	1	3	—	4	6	—	3	10	1
TOTAL	10	35	1	5	2	5	10	1	3	10	5
COMBINED TOTAL	16	53	1	5	2	7	12	1	3	16	7

[1] Transferred from GHQ Reserves on October 13, 1944.
[2] Transferred from 1st Baltic Army Group on December 20, 1944.
[3] Transferred from GHQ Reserves on October 16, 1944.
[4] Transferred from 1st Byelorussian Army Group on November 19, 1944.
[5] Transferred from GHQ Reserves on January 8, 1945.

Table 7

Soviet Artillery Buildup
Before January 10, 1945

Armies	Breakthrough Corps	Divs	Bdes	Rgts	TD Bdes	TD Rgts	Mortar Bdes	Mortar Rgts	MRL Divs	MRL Bdes	MRL Rgts	AAA Divs	AAA Rgts
3d Byelorussian Army Group													
Twenty-eighth[1]	—	—	1	—	—	1	—	1	—	—	1	—	1
Second Guards[2]	—	1	1	2	—	1	—	—	—	—	—	—	1
Ind elements	—	—	5	—	—	1	1	—	—	—	—	—	—
TOTAL	—	1	7	2	—	3	1	1	—	—	1	—	2
2d Byelorussian Army Group													
Second Strike[3]	—	—	1	1	—	1	—	1	—	—	—	—	1
Sixty-fifth[4]	—	—	1	—	—	1	—	1	—	—	1	1	1
Seventieth[4]	—	—	1	—	—	1	—	1	—	—	—	1	1
Fifth Tank[5]	1	—	1	—	1	1	—	—	1	—	1	1	—
Ind elements	—	5	25	—	—	—	5	—	—	5	3	—	—
TOTAL	1	5	29	1	1	4	5	3	1	5	5	3	3
COMBINED TOTAL	1	6	36	3	1	7	6	4	1	5	6	3	5

[1] Transferred from GHQ Reserves on October 13, 1944.
[2] Transferred from 1st Baltic Army Group on December 20, 1944.
[3] Transferred from GHQ Reserves on October 16, 1944.
[4] Transferred from 1st Byelorussian Army Group on November 19, 1944.
[5] Transferred from 1st Byelorussian Army Group on January 8, 1945.

Table 8

Operational Density of Soviet Forces
January 10, 1945

| Armies | Width of Front (km) | Breakthrough Sector (km) | Number of Divisions | | | Mobile Groups |
			First Echelon	Second Echelon	Reserves	
3d Byelorussian Army Group						
Thirty-ninth	46	8	9	—	1	—
Fifth	9	9	8	—	1	—
Twenty-eighth	21	7	8	—	1	—
Second Guards	22	—	—	—	—	—
Thirty-first	72	—	—	—	—	—
2d Byelorussian Army Group						
Fiftieth	155	—	—	—	—	—
Forty-ninth	50	—	—	—	—	—
Forty-eighth	18	6	8	—	1	VIII Mech Corps
Third	17	6	9	—	1	—
Second Strike	19	6	7	2	—	VIII Gds Tank Corps
Sixty-fifth	14	7	8	—	1	I Guards Tank Corps
Seventieth	12	3	6	3	—	—

Table 9

Width of Front and Density of Artillery and Tanks
January 10, 1945

	3d Byelorussian Army Group	2d Byelorussian Army Group
Width of front (km)		
Total	170	285
Breakthrough sector	24	28
Percent of total	14.1	9.8
Guns and mortars		
Total front	8,703	11,204
Breakthrough sector	4,805	6,682
Percent of total	55.2	59.6
Guns and mortars/kilometer		
Total front	51	39
Breakthrough sector	160–200	238
Tanks and assault guns		
Total front	1,598	2,195
Breakthrough sector	1,493	2,115
Percent of total	93.4	96.3
Tank and assault guns/kilometer*		
Total front	8.8	7.7
Breakthrough sector	87	74

* Includes mobile groups of armies and army groups.

Table 10

Soviet Advance Rates
January 13–26, 1945

Army Groups	Soviet Breakthrough January 13–18		Exploitation of Breakthrough, January 19–26			
			Combined Arms Armies		Mobile Troops	
	Adv (km)	Daily Adv (km)	Adv (km)	Daily Adv (km)	Adv (km)	Daily Adv (km)
3d Byelorussian	20–30	3.3–5.0	80–100	10–13	100–120	12–15
2d Byelorussian	30–60	6.0–12.0	150–170	18–20	170–250	28–40

Table 11
Soviet Supply Levels
January 10, 1945

Army Groups	Ammunition (units of fire)						Fuel (refueling units)			Food (daily rations)
	Small Arms	Mortar	AT Arty	76mm	122mm	152 and 203mm	Aviation	Vehicle	Diesel	
3d Byelorussian	1.5	4.6	2.00	3.6	4.1	5.0	10.3	3.8	4.4	31
2d Byelorussian	2.1	3.6	2.65	3.1	4.2	5.0	7.1	4.0	3.1	30

Table 12
German Divisions Destroyed and Defeated
January 13–April 26, 1945

Formation and Month	Divisions				
	Inf	Lt Inf	Motorized	Panzer	Total
January					
Third Panzer Army[1]	5	—	—	—	5
Fourth Army	—	—	—	—	—
Second Army[2]	3	—	—	—	3
February					
Operational Group "Samland"	—	—	—	—	—
Fourth Army	11	—	—	—	11
March					
Operational Group "Samland"	3	—	—	—	3
Fourth Army	5	1	2	1	9
April					
Operational Group "Samland"	9	—	1	1	11
TOTAL	36	1	3	2	42[3]

[1] February 2, 1945, name changed to Operational Group "Samland."

[2] January 26, 1945, attached to Army Group "Vistula."

[3] 37 divisions were destroyed.

The Vistula-Oder Offensive

January 12–February 3, 1945

The Vistula-Oder offensive, one of the great strategic operations on the Eastern Front, was aimed at destroying German forces between the Vistula and Oder rivers, liberating Polish territories still under German occupation, plunging into the heart of Germany, and establishing the basis for a final assault on Berlin.

The Soviet Supreme Command assigned this mission to the 1st Byelorussian and 1st Ukrainian army groups, which were to launch the operation from bridgeheads on the western bank of the Vistula. The attacking force numbered 1,565,000 men (2,200,000 with rear services) and had 6,500 tanks and assault guns, some 34,000 artillery pieces and mortars, and 5,000 aircraft.

The 1st Byelorussian Army Group, commanded by Marshal Zhukov and composed of eight combined arms armies, two tank armies, one air army, and several independent tank, mechanized, and cavalry formations, was to break through the German defenses on two axes. The main blow was to be launched from the Magnushev bridgehead south of Warsaw toward Kutno and Poznan. The secondary effort was to be an advance from the Pulawy bridgehead farther to the south, toward Radom and Lodz. One army was to cross the Vistula north of Warsaw and envelop the city from the north and northwest.

After achieving its first objective, the army group would continue toward the Oder River, cross it, and establish bridgeheads on its left bank.

The 1st Ukrainian Army Group, commanded by Marshal Konev, had approximately the same organizational structure and strength as the 1st Byelorussian Army Group. It was to jump off from the Sandomierz bridgehead toward Chmielnik and Radomsko and continue to Breslau, the capital of Silesia. Two secondary attacks were envisioned—on the northern flank toward

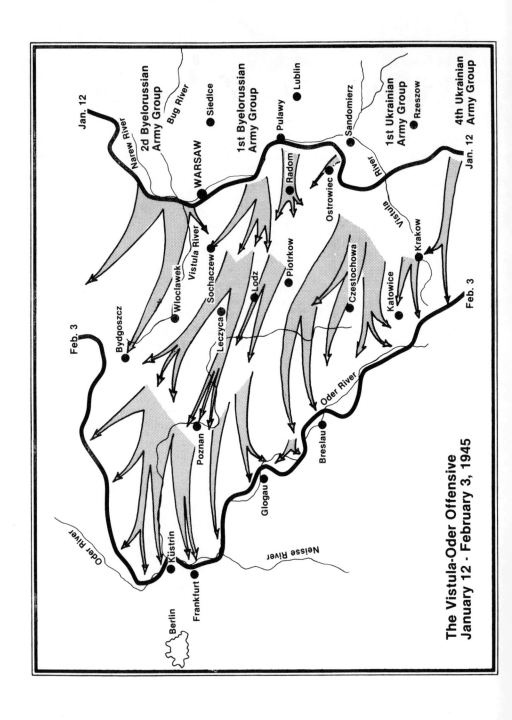

The Vistula-Oder Offensive
January 12 - February 3, 1945

Szydlowiec, Ostrowiec, and Opatow, and on the southern toward Krakow, along the western bank of the Vistula.

Facing the Soviet forces along a front of nearly 500 kilometers was German Army Group A, under Field Marshal Josef Harpe (replaced on January 16 by Field Marshal Ferdinand Schorner), composed of the Ninth and Seventeenth field armies and the Fourth Panzer Army, a total of twenty-two infantry, four panzer, and two motorized divisions, and numerous smaller independent units, numbering 560,000 men, 1,220 tanks and assault guns, over 4,000 artillery pieces and mortars, and nearly 650 aircraft. Most of these forces were deployed against the Soviet bridgeheads.

The ratio of forces favored the Russians 2.8:1 in men, 5:1 in armor, 6.8:1 in artillery, and 7:1 in aircraft.

The 1st Ukrainian Army Group began the offensive from the Sandomierz bridgehead on the morning of January 12, against General Fritz Graeser's Fourth Panzer Army. After a two-hour artillery preparation the XLII and XLVIII panzer corps were overwhelmed by the powerful Soviet barrages and determined infantry attacks. They began to withdraw and disintegrate. During the first day of operation the Russians advanced as much as 20 kilometers. In an attempt to close the penetration, Graeser committed his reserve, the XXIV Panzer Corps; but after several unsuccessful attempts to counterattack, it too was defeated and retreated toward Kielce. Konev brought in his second echelon, and on January 15, in a skillful enveloping maneuver from the northeast, south, and west, liberated Kielce. Soviet tank armies reached the open country and raced almost unopposed toward the Oder.

The capture of Kielce, and the successful operations of the 1st Byelorussian Army Group to the north, forced the German forces still holding the line along the Vistula to withdraw westward. The withdrawal turned into flight. Communications were disrupted and the troops were in disorder. Only a few managed to escape.

In four days of operation the main force of the Fourth Panzer Army was defeated and destroyed. Only a few groups were able to elude the pursuing Russians and organize a hasty defense farther to the west.

Heavy fighting took place on the Krakow axis. Despite stubborn resistance by elements of the German Seventeenth Army, Russian troops pushed forward and captured Krakow on January 19. To the west of the city, the advance of the left wing of the army was slowed as it approached the industrial area of Upper Silesia. The Germans decided to hold this important coal and steel region at all costs, and so committed about ten infantry and panzer divisions to its defense.

In the center and on the right flank the going was easier. The Third Guards Tank Army and the Fifth Guards and Fifty-second armies, in pursuit of the disorganized German troops, crossed the former Polish-German border on

January 19 and pushed rapidly toward the Oder River. To ease the situation on the left flank, on January 21 Konev turned General P. S. Rybalko's Third Guards Tank Army southward toward Oppeln in the rear of the German Upper Silesia Group of Forces. Oppeln was captured two days later, and the Soviet tanks continued to press forward.

The appearance of Soviet tanks deep in the rear stunned the defenders. Fearful of encirclement, they quickly retreated. In the course of the next several days most of the Upper Silesia industrial region changed hands. Between January 30 and February 3 Konev reached the Oder and established several bridgeheads on its western bank. Breslau was bypassed and encircled.

The 1st Byelorussian Army Group launched its operations from the Pulawy and Magnuszew bridgeheads against General Freiherr S. von Lüttwitz's Ninth Army on January 14. The main German defense line was breached the same day, and the Soviets advanced from 12 to 22 kilometers. The LVI Panzer Corps and the VIII Army Corps were scattered, and retreated in disorder. In an effort to halt the advance, von Lüttwitz counterattacked with his reserve, General S. Henrici's XL Panzer Corps, but the German tanks were repulsed and withdrew hastily.

On January 15 Zhukov committed General M. E. Katukov's First Tank Army. During that day Katukov advanced 40 to 50 kilometers and reached the Pilica River. On January 16, the Pilica was crossed, and General Kolpakchiy's Sixty-ninth Army took Radom and moved quickly toward Lodz. North of Warsaw the Forty-seventh Army, under General F. I. Perkhorovich, crossed the Vistula and enveloped the city from the north.

Taking advantage of the gap that had been created on the Pilica front, Zhukov sent in the Second Guards Tank Army, commanded by General S. I. Bogdanov, and General V. V. Kryukov's II Guards Cavalry Corps. Not encountering any serious resistance, the tank army advanced some 80 kilometers during the first day, taking Sochaczew, a town in the rear of the German forces defending Warsaw. By that time Warsaw was enveloped from north and south. Threatened by encirclement, the Germans abandoned the defenses and retreated. Warsaw was liberated on January 17. The next day, forces of the 1st Byelorussian and 1st Ukrainian Army Groups met in the Szydlowiec area, forming a continuous front of 500 kilometers.

The tempo of the offensive increased, and the drive to the Oder developed into a race. The German defense collapsed totally. The remnants of the Ninth Army were left far behind the advancing Soviet troops. Lodz was taken on January 19, the Warta River was crossed, and on January 22 Poznan, which Hitler had declared a fortress to be defended to the last, was surrounded by Katukov's tanks. Unable to take the city immediately, Katukov left the Eighth Guards and Sixty-ninth armies, which were following close behind, to take it, and forged rapidly westward. The First Guards Tank Army broke through the Meseritz fortified zone, and on February 3 in a spectacular thrust reached the Oder River. Soviet forces seized a bridgehead on its west bank near Küstrin. Berlin was only 70 kilometers away.

The Vistula-Oder offensive was completed on February 3. In 23 days, the 1st Byelorussian and 1st Ukrainian army groups had overrun German forces between the Vistula and the Oder, reached the Oder River, established several bridgeheads on its left bank, and laid the foundation for the final campaign of the war, the Battle of Berlin.

Soviet Order of Battle
January 12, 1945

1st Byelorussian Army Group
  First echelon
    Forty-seventh Combined Arms Army
    First Polish Army
    Sixty-first Combined Arms Army
    Fifth Strike Army
    Eighth Guards Army
    Sixty-ninth Combined Arms Army
    Thirty-third Combined Arms Army
  Second echelon
    Third Strike Army
  Mobile groups
    First Guards Tank Army
    Second Guards Tank Army
    II Guards Cavalry Corps
  Army group reserve
    VII Guards Cavalry Corps

1st Ukrainian Army Group
  First echelon
    Sixth Combined Arms Army
    Third Guards Army
    Thirteenth Combined Arms Army
    Fifty-second Combined Arms Army
    Fifth Guards Army
    Sixtieth Combined Arms Army
  Second echelon
    Fifty-ninth Combined Arms Army
    Twenty-first combined Arms Army
  Mobile groups
    Third Guards Tank Army
    Fourth Tank Army
  Army group reserve
    VII Guards Mechanized Corps
    I Guards Cavalry Corps

Table 1

Composition of the Soviet Forces
January 12, 1945

Formations and Independent Units	1st Byelorussian Army Group	1st Ukrainian Army Group	Total
Combined arms armies	8	8	16
Tank armies	2	2	4
Air armies	1	1	2
Rifle corps	21	22	43
Rifle divisions	68	66	134
Fortified areas	2	1	3
Cavalry corps	2	1	3
Cavalry divisions	6	3	9
Tank corps	5	6	11
Mechanized corps	2	3	5
Ind tank and assault gun brigades	7	6	13
Ind tank and assault gun regiments	35	28	63
Artillery corps	2	2	4
Artillery divisions	6	6	12
AA artillery divisions	11	7	18
Ind artillery brigades	11	10	21
TD artillery brigades	9	7	16
Ind mortar brigades	1	1	2
Ind artillery regiments	4	4	8
Ind TD artillery regiments	7	21	28
Ind AA artillery regiments	13	10	23
Ind mortar regiments	9	11	20
MRL divisions	1	1	2
Ind MRL brigades	2	1	3
Ind MRL regiments	13	12	25
Engineer brigades	15	16	31

Table 2

Men and Equipment
January 12, 1945

Men and Equipment	1st Byelorussian Army Group		1st Ukrainian Army Group		Totals	
	Total	In Combat Units	Total	In Combat Units	Total	In Combat Units
Men	1,119,838	809,648	1,083,848	755,283	2,203,686	1,564,931
Tanks	2,102	1,975	2,427	2,255	4,529	4,230
Assault guns	1,279	1,245	1,234	989	2,513	2,234
AT guns (45mm, 57mm)	2,490	2,374	2,446	2,346	4,936	4,720
Field artillery (76mm and larger)	7,015	6,526	6,748	6,679	13,763	13,205
Mortars (82mm, 120mm)	7,595	7,180	7,217	7,038	14,812	14,218
MRLs	1,114	1,114	1,084	1,031	2,198	2,145
AA guns	1,676	1,117	1,846	1,031	3,522	2,148
Trucks and cars	65,120	37,474	56,443	31,077	121,563	68,551

Table 3

Operational Density of Soviet Forces
January 12, 1945

	1st Byelorussian Army Group			1st Ukrainian Army Group		
		Breakthrough Sector			Breakthrough Sector	
	Total	Width	% of Total	Total	Width	% of Total
Width of front (kms)	230	30[1]	13.0	250	36[2]	14.4
Rifle divisions						
Total	68	37	54.4	66	34	51.5
Kilometers/ division	3.4	0.8		3.8	1.06	
Guns and mortars[3]						
Total	13,706	7,318	53.4	13,717	8,626	62.9
Per kilometer	60	244		54.9	239.6	
Tanks and assault guns						
Total	3,220	2,942	91.4	3,244	3,181	98.1
Per kilometer	14	98		13	88	

[1] Does not include the 4-kilometer breakthrough sector of the Forty-seventh Army.

[2] Does not include the 3-kilometer breakthrough sector of the Sixtieth Army.

[3] Does not include 45mm and 57mm AT guns, MRLs, and AA artillery.

Table 4

Composition and Strength of Soviet Air Force
January 12, 1945

	Sixteenth Air Army 1st Byelorussian Army Group	Second Air Army 1st Ukrainian Army Group	Total
Corps			
Fighter	3	3	6
Ground attack	2	3	5
Bomber	1	2	3
TOTAL	6	8	14
Divisions			
Fighter	9	10	19
Ground attack	6	6	12
Bomber	6	5	11
TOTAL	21	21	42
Aircraft*			
Fighter	1,131	1,172	2,303
Ground attack	735	775	1,510
Bomber	327	417	744
Night bomber	172	120	292
Reconnaissance	94	104	198
TOTAL	2,459	2,588	5,047

* Operational only.

Table 5

Composition of German Army Group A[1]
January 12, 1945

Armies	Divisions				Bdes	Front (km)	Km/Div
	Inf[2]	Panzer	Motorized	Total			
Ninth	8	—	—	8	1	230	27
Fourth Panzer	7	—	—	7	1	160	21
Seventeenth[3]	5	—	—	5	—	90	18
Reserve	2	4	2	8	—	—	—
TOTAL	22	4	2	28	2[4]	480	17

[1] Strength: 400,000 men, 4,103 guns and mortars, 1,136 tanks and assault guns. The First Panzer and First Hungarian armies were deployed in another sector.

[2] Includes light infantry, mountain, and security divisions.

[3] Five divisions defended a 90-kilometer sector facing the Soviet 1st Ukrainian Army Group; one division defended a 20-kilometer sector facing the 4th Ukrainian Army Group.

[4] Two brigades equal one division.

Table 6

Operational Deployment of Soviet Armies
January 12, 1945

Armies	Frontage (kms)		Number of Formations			
	Total	Breakthrough Sector	First Echelon	Second Echelon	Reserve	Mobile Groups
1st Byelorussian Army Group						
Forty-seventh[1]	14	4	9 rifle divs	—	—	—
First Polish	53	—	2 inf divs	3 inf divs / 1 cav bde	—	—
Sixty-first[1]	30	4	7 rifle div / 1 FA[2]	—	2 rifle divs	—
Fifth Strike	12	6	8 rifle divs	—	1 rifle div	—
Eighth Guards	30	7	9 rifle divs	—	1 rifle div	—
Sixty-ninth[1]	54	7	9 rifle divs	—	1 rifle div	XI Tank Corps
Thirty-third[1]	36	6	8 rifle divs / 1 FA[2]	—	1 rifle div	IX Tank Corps
1st Ukrainian Army Group						
Sixth[1]	94	—	4 rifle divs / 1 FA[2]	—	1 rifle div	—
Third Guards	12	2	3 rifle divs	3 rifle divs	3 rifle divs	XXV Tank Corps
Thirteenth[1]	11	11	6 rifle divs	3 rifle divs	—	—
Fifty-second[1]	10	10	6 rifle divs	3 rifle divs	—	IV Guards Tank
Fifth Guards	13	13	9 rifle divs	—	—	XXXI Tank Corps
Sixtieth[1]	110	3	6 rifle divs	3 rifle divs	—	—

[1] Combined arms armies.
[2] Fortified areas.

Table 7

Reinforcements Sent to 1st Byelorussian Army Group October–December 1944

Armies	1st Byelorussian Army Group						
	Thirty-third*	Fifth Strike	Third Strike	Second Guards Tank	First Guards Tank	Independent Units	Total
Arrival Dates	Oct 19	Oct 30	Dec 31	Oct 30	Nov 22	Various	Total
Rifle corps	3	3	3	—	—	—	9
Rifle divisions	9	9	9	—	—	—	27
Fortified areas	—	—	—	—	—	—	—
Tank corps	—	—	—	2	1	—	3
Mechanized corps	—	—	—	1	1	—	2
Tank brigades	—	—	—	—	1	—	1
Assault gun brigades	—	—	—	—	1	—	1
Ind tank regiments	—	—	—	—	1	6	7
Assault gun regiments	—	—	—	—	—	5	5
Motorcycle regiments	—	—	—	1	1	—	2
Artillery							
Breakthrough corps	—	—	—	—	—	1	1
Divisions	—	—	—	—	—	2	2
Brigades	1	1	1	1	1	8	13
Independent regiments	—	—	—	—	—	—	—
Independent TD rgts	1	1	1	—	—	—	3
Mortar brigades	—	—	—	—	—	4	4
Mortar regiments	1	1	1	—	—	—	3
MRL divisions	—	—	—	—	—	—	—
Independent MRL bdes	—	—	—	—	—	4	4
MRL regiments	—	—	—	1	1	3	5
AAA divisions	—	—	—	—	—	1	1
Ind AAA regiments	1	1	1	—	—	—	3
Engineer brigades	1	1	1	1	1	1	6
Air Force							
Corps	—	—	—	—	—	2	2
Divisions	—	—	—	—	—	6	6

* Combined arms army.

Table 8

Reinforcements Sent to 1st Ukrainian Army Group
October–December 1944

	1st Ukrainian Army Group						
Armies	Fifty-sec-ond*	Sixth*	Twenty-first*	Fifty-ninth*	Third Guards Tank	Inde-pendent Units	Total
Arrival Date	Oct 30	Dec 7	Dec 12	Dec 20	Oct 28	Various	Total
Rifle corps	3	2	3	2	—	—	10
Rifle divisions	9	5	9	7	—	—	30
Fortified areas	—	—	—	—	—	1	1
Tank corps	—	—	—	—	2	—	2
Mechanized corps	—	—	—	—	1	1	2
Tank brigades	—	—	—	—	—	—	—
Assault gun brigades	—	—	—	—	1	1	2
Ind tank regiments	—	—	—	—	1	5	6
Assault gun regiments	—	—	—	—	—	11	11
Motorcycle regiments	—	—	—	—	1	—	1
Artillery							
Breakthrough corps	—	—	—	—	—	1	1
Divisions	—	—	—	—	—	2	2
Brigades	1	1	1	1	1	8	13
Independent regiments	—	—	1	1	—	—	2
Independent TD rgts	1	1	1	1	—	—	4
Mortar brigades	—	—	—	—	—	4	4
Mortar regiments	1	1	1	1	—	—	4
MRL divisions	—	—	—	—	—	1	1
Independent MRL bdes	—	—	—	—	—	5	5
MRL regiments	—	—	—	—	1	1	2
AAA divisions	—	—	—	—	—	—	—
Ind AAA regiments	1	1	1	1	2	—	6
Engineer brigades	1	1	1	1	1	1	6
Air Force							
Corps	—	—	—	—	—	3	3
Divisions	—	—	—	—	—	7	7

* Combined arms army.

Table 9
German Reinforcements
January 15–February 8, 1945

Dates	Inf	Motor-ized	Panzer	Special Purpose	Ski	Air-borne	Marines	Total	Fortress Groups	Bdes
January 15–20	5	1	1	1	—	—	—	8	—	—
January 21–31	1	—	2	—	1	—	—	4	—	1
February 1–8	13	3	2	3	—	1	1	23	4	1
TOTAL	19	4	5	4	1	1	1	35	4	2

Table 10
Ammunition, Fuel and Rations
January 1945

Type	1st Byelorussian Army Group	1st Ukrainian Army Group
Units of fire		
Small arms	1.5–2.5	1.5–2.0
Artillery	3.1–9.8	3.5–4.0
POL refueling units		
Aviation	14.1	9.4
Vehicle	4.3	5.1
Diesel	3.4	4.6
Rations (days)		
Bread	140.0	21.8
Groats	65.0	20.0
Fats	33.0	28.8
Sugar	66.0	35.5

Table 11

Minimum/Maximum Daily Advance Rates (Kilometers)
January 12–February 3, 1945

| Date | 1st Byelorussian Army Group | | 1st Ukrainian Army Group | |
	Combined Arms Armies	Tank Armies	Combined Arms Armies	Tank Armies
January 12	—	—	15–20	14–15
January 13	—	—	18–20	25
January 14	12–18	—	10–25	15–35
January 15	11–28	11	12–25	15–40
January 16	15–20	30–70	20–35	35
January 17	25–35	15–55	30–40	40
January 18	20–30	35–45	10–30	15–20
January 19	20–35	45–70	17–30	35–40
January 20	20–40	20–45	25–35	35–40
January 21	25–35	45–50	28–35	25–30
January 22	25–40	40–60	20–32	15–40
January 23	25–45	10–45	20–28	30–50
January 24	25–40	0–50	25–32	30–40
January 25	20–35	20–40	5–50	25–40
January 26	10–40	12–30	5–25	25–35
January 27	15–40	5–10	4–25	12–25
January 28	10–35	25	3–25	0–10
January 29	5–15	15–25	8–15	0–8
January 30	10–30	30	2–20	5
January 31	10–55	25–50	0–8	0–5
February 1	15–20	0–40	—	—
February 2	10–30	20	—	—
February 3	10–20	—	—	—

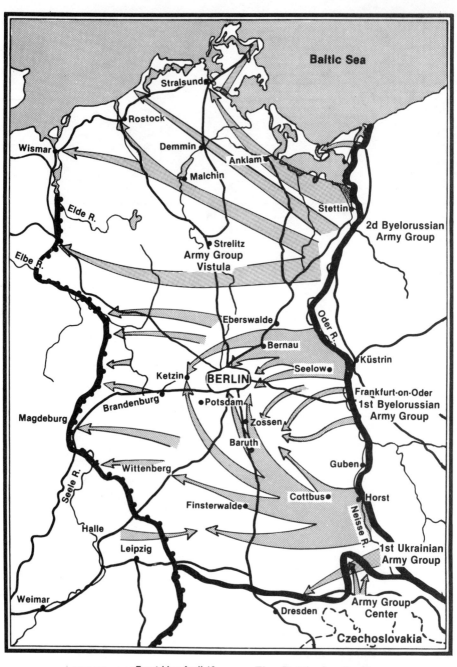

The Battle for Berlin
April 16 - May 8, 1945

Front Line April 16
Allied-Soviet Line May 8

Baltic Sea

Stralsund
Rostock
Demmin
Anklam
Malchin
Wismar
Elde R.
Stettin
2d Byelorussian
Army Group
Elbe R.
Strelitz
Army Group
Vistula
Eberswalde
Oder R.
Bernau
Küstrin
Ketzin
BERLIN
Seelow
Brandenburg
Potsdam
Frankfurt-on-Oder
1st Byelorussian
Army Group
Magdeburg
Zossen
Baruth
Wittenberg
Guben
Seele R.
Finsterwalde
Cottbus
Horst
Halle
Neisse R.
Leipzig
1st Ukrainian
Army Group
Weimar
Dresden
Army Group
Center
Czechoslovakia

The Battle for Berlin

April 16–May 2, 1945

As a result of the Red Army's offensive in the winter of 1945, Soviet troops reached the Oder and the Neisse rivers, established several bridgeheads on the western bank of the Oder, and took up advantageous positions in preparation for an attack on Berlin. The Soviet Supreme Headquarters planned to launch the operation in mid-April with the 1st and 2d Byelorussian army groups and the 1st Ukrainian Army Group. Berlin was to be assaulted from several directions; German forces were to be split into isolated groups and destroyed piecemeal. The Soviets planned to take Berlin on the sixth day of the operation. Next they intended to advance on a broad front to the Elbe River and link up with US and British forces no later than 15 days after the commencement of the offensive.

The 1st Byelorussian Army Group, commanded by Marshal Zhukov, was deployed in the center. It was composed of nine combined arms armies, two tank armies, one air army, and numerous independent formations and units. It was also supported by one long range air army and, during the first four days of the operation, one additional air army detached from the 2d Byelorussian Army Group.

Zhukov planned to launch the main attack with four combined arms armies and two tank armies from the Küstrin bridgehead on the left bank of the Oder River directly toward Berlin, 70 kilometers away. The tank armies were to exploit breakthroughs by the infantry and quickly envelop the city from the north and northeast. Other armies would close in from the east and southeast.

Two secondary blows were to be delivered, one from the north and the other from south of Küstrin. In the north, General Pavel Batov's Sixty-first Army and General Stanislaw Poplawski's First Polish Army, after crossing

219

the Oder, would advance toward Eberswalde and Sandau. In the south, Generals V. Y. Kolpakchiy's Sixty-ninth and V. D. Tsvetayev's Thirty-third army would cross the Oder and move on Furstenwalde and Brandenburg. After taking its initial objectives, the army group would advance to the Elbe.

Deployed on the left flank, the 1st Ukrainian Army Group under Marshal Konev consisted of six combined arms armies, two tank armies, one air army, and numerous independent formations. It was to deliver its main attack on the Cottbus-Wittenberg-Beelitz axis, and to assault Berlin from the southwest. A secondary attack was to be launched toward Dresden.

On the right flank, bordering the Baltic Sea, was the 2d Byelorussian Army Group commanded by Marshal Rokossovskiy. It had four combined arms armies, one air army, three independent tank corps, one mechanized corps, and one cavalry corps. The army group was to assault across the lower Oder River, take Stettin, and reach Anklam, Demmin, Malchin, and Wittenberg no later than the twelfth day of the operation. The main effort would be directed north of Schwedt toward Strelitz.

The three army groups together had 1,600,000 combat troops (2,500,000 including support troops), 6,200 tanks and assault guns, some 42,000 artillery pieces and mortars, and nearly 7,500 aircraft. April 16 was set for the attack of the 1st Byelorussian and 1st Ukrainian army groups, and April 20 for that of the 2d Byelorussian Army Group.

Opposing the Soviet onslaught was Army Group Vistula under General Gotthard Heinrici. It included General Hasso von Manteuffel's Third Panzer Army, General Theodor Busse's Ninth Field Army, and Army Group Center's Fourth Panzer Army, commanded by General Graeser. Manteuffel faced Rokossovskiy with ten divisions; Busse confronted Zhukov with fifteen; and Graeser opposed Konev with fourteen divisions. In reserve, the Germans had eight divisions, of which four were panzer. These forces numbered about 1,000,000 men, 10,400 guns and mortars, 1,500 tanks and assault guns, and nearly 3,300 aircraft. The ratio of forces was in the Soviets' favor—2.5:1 in men, 4.0:1 in artillery, 4.1:1 in tanks and assault guns, and 2.3:1 in aircraft. In the main effort sectors this superiority was even greater.

In the early hours of April 16, long before sunrise, the 1st Byelorussian and the 1st Ukrainian army groups moved out almost simultaneously. After a devastating artillery and air preparation, Zhukov's forces advanced from the Küstrin bridgehead to assault the forward defenses of the German Ninth Army. Strong resistance was encountered, and the advance was slow. German troops repeatedly counterattacked, but each time they were repelled. Soviet progress was much slower than expected, and it appeared that the 1st Ukrainian Army Group, approaching from the south, would reach Berlin first. Only the Third Strike Army managed to break through the first line of resistance and make steady headway. General V. Chuikov's Eighth Guards Army, on the main axis of the army group, was halted below the Seelow Heights. This feature, with its steep slopes and strong fortifications, including many anti-tank ditches and strongholds, represented a formidable obstacle.

By midday Zhukov realized that he could not break through Busse's defenses quickly. In order to achieve a breakthrough of the tactical defense zone he would have to commit his two tank armies immediately.

Thus, in the afternoon General M. E. Katukov's First Guards Tank Army went into action in Chuikov's sector. However, despite the combined efforts of tanks and infantry, the defenses of Seelow Heights still held.

The Second Guards Tank Army, under General S. I. Boghdanov, fared no better. Attacking toward Bernau in the sectors of General V. I. Kuznetsov's Third Strike Army and General N. E. Berzarin's Fifth Strike Army, Boghdanov's tanks encountered stubborn resistance and were halted.

Heavy fighting ensued on April 17 along the entire front, reaching a peak in the direct assault on the Seelow Heights. By nightfall the defenses were penetrated, and the Germans started to withdraw. The staunch resistance of the defenders, many of them inexperienced recruits and Volkssturm members, had surprised the Soviets and put Zhukov two days behind his schedule.

Despite German tenacity, spearheads of the 1st Byelorussian Army Group drew relentlessly closer to Berlin. On April 21 they crossed the main autobahn ring and entered the city's suburbs. Part of the Second Guards Tank Army and the Forty-seventh Army bypassed and enveloped Berlin from the north. Immediately to the east of Berlin, in the Furstenwalde, Erkner, and Petershagen areas, Katukov's tanks and Chuikov's infantry units were engaged in heavy fighting against counterattacking panzer and infantry units.

Berlin was also threatened from the south. Konev's 1st Ukrainian Army Group had also launched its offensive on April 16. The striking task force was composed of the Third Army, Fifth Guards Army, and Thirteenth Army, commanded respectively by Generals V. N. Gordov, A. S. Zhadov, and N. P. Pukhov. The assault elements crossed the Neisse River and penetrated the first defense zone to a depth of up to 15 kilometers. Although initially shocked by the strength and impetus of the attack, the German Fourth Panzer Army rallied, brought up reserves, and began to offer stiff resistance. So as not to lose momentum, Konev committed the IV and XXV Guards tank corps, followed shortly by General P. S. Rybalko's Third Guards Tank Army and General D. D. Lelyushenko's Fourth Guards Tank Army. The tanks advanced rapidly and on April 18 crossed the Spree River. Then Rybalko continued toward Baruth, Zossen, Teltov, and the southern suburbs of Berlin, while, to his left, Lelyushenko moved toward Luckenwalde, Beelitz, and Ketzin.

The advance of the Third and Fourth Guards tank armies, followed by the Thirteenth Army, separated German Army Group Vistula from Army Group Center. On April 20 Rybalko captured the Zossen defense area and cut off the withdrawal routes of the German forces still in the Frankfurt-Guben area. Meanwhile, the Fourth Guards Tank Army was speeding northwestward to meet with Boghdanov's tanks west of Berlin, closing the encirclement ring around the city.

As planned, Rokossovskiy's 2d Byelorussian Army Group, after crossing the marshy lowlands between the East and the West Oder on April 18 and 19, assaulted across the West Oder on April 20 and penetrated the main defenses of the Third Panzer Army. This operation pinned down German forces north of Berlin, preventing them from turning south against the 1st Byelorussian Army Group, which was attacking the city.

By April 21 all three army groups were progressing in their respective sectors. The Germans were in retreat along the entire front. Those troops that did not withdraw in time were surrounded and were either taken prisoner or destroyed.

On April 24 Konev's Third Guards Tank Army and Twenty-eighth Army met with Zhukov's Eighth Guards Army, Third Army, and Sixty-ninth Army southeast of Berlin, and one day later elements of the Forty-seventh and Second Guards Tank armies of the 1st Byelorussian Army Group linked with the 1st Ukrainian Army Group's Fourth Guards Tank Army at Ketzin, west of Berlin. The German troops in Berlin found themselves not only surrounded, but also split from the Frankfurt-Guben forces southeast of Berlin. The German situation had become hopeless.

The Frankfurt-Guben Group, some 200,000 men strong, made several attempts to break out, but all were unsuccessful. By May 1, the entire force, except for a few small groups that made their way westward through swamps and forests, was annihilated.

Overcoming fierce resistance from the encircled Berlin garrison, the troops of the 1st Byelorussian and 1st Ukrainian army groups drew closer to the center of the city. The ring tightened with each passing day. Particularly vicious were the battles in the heart of the city, where the defenders fought with desperation for each street and building. By April 29 most of the city was in Soviet hands. The Reichstag, the symbol of the Third Reich, fell on April 30 to the 171st Rifle Division of Colonel A. T. Negoda. On that day Hitler committed suicide, leaving Grand Admiral Karl Dönitz in power.

By the morning of May 2 there were only scattered minor pockets of resistance. At 3:00 PM all resistance in Berlin ceased. Soviet forces continued to advance westward toward the Allied armies. On May 8, representatives of vanquished Nazi Germany signed the instrument of unconditional surrender.

Soviet Order of Battle
April 15, 1945

2d Byelorussian Army Group
  First echelon
    Second Strike Army
    Sixty-fifth Combined Arms Army
    Seventieth Combined Arms Army
    Forty-ninth Combined Arms Army
  Mobile groups
    I Guards Tank Corps
    III Guards Tank Corps
    VIII Mechanized Corps
    III Guards Cavalry Corps
1st Byelorussian Army Group
  First echelon
    Sixty-first Combined Arms Army
    First Polish Army
    Sixty-ninth Combined Arms Army
    Thirty-third Combined Arms Army
    Forty-seventh Combined Arms Army
    Third Strike Army
    Fifth Strike Army
    Eighth Guards Army
    IX Tank Corps
    XI Tank Corps
    II Guards Cavalry Corps
  Second echelon
    Third Combined Arms Army

  Mobile groups
    First Guards Tank Army
    Second Guards Tank Army
  Army group reserves
    VII Guards Cavalry Corps
1st Ukrainian Army Group
  First echelon
    Third Guards Army
    Fifth Guards Army
    Thirteenth Combined Arms Army
    Fifty-second Combined Arms Army
    Second Polish Army
    IV Guards Tank Corps
    XXV Tank Corps
    VII Guards Mechanized Corps
    I Polish Tank Corps
  Second echelon
    Twenty-eighth Combined Arms Army
  Mobile groups
    Third Guards Tank Army
    Fourth Guards Tank Army
  Army group reserves
    I Guards Cavalry Corps

Table 1

Composition of Soviet Forces
April 15, 1945

Formations and Units	Army Groups			Total
	2d Byelorussian[1]	1st Byelorussian	1st Ukrainian[2]	
Armies				
Combined arms	4	9	6	19
Tank	—	2	2	4
Air	1	1	1	3
Corps				
Rifle	10	24	15	49
Cavalry	1	2	1	4
Mechanized	1	2	4	7
Tank	3	5	6	14
Artillery	1	3	2	6
Air	3	8	8	19
Divisions				
Rifle	33	77	49	159
Cavalry	3	6	3	12
Artillery	3	8	7	18
MRL	1	2	1	4
AAA	5	13	7	25
Air	15	29	21	65
Fortified areas	—	2	—	2
Cavalry bde	—	1	—	1
Ind tank and assault gun bde	2	8	6	16
Ind tank and assault gun rgt	19	42	22	83
Ind artillery bde	5	14	7	26
Ind artillery rgt	9	5	2	16
TD artillery bde	6	12	7	25
TD artillery rgt	4	8	13	25
Ind mortar bde	2	2	1	5
Ind mortar rgt	6	10	7	23
Ind MRL bde	1	2	1	4
MRL rgt	7	17	8	32
Ind AAA rgt	12	11	8	31
River boat bde	—	3	—	3
Engineer bde	11	17	16	44
Flotillas	—	1	—	1

[1] As of April 20, 1945. Excludes the Fifth Guards Tank and Nineteenth Combined Arms armies, deployed in another sector.

[2] Excludes Sixth, Twenty-first, Thirty-first, and Fifty-ninth Combined Arms armies, deployed on another axis.

Table 2

Soviet Equipment and Strengths
April 15, 1945

Men and Equipment	Army Groups			Total
	2d Byelorussian	1st Byelorussian	1st Ukrainian	
Men[1]	314,000	768,100	511,700	1,593,800
Tanks	644	1,795	1,388	3,827
Assault guns	307	1,360	667	2,334
AT guns	770	2,306	1,444	4,520
Field guns (76mm and larger)	3,172	7,442	5,040	15,654
Mortars (82mm and larger)	2,770	7,186	5,225	15,181
MRLs	807	1,531	917	3,255
AAA guns	801	1,665	945	3,411[2]
Vehicles	21,846	44,332	29,205	95,383
Operational aircraft				
Fighters	602	1,567	1,106	3,275
Ground attack	449	731	529	1,709
Bombers	283	762	422	1,467[3]
Reconnaissance	26	128	91	245
TOTAL	1,360	3,188	2,148	6,696

[1] Combat troops only. With rear elements, total 2,500,000.

[2] Excludes IV, V, and X AA artillery corps of the Air Defense of the Country, covering rear areas of army groups.

[3] Excludes 800 long range bombers of the Eighteenth Air Army supporting the 1st Byelorussian Army Group.

Table 3

Composition of German Forces
April 15, 1945

Formations	Divisions								Inf Bde	Width of Front (km)	Km/ Div
	Inf	Panzer	Motorized	Special	Field Training	Airborne	Marine	Total			
Third Panzer Army	6	—	2	1	1	—	2	12	1	157	12.5
Ninth Field Army	9	1	4	1	—	1	—	16	—	115	7.2
Army Group Vistula Reserves	3	1	1	—	1	—	—	6	—	—	—
TOTAL	18	2	7	2	2	1	2	34	1	272	7.9
Fourth Panzer Army[1]	9	1	1	2	—	—	—	13	—	116[2]	8.9
GRAND TOTAL	27	3	8	4	2	1	2	47	1	388	8.2

[1] Army Group Center.
[2] Only sector facing the right flank of the Soviet 1st Ukrainian Army Group advancing on Berlin.

Table 4

German Reinforcements[1]

Reinforced Formations	Reinforcements										Total Division Equivalent[3]
	Divisions							Brigades			
	Inf	Panzer	Motorized	Special	Field Training	Airborne	Total	Inf	Airborne	Total	
Third Panzer Army	3	1	1	1	1	—	7	2	1	3	8.5
Ninth Field Army	1	—	—	—	—	—	1	—	—	—	1
Army Group Vistula Reserves	10	—	1	—	—	1	12	—	—	—	12
TOTAL	14	1	2	1	1	1	20	2	1	3	21.5
Fourth Panzer Army[2]	5	4	1	2	—	—	12	—	—	—	12
GRAND TOTAL	19	5	3	3	1	1	32	2	1	3	33.5

[1] Deployed during the course of the operation.
[2] Army Group Center.
[3] Two brigades equal one division.

Table 5
First Echelon Deployment of Soviet Army Groups

Army Groups/ Armies	Front (km) — Total	Front (km) — Bkth Sector	Formations — Total	Formations — Bkth Sector	Formations — % of Div	Deployment of Rifle Divisions in Armies — First Echelon	Second Echelon	Mobile Group	Army Reserves	Deployment of Rifle Divisions in Corps — First Echelon	Second Echelon
2d Byelorussian											
Second Strike	73	7.0	6 rifle div	3	50.0	6	—	—	—	3	3
Sixty-fifth[1]	17	4.0	9 rifle div	7	77.7	8	—	—	1	6	2
Seventieth[1]	14	4.0	9 rifle div	7	77.7	6	3	—	—	4	2
Forty-ninth[1]	16	6.0	9 rifle div	9	100.0	6	3	—	—	5	1
TOTAL	120	21.0	33 rifle div	26	78.7	26	6	—	1	18	8
1st Byelorussian											
Sixty-first[1]	37	2.5	9 rifle div	6	66.6	8	1 inf div	—	1	5	3
First Polish	12	5.0	5 inf div / 1 cav bde	4	80.0	4	—	—	—	4	—
Forty-seventh[1]	9	4.3	9 rifle div	8	88.8	9	1 cav bde	—	—	6	3
Third Strike	13	6.0	9 rifle div	7	77.7	6	3	IX Tank Corps	—	6	—
Fifth Strike	9	7.0	9 rifle div	6	66.6	8	—	—	—	5	3
Eighth Guards	13	7.0	9 rifle div	6	66.6	9	—	XI Tank Corps	1	6	3
Sixty-ninth[1]	18	6.0	10 rifle div	6	60.0	9	—	II Guards Cavalry Corps	1	8	1
Thirty-third[1]	64	6.5	10 rifle div / 2 FA[2]	9	90.0	9 / 2 FA	4 rifle div / 1 cav bde	2 tank corps / 1 cavalry corps	1	6 / 2 FA	3
TOTAL	175	44.3	70 rifle div / 2 FA / 1 cav bde	52	74.3	62 / 2 FA	4 rifle div / 1 cav bde		4	46 rifle div / 2 FA	16
1st Ukrainian											
Third Guards	28	9.0	9 rifle div	6	66.6	8	—	XXV Tank Corps	1	6	2
Thirteenth	10	10.0	8 rifle div	8	100.0	6	2	—	—	5	1
Fifth Guards	13	8.0	9 rifle div	8	88.8	6	3	IV Gds Tank Corps / I Tank Corps	—	5	1
Second Polish[1]	33	4.0	5 rifle div	3	60.0	4	1	VII Gds Mech Corps	—	4	—
Fifty-second[1]	106	5.0	9 rifle div	4	44.4	8	—	—	1	7	1
TOTAL	190	36.0	40 rifle div	29	72.5	32	6	3 tank corps / 1 mech corps	2	27	5

[1] Combined Arms Army.
[2] FA = fortified area.

Table 6

Soviet Ammunition, Fuel and Rations
April 15, 1945

| | Army Groups | | | Total/ |
	2d Byelorussian	1st Byelorussian	1st Ukrainian	Average
Ammunition (shells)				
Field artillery	361,200	793,600	733,100	1,887,900
AA artillery	99,000	226,100	176,400	501,500
Mortars	275,500	761,400	670,200	1,707,100
TOTAL	735,700	1,781,100	1,579,700	4,096,500
Ammunition (units of fire)				
76–100mm	1.80	2.90	1.85	2.18
122mm	1.25	3.00	2.70	2.32
152–203mm	2.20	3.00	2.95	2.71
AA artillery	2.80	3.00	2.75	2.85
Mortar	1.20	4.25	2.00	2.48
Fuel (refueling units)				
Aviation	6.80	8.70	6.50	7.33
Vehicle	3.10	5.80	4.70	4.53
Diesel	5.20	5.50	5.00	5.23
Daily rations	30	70	50	50

Table 7
Density of Soviet Forces
April 15, 1945

| Army Group | Width of Front (km) | | | | | Divisions | | | | | | |
| | Total | Main Effort Sector | % of Total | Bkth Sector | % of Total | Front | | Main Effort | | Breakthrough | |
						Divs	Km/Div	Divs	Km/Div	Divs	Km/Div
2d Byelorussian[1]	120	47	39.2	14	11.7	36	3.3	30	1.6	23	0.6
1st Byelorussian	175	44	25.1	24	13.7	83	2.1	46	1.0	27	0.9
1st Ukrainian[2]	90	51	56.6	27	30.0	48[3]	1.9	38	1.3	22	1.2
TOTAL	385	142	36.9	65	16.9	167	2.3	114	1.2	72	0.9

[1] Excludes Nineteenth Combined Arms Army and Fifth Guards Tank Army.
[2] Right wing only.
[3] Four divisions deployed in defensive.

Table 8

Deployment of Soviet Forces
April 15, 1945

	Army Groups			
	2d Byelorussian[1]	1st Byelorussian	1st Ukrainian[2]	Total
Total armies				
Combined arms	4	9	6	19
Tank	—	2	2	4
Total	4	11	8	23
Armies in main effort				
Combined arms	3	5	4	12
Tank	—	2	2	4
Total	3	7	6	16
% of total	75.0	63.6	75.0	69.5
Independent corps				
Total	5	4	5	14
Main effort	5	3	3	11
% of total	100.0	75.0	60.0	78.5

[1] Excluded are the Nineteenth Combined Arms Army and Fifth Guards Tank Army.

[2] Right wing only.

Table 9

Tactical Density of Soviet Artillery[1] and Tanks
April 15, 1945

	2d Byelorussian[2] Army Group	1st Byelorussian Army Group	1st Ukrainian[3] Army Group	Total
Width of front				
Total	120	175	90	385
Main effort sector	47	44	51	142
Percent of total	39.2	25.1	56.7	36.9
Breakthrough sector	14	24	27	65
Percent of total	11.7	13.7	30	16.9
Guns and mortars				
(76mm and larger)				
Total	5,942	14,628	10,265	30,835
Main effort sector	4,287	8,983	7,733	21,003
Percent of total	72.1	61.4	75.3	68.1
Breakthrough sector	3,270	7,087	7,170	17,527
Percent of total	55.0	48.4	69.8	56.8
Per kilometer				
Total front	49.5	83.6	114.1	80.1
Main effort sector	91.2	204.2	151.6	147.9
Breakthrough sector	233.6	295.3	265.6	269.6
Tanks and assault guns				
Total	951	3,155	2,055	6,161
Main effort sector	917	2,519	1,594	5,030
Percent of total	96.4	79.8	77.6	81.6
Breakthrough sector	287	731	302	1,320
Percent of total	30.2	23.2	14.7	21.4
Per kilometer				
Total front	7.9	18	22.8	16.0
Main effort sector	19.5	57.2	31.3	35.4
Breakthrough sector	20.5	30.5	11.2	20.3

[1] Excludes antiaircraft and antitank artillery and multiple rocket launchers.

[2] Excludes Nineteenth Combined Arms Army and Fifth Guards Tank Army.

[3] Right wing only.

Table 10

Tactical Density of Soviet MRLs, AAA, and AT Artillery
April 15, 1945

	2d Byelorussian[1] Army Group	1st Byelorussian Army Group	1st Ukrainian[2] Army Group	Total
Width of front (km)				
Total	120	175	90	385
Main effort sector	47	44	51	142
Breakthrough sector	14	24	27	65
MRLs				
Total	807	1,531	917	3,255
Main effort sector	807	1,401	764	2,972
Breakthrough sector	729	1,267	599	2,595
Per kilometer				
Total front	6.7	8.7	10.2	8.5
Main effort sector	17.2	31.8	15.0	20.9
Breakthrough sector	52.1	52.8	22.2	39.9
AAA				
Total[3]	801	1,665	945	3,411
Main effort sector	785	1,206	741	2,732
Breakthrough sector	306	524	310	1,140
Per kilometer				
Total front	6.7	9.5	10.5	8.9
Main effort sector	16.7	27.4	14.5	19.2
Breakthrough sector	21.9	21.8	11.5	17.5
AT artillery				
Total	770	2,306	1,444	4,520
Main effort sector	695	1,221	883	2,799
Per kilometer				
Total front	6.4	13.2	16.0	11.7
Main effort sector	14.8	27.8	17.3	19.7

[1] Excludes Nineteenth Combined Arms Army and Fifth Guards Army.

[2] Right wing only.

[3] Excludes AA Artillery of the Air Defense of the Country deployed in rear areas.

234

GREAT BATTLES ON THE EASTERN FRONT

Table 11

Number of Soviet Sorties
April 16–May 2, 1945

	Air Armies			
	Sixteenth, Eighteenth and Fourth[1]	Second[2]	Fourth[3]	Total
Phase I sorties (April 16–18)				
Total	12,484	7,517	—	20,001
Day	10,409	6,959	—	17,368
Night	2,075	558	—	2,633
Average				
Day	3,470	2,320	—	5,790
Night	692	186	—	878
Phase II sorties (April 19–25)				
Total	20,424	10,285	15,046	45,755
Day	16,813	8,911	10,493	36,217
Night	3,611	1,374	4,553	9,538
Average				
Day	2,402	1,273	1,499	5,174
Night	516	196	650	1,362
Phase III (April 26–May 2)				
Total	6,651	8,533	10,444	25,628
Day	5,491	7,927	8,544	21,962
Night	1,160	606	1,900	3,666
Average				
Day	785	1,132	1,221	3,138
Night	166	86	271	523
Total (April 16–May 2)				
Total	39,559	26,335	25,490[4]	91,384
Day	32,713	23,797	19,037	75,547
Night	6,846	2,538	6,453	15,837
Average				
Day	1,924	1,400	1,464	4,788
Night	403	149	496	1,048

[1] In the zone of the 1st Byelorussian Army Group. The Fourth Air Army April 16–19 only.

[2] In the zone of the 1st Ukrainian Army Group.

[3] In the zone of the 2d Byelorussian Army Group from April 20, 1945.

[4] For 13 days only (April 20–May 2, 1945).

Soviet Campaign in Manchuria

August 1945

At the outbreak of the Soviet-German war, Japan—which was allied with Germany and Italy in the Tripartite Pact, or Rome-Berlin-Tokyo Axis— assumed a position of "hostile" neutrality toward the Soviet Union. This forced the Soviet Supreme Command to keep a considerable force along the USSR's Far Eastern borders in order to repulse any possible Japanese attack. Despite the fact that the danger of Japanese aggression decreased somewhat after Pearl Harbor, and dropped sharply after the German defeats at Stalingrad and Kursk toward the end of the war in Europe, the USSR still had some 40 combat divisions deployed defensively on the Manchurian border.

In February 1945, at the Yalta Conference, Stalin assured the Western Allies, who for a long time had been trying to persuade him to ease pressure on them in the Far East by declaring war on Japan, that the Soviet Union would enter the war against Japan within two or three months after the defeat of Germany. On April 5, 1945, the Kremlin abrogated the Soviet-Japanese neutrality treaty of 1941, paving the way for the forthcoming war. At the same time the Soviets started to transfer troops to the Far East.

Between April and August 1945, the Soviet Supreme Command assembled a sizable force in the Far East, consisting of eleven combined arms armies, one tank army, three air armies, and three air defense armies, with an aggregate strength of over 1,500,000 men, over 26,000 guns and mortars, 5,500 tanks and self-propelled guns, and about 3,800 aircraft. These forces were organized into three fronts or army groups: the Transbaikal, and the 1st and 2d Far Eastern. In addition, the Pacific Fleet and the Amur Flotilla had some 650 vessels and nearly 1,500 aircraft. All the Soviet forces in the area were subordinated to the newly established Far Eastern Theater of Operations, commanded by Marshal Aleksander M. Vasilevskiy.

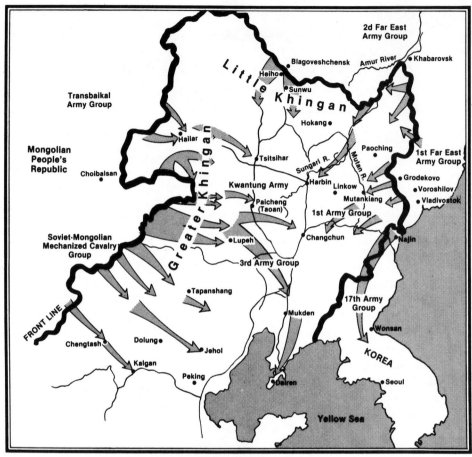

Soviet Campaign in Manchuria
August 1945

The Soviet strategic plan for the war against Japan called for several pincer strikes to converge on the center of Manchuria, aiming at enveloping and then destroying the Japanese forces in northern and central Manchuria. The scope of the planned combined operation by the three Soviet army groups was immense. The Soviet forces were to advance on a front of nearly 3,000 kilometers to a depth of up to 800 kilometers. The two main converging strikes were some 1,500 kilometers apart. The terrain was difficult. Numerous mountain ranges formed natural barriers. Wide rivers, including the Amur, the Ussuri, and the Sungari, flowed parallel to the borders and would present formidable obstacles.

Deployed on the left flank of the theater of operations, the 1st Far Eastern

Army Group under Marshal Kiril Meretzkov was to launch its main attack from Grodekovo and Voroshilov toward Changchun and Mukden (Shenyang), breach the Japanese fortified areas, and cut the Japanese Kwantung Army in two.

On the right flank, the Transbaikal Army Group under Marshal Malinovskiy was also to strike toward Changchun and Mukden, delivering its main blow from the Tamtsag-Bulago salient in the Mongolian People's Republic and, together with the 1st Far Eastern Army Group, closing the circle around the Japanese forces. Secondary attacks were to be launched toward Hailar and Kalgan.

Between the 1st Far Eastern Army Group and the Transbaikal Army Group was the 2d Far Eastern Army Group, whose mission was to pin down opposing enemy forces and deliver its main strike toward Harbin. The army group was commanded by General of the Army M.A. Purkhayev. The operations of the 2d Far Eastern Army Group were to be supported by the Amur Flotilla along the Sungari River.

The Japanese armed forces, despite the critical situation in the Pacific theater of operations, maintained a strong force in Manchuria, Korea, and Inner Mongolia. The mainstay of the Japanese forces was the Kwantung Army, under General Otozo Yamada. It was about 1,000,000 men strong, 700,000 of whom were Japanese, the remainder being local satellite troops of Manchoukuo, Inner Mongolia, and the province of Suiyuan. It had some 1,200 tanks, 6,000 guns and mortars, and about 1,900 aircraft. The Kwantung Army consisted of three army groups, one independent army, and two air armies. The 1st (Eastern Manchurian) Army Group, deployed in the Mutankiang region, faced the Soviet Maritime Provinces. The 3d Army Group had its main forces concentrated around the Mukden area in the heart of Manchuria, and its remaining troops near the Mongolian frontier. The 17th Army Group was in Korea, and the Fourth Independent Army was spread out over the vast territories of northern Manchuria. The Second and Fifth air armies were located in Manchuria and Korea, respectively.

The Kwantung Army was deployed within a huge arc formed by the borders of the Soviet Union and the Mongolian People's Republic, over a distance of nearly 4,500 kilometers. Remote from Japan proper, the army suffered from extended communication lines, and contact with Japan was poor. Railroad lines in the northern and western areas of Manchuria were almost nonexistent, and those in the central and eastern areas were within range of Soviet aircraft. Additional problems were caused by the Chinese population of the Manchoukuo puppet state, which was hostile to the occupying forces.

General Yamada had to rely on Korea for base support. The Japanese had long been established in Korea, which was both the main source of food and an operational base in case of emergency. But Korea was also a long way from most of the Japanese forces in Manchuria and could be cut off with relative ease by a thrust from the Soviet Maritime Provinces. The rear of the Kwantung Army was thus vulnerable to encirclement from the north and east.

The Japanese defense system was organized in three belts. The first, just behind the border, was for covering purposes only and, despite numerous concrete, log, and earth bunkers, contained only a small garrison. The second belt (the main line of resistance) was organized between the Mutan and Muling rivers, and followed the Tumen River in the south. The third belt (rear defense line), not yet complete, was being built in the area extending from Lake Tsinpo Hu to Yenki and the Tumen River.

The Japanese built 17 fortified zones, covering the main routes leading into the Manchurian interior from the USSR and Mongolia. These zones, with defenses sited to take advantage of the rugged terrain, extended over a frontage of more than 1,000 kilometers and included about 8,000 pillboxes, underground communication passages, and a system of observation and command posts with shelters. In addition, all border villages were turned into strong points, with embrasures in every house.

In so vast an operational theater, Japan could not possibly deploy enough forces to man the whole frontier. The Japanese command had to concentrate its defenses and manpower on what seemed to be the most likely avenues for attack. On several extensive sections of the frontier between Manchuria and the Mongolian People's Republic, there were neither defense works nor covering forces. On the extreme left flank of the Kwantung Army the defense lines protecting the approaches toward Dolung and Kalgan were particularly weak.

In the spring of 1945, expecting a Soviet attack, the Japanese command prepared a detailed plan of defense operations. Japanese troops were to offer stubborn resistance to the Red Army in the border regions, and to try to repulse the Soviet assault along a line running from the Laoling Range to Pehanchen and Mehen and then along the Greater Khingan Range to Kailu and Chengteh. If, despite Japanese resistance, the Red Army should break through, the Japanese forces were to withdraw to, but not beyond, the Changchun-Tumen and Changchun-Dairen lines to protect the approaches to their main bases in Korea.

Redeployment of Soviet troops from Europe to the Far East was finished early in August, and by August 7 Soviet forces deployed offensively were ready to attack. Late on the evening of August 8 the Soviet Government informed the Japanese that as of the following day the USSR would consider itself in a state of war with Japan. Following this announcement, and shortly after midnight (local time) August 9, all three Soviet army groups crossed the border and attacked the Kwantung Army. The Transbaikal Army Group moved from Transbaikal and Mongolia, the 2d Far Eastern Army Group from Blagoveshchensk and Khabarovsk, and the 1st Far Eastern Army Group from the Maritime Provinces.

The Transbaikal Army Group advanced fanwise from the area of Tamtsag-Bulago. The attack was spearheaded by the Sixth Guards Tank Army, pushing toward the Greater Khingan Mountains, an area extremely difficult for tank operations. The Japanese, who did not expect a Soviet main thrust in this sector, had kept only a small force there, and it was easily overrun. By noon on August 10 forward elements of the tank army had advanced some 250 kilometers, reached the mountain range, and started to cross it. It was a dangerous maneuver. The mountain roads, running along ledges between high cliffs and sheer declivities, abounded in hairpin turns and steep gradients. Despite darkness and rain, by the morning of August 11 the first tank units had crossed the mountain range. They continued to advance, and in the evening they took Lupeh. On August 12 Lichuan fell to the Soviet spearheads.

The main forces of the Sixth Guards Tank Army, after advancing over 450 kilometers, reached the Central Manchurian Plain on August 13, threatening a strategic envelopment of the main forces of the Kwantung Army.

To the right of the tank army, the Soviet-Mongolian Cavalry and Mechanized Group negotiated the Gobi Desert and, after covering some 300 kilometers in five days, on August 14 took Dolung, a trading center northeast of Kalgan.

On the left flank of the Transbaikal Army Group, the Thirty-sixth and Thirty-ninth armies, despite moderate to heavy resistance, advanced rapidly and pushed into the center of Manchuria. Hailar was taken on August 11; Japanese garrisons in fortified areas were blockaded, and the main forces of the two Soviet armies proceeded toward Lunkiang (Tsitsihar).

The 1st Far Eastern Army Group, which had launched its assault from the Maritime Provinces, was faced with formidable Japanese fortifications. The main effort was delivered in the general direction of the Mutan River and the city of Mutankiang. Initial Soviet plans were disrupted by a sudden tropical storm, which caused the Soviets to move out without artillery preparation. The surprised Japanese offered only token resistance. Taking advantage of the downpour and pitch-dark night, the assault units reached their first objectives on schedule. The Japanese began a hasty retreat, followed closely by Soviet troops. Protracted and bitter fighting developed along the approaches to Mutankiang, where the Japanese had prepared several rings of strong fortifications. Unable to breach the defenses, Marshal Meretzkov decided to bypass Mutankiang and advance toward Kirin, Harbin, and Changchun, to link up with the advance elements of the Transbaikal Army Group.

The 2d Far Eastern army group, supported by the Amur Flotilla and advancing on a secondary axis, successfully crossed the Amur and Ussuri rivers and drove toward Harbin, supplementing the operations of the Trans-baikal and 1st Far Eastern army groups. The Japanese put up strong resistance, based on well-prepared fortifications that somewhat slowed the Soviet advance.

On August 14, with the Kwantung Army facing total collapse, the Japanese Government announced its acceptance of unconditional surrender. At that time the situation on the Soviet-Japanese front was as follows:

The Transbaikal Army Group had advanced from 250 to 450 kilometers into the Manchurian heartland and had reached the line Dolung-Tapanshang-Taoan.

The 1st Far Eastern Army Group had advanced 120 to 150 kilometers and had reached the line Linkow–east of Mutankiang–Najin (Korea).

The 2d Far Eastern Army Group had advanced from 50 to 200 kilometers and approached the towns of Heiho, Sunwu, Hokang, and Paoching.

Despite the official Japanese capitulation, many units of the Kwantung Army did not cease resistance. Heavy fighting continued, while local commanders negotiated surrender terms. On August 17 the Japanese Command finally ordered an immediate ceasefire, and Japanese troops began to surrender en masse.

Table 1

Soviet Forces in the Far East
1941–1945

	June 22 1941	December 1 1941	July 1 1942	November 19 1942	July 1 1943	January 1 1944	May 9 1945
Divisions							
Rifle	23	24	29	20	20	31	45
Cavalry	1	2	3	3	3	2	2
Tank	8	4	2	2	2	2	2
Air	13	23	10	24	27	29	29
AAA	—	—	—	—	—	—	6
Brigades							
Rifle	3	11	20	31	30	26	6
Tank	1	7	20	22	25	26	27
Air	4	4	4	3	4	—	—
AAA	1	—	—	—	1	4	4
Fortified areas	13	15	15	15	15	18	19

Table 2

Combat Strength of the Soviet Forces in the Far East
1941–1945

	Personnel	Guns and Mortars[1]	Tanks and Assault Guns[2]	Combat Aircraft
June 22, 1941	703,714	10,080	3,188	4,140
December 1, 1941	1,343,307	8,777	2,124	3,193
July 1, 1942	1,446,012	11,759	2,589	3,178
November 19, 1942	1,296,822	12,728	2,526	3,357
July 1, 1943	1,156,961	13,843	2,367	3,949
January 1, 1944	1,162,991	16,827	2,069	4,006
May 9, 1945	1,185,085	20,695	2,338	4,314

[1] Excluding 50mm mortars.

[2] Assault guns (137) first deployed in May 1945.

Table 3

Men and Materiel Transferred from Europe to the Far East
May–August 1945

	May	June	July	August 1–8	Total
Men	33,456	152,408	206,042	11,449	403,355
Rifles and carbines	13,343	79,295	83,334	4,644	180,616
Submachine guns	4,041	37,802	38,061	3,073	82,977
Light and heavy machine guns	1,177	5,800	3,482	164	10,623
Guns and mortars	504	2,624	3,723	286	7,137
Tanks and assault guns	156	564	1,229	170	2,119
Trucks	1,059	4,475	10,424	1,416	17,374
Tractors and prime movers	77	477	895	33	1,482
Horses	4,983	18,533	12,764	—	36,280

Table 4

Composition of the Soviet Ground Forces
August 9, 1945

	Transbaikal Army Group	1st Far Eastern Army Group	2d Far Eastern Army Group	Total
Combined arms armies	4	4	3	11
Tank armies	1	—	—	1
Air defense armies	1	1	1	3
Cavalry-mechanized groups	1	—	—	1
Rifle corps	8	9	2	19
Mechanized and tank corps	3	1	—	4
Rifle and motorized rifle divisions	30	31	11	72
Cavalry divisions	5[1]	1	—	6
Tank divisions	2	—	—	2
Fortified areas	2	12	6	20
Rifle, motorized rifle, mechanized and tank brigades	20[2]	14	12	46
Rifle, motorcycle, tank, and assault gun regiments	10[3]	15	4	29
Artillery divisions	2	—	—	2
AAA divisions	3	5	1	9
Independent artillery brigades	15	26	2	43
Independent artillery regiments	36	15	26	77
Engineer brigades	7	8	3	18

[1] Including four divisions of the Mongolian People's Republic.

[2] Including one armored brigade of the Mongolian People's Republic.

[3] Including one tank regiment of the Mongolian People's Republic.

Table 5

Soviet Men and Materiel
August 8, 1945

	Transbaikal Army Group	1st Far Eastern Army Group	2d Far Eastern Army Group	Total
Men (total)	654,040	586,589	337,096	1,577,725
Men (in combat units)	416,000	404,056	238,926	1,058,982
Rifles and carbines	283,608	294,826	158,451	736,885
Submachine guns	117,447	120,291	54,197	291,935
Light and heavy machine guns	19,603	25,789	12,564	57,956
Tanks	1,751	1,201	752	3,704
Assault guns	665	659	528	1,852
AT guns (45 and 57mm)	1,360	1,539	808	3,707
Field artillery (76mm and larger)	3,075	3,743	1,604	8,422
Mortars	3,922	4,879	2,829	11,630
MRLs	583	516	72	1,171
AA guns	601	504	1,280	2,385

Table 6

Composition, Strength, and Performance of the Soviet Air Force August 1945

	Twelfth Air Army (Transbaikal Army Group)	Ninth Air Army (1st Far Eastern Army Group)	Tenth Air Army (2d Far Eastern Army Group)	Aviation of the Pacific Fleet	Aviation of the North Pacific Fleet	Total
Air divisions						
Fighter	3	3	3	1	—	10
Mixed	—	—	2	1	1	4
Ground attack	2	2	2	1	—	7
Bomber	6	3	1	1	—	11
Torpedo bomber	—	—	—	1	—	1
Transport	2	—	—	—	—	2
Independent air regiments	1	4	5	6	5	21
Aircraft						
Fighters	499	536	823	461	178	2,497
Ground attack	197	193	178	194	46	808
Bombers	440	352	198	312	62	1,364
Torpedo bombers	—	—	—	138	—	138
Reconnaissance	40	62	40	84	31	257
Aerial spotters	—	35	39	—	—	74
Transport	189	15	24	—	—	228
Sorties						
Combat	2,361	4,442	3,297	3,049	881	14,030
Non-combat*	3,167	2,329	1,323	608	—	7,427
Ammunition expenditure						
Bombs (tons)	710.7	1,032.6	340.3	689.5	—	2,773.1
Guns (thousands)	14,746	221,730	79,494	45,109	—	361,079
Machine guns (thousands)	42,134	574,635	179,085	227,843	—	1,023,697
Transported by air						
Men	7,200	2,487	6,810	—	—	16,497
Fuel (tons)	2,456.5	90.5	230	—	—	2,777
Ammunition (tons)	172.3	75.3	301.7	—	—	549.3
Miscellaneous (tons)	671.3	132.8	691.9	—	—	1,496

* Includes transport, communication, and evacuation.

Table 7

Composition of the Soviet Naval Forces
August 8, 1945

Ships	Pacific Fleet	Amur Flotilla	Other	Total
Cruisers	2	—	—	2
Destroyers	11	—	—	11
Torpedo boats	2	—	—	2
Escort ships	19	—	—	19
Submarines	78	—	—	78
Gunboats	—	9	5	14
Armored cutters	—	52	23	75
Minelayers	10	1	—	11
Minesweepers	52	12	4	68
Minesweeper cutters	—	43	6	49
Netlayers	—	1	—	1
Floating AA batteries	—	5	—	5
Hydrogliders	—	15	11	26
Submarine chasers	49	—	—	49
Torpedo cutters	204	—	—	204
Patrol boats	—	3	—	3
Floating bases	—	3	—	3
Command and staff ships	—	1	—	1

Table 8

Composition and Strength of the Japanese Force
August 8, 1945

	Manchuria and Inner Mongolia					Southern Sakhalin Group	Kurile Islands Group	Grand Total
	Kwantung Army	Manchoukuo Army	Inner Mongolian Army	Army Group Suiyuan	Total			
Army groups	3	—	—	—	3	—	—	3
Armies or equivalents	7	1	1	1	10	—	—	10
Infantry divisions	31	2	4	—	37	1	2	40
Cavalry divisions	—	2	—	5	7	—	—	7
Infantry brigades	10	12	—	—	22	—	1	23
Cavalry brigades	—	—	—	2	2	—	—	2
Tank brigades	2	—	—	—	2	—	—	2
Independent infantry and marine regiments	3	—	—	—	3	—	1	4
Independent cavalry regiments	—	4	—	—	4	—	—	4
Independent tank regiments	—	—	—	—	—	—	1	1
Air armies	2	—	—	—	2	—	—	2
Men (thousands)	1,040	170	44	66	1,320	20	80	1,420
Tanks	1,155	—	—	—	1,155	—	60	1,215
Guns and mortars	5,360[1]	800	40	60	6,260	120	320	6,700
Ships[2]	25	—	—	—	25	—	—	25
Aircraft	1,800	100	—	—	1,900	—	7	1,907

[1] Guns only.
[2] Sungari Flotilla.

Table 9

Rate of Advance
August 8–19, 1945

	Width (km)	Advance of front (km)	Rate (km/day)
Transbaikal Army Group armies[1]			
Sixth Guards Tank	100	820	82
Thirty-ninth Combined Arms	120	380	38
Seventeenth Combined Arms	90	450	45
Thirty-sixth Combined Arms	20	450	45
Soviet-Mongolian Cavalry-Mechanized Group	250	420–550	42–55
1st Far Eastern Army Group armies[2]			
First Red Banner Combined Arms	135	300	30
Fifth Combined Arms	65	300	30
Thirty-fifth Combined Arms	215	250	25
Twenty-fifth Combined Arms	285	200	20
2d Far Eastern Army Group armies[3]			
Fifteenth Combined Arms	330	300	30
Second Red Banner Combined Arms	150	200	20

[1] Total frontage: 2,300km; active sector: 1,500km.

[2] Total frontage: 700km; active sector: 700km.

[3] Total frontage: 1,610km; with the Kamchatka and Sakhalin sectors: 2,130km; active sector: 500km.

Table 10

Ammunition, Fuel and Food Supplies
August 8, 1945

	Transbaikal Army Group	1st Far Eastern Army Group	2d Far Eastern Army Group	Average in Army Groups
Ammunition (units of fire)				
Small arms	4.0	4.6	4.0	4.2
AAA and 45 and 76mm guns	6.5	7.9	6.5	7.0
122 and 152mm guns	17.0	7.9	18.0	14.3
Mortar	11.0	8.4	10.0	9.8
Aircraft	60.0	76.0	60.0	65.3
Fuel (refuelings)				
High octane gasoline	4.7	1.9	2.0	2.9
KB–70 gasoline	6.9	2.0	0.7	3.2
Gasoline for cars and trucks	4.3	1.7	2.0	2.7
Diesel fuel	4.0	1.5	2.6	2.7
Food and forage (daily rations)				
Flour and barley	33.4	65.4	122.0	73.6
Meat	35.7	64.9	73.0	57.9
Sugar	72.0	67.4	237.0	125.5
Forage	6.3	7.0	25.0	12.8

Table 11

Prisoners of War and Materiel
Captured by the Soviet Forces
August 1945

	Transbaikal	1st Far Eastern	2d Far Eastern	Total
Men	220,135	107,891	265,964	593,990
Tanks	480	120	86	686
Artillery pieces	860	705	271	1,836
Assault guns	—	—	15	15
Mortars	1,022	1,117	335	2,474
Rifles	n/a	n/a	n/a	300,000 (about)
Submachine and machine guns	9,456	2,532	1,111	13,099
Cars and trucks	712	1,417	192	2,321
Aircraft	502	359	—	861
Artillery and mortar shells	578,146	n/a	195,960	774,106
Depots	233	441	43	717

Units of Fire for Principal Soviet Weapons*

	Rounds per Weapon	Weight (short tons)
7.62mm rifle	100	0.038
7.62mm semiautomatic rifle	120	0.046
7.62mm sub-mach gun	300	0.044
7.62mm light mach gun	800	0.270
7.62mm heavy mach gun	2,500	0.100
7.62mm tank mach gun	3,000	0.100
12.7mm AA mach gun	2,000	0.370
14.5mm AT rifle	120	0.160
50mm mortar	120	0.190
82mm mortar	120	0.510
120mm mortar	80	2.200
160mm mortar		
37mm AA gun	200	
45mm AT gun	200	0.700
57mm AT gun	200	0.690
76mm how	140	0.790
76mm gun	140	1.790
85mm AA gun	150	3.390
85mm gun (tank)	48	1.100
100mm gun		
122mm how	80	2.990
122mm gun	80	3.660
152mm how	60	6.330
152mm gun/how	60	3.950
152mm gun	40	3.560
203mm how	40	5.850

* Source: US Army TM30–430, March 1, 1946.

Glossary of Abbreviations

AA	Antiaircraft	Lt	Light
AAA	Antiaircraft Artillery	Lt Inf	Light Infantry
Adv	Advance	Mach gun	Machine gun
Arty	Artillery	Max	Maximum
AT	Antitank	Med	Medium
Atk	Attack	mm	Millimeter
Bde	Brigade	Mot	Motorized
Bkth Sect	Breakthrough Sector	MRL	Multiple Rocket Launcher
Bn	Battalion	Mtn	Mountain
Brty	Battery	n/a	Not available
Cav	Cavalry	No	Number
Czech	Czechoslovakia	Op	Operational
Div	Division	OKH	Oberkommando des Heeres
Div Equ	Division Equivalent		(German Army High Command)
FA	Fortified area		Soviet Air Defense of the Country
Ftr	Fighter (aircraft)	Pz	Panzer
Gds Tank	Guards Tank	Recon	Reconnaissance
Gds Mech	Guards Mechanized	Rgt	Regiment
GHQ	General Headquarters	Sec	Security
How	Howitzer	S/G	Soviet/German
Hvy	Heavy	SS	Special Security
Ind	Independent	TD	Tank Destroyer
Inf	Infantry	Tk	Tank
Km	Kilometer	Tot	Total